WANDERINGS IN INDIA

WANDERINGS IN INDIA

AUSTRALIAN PERCEPTIONS

Edited by Rick Hosking and Amit Sarwal

© Copyright 2012
All rights reserved. Apart from any uses permitted by Australia's Copyright Act 1968, no part of this book may be reproduced by any process without prior written permission from the copyright owners. Inquiries should be directed to the publisher.

Monash University Publishing
Building 4, Monash University
Clayton, Victoria 3800, Australia
www.publishing.monash.edu
www.publishing.monash.edu/books/wi-9781921867323.html

Monash University Publishing brings to the world publications which advance the best traditions of humane and enlightened thought. Monash University Publishing titles pass through a rigorous process of independent peer review.

Design: Les Thomas
Cover image: 'Nena Sahib's Turn-out', an illustration from Lang, John 1861 *Wanderings in India and other sketches from life in Hindostan*, Routledge, Warne & Routledge, London.

This book is part of the Monsh Asia Series.

The Monash Asia Series comprises works that make a significant contribution to our understanding of one or more Asian nations or regions. The individual works that make up this multi-disciplinary series are selected on the basis of their contemporary relevance. The Monash Asia Series of the Monash Asia Institute replaces Monash University's MAI Press imprint, which, from the early 1970s, has demonstrated this University's strong interest and expertise in Asian studies.

Monash Asia Series Editorial Board
Professor Marika Vicziany, Chair, Professor of Asian Political Economy, Monash Asia Institute, Faculty of Arts
Professor Greg Barton, School of Political and Social Inquiry, Faculty of Arts
Associate Professor Gloria Davies, School of Languages, Cultures and Linguistics, Faculty of Arts
Dr Julian Millie, School of Political and Social Inquiry, Faculty of Arts
Dr Jagjit Plahe, Department of Management, Faculty of Business and Economics
Dr David Templeman, School of Philosophical, Historical and International Studies, Faculty of Arts

National Library of Australia Cataloguing-in-Publication entry:
  Title: Wanderings in India : Australian perceptions / Rick Hosking and Amit Sarwal (editors).
  ISBN: 9781921867323 (pbk.)
  Notes: Includes index.
  Subjects: Public opinion--Australia; India--Foreign public opinion, Australian; India--Relations--Australia; Australia--Relations--India.
  Dewey Number: 305.895

Printed in Australia by Griffin Press

Dedicated to John George Lang (1816–1864), first Australian-born author and Bruce Bennett (1941–2012), a champion of Australia-India connections.

Contents

Preface ix
Who was John Lang?
Rick Hosking

Acknowledgments xv

Introduction. xvii

Section I: Encounters and Interactions

India. 3
The Antique Orient
David Walker

India in Australia 20
A Recent History of a Very Long Engagement
Kama Maclean

'White Already to Harvest'. 36
South Australian Women Missionaries in India
Margaret Allen

Almost Forgotten, if Not Unknown 52
Australian and Indian Capital Connections
Christopher Vernon

Australia–India Cricket 65
A Bridge in Cultural Relations
Bernard Whimpress

India Through Australian Eyes, 1850–1950. 75
Bruce Bennett

A Traveller's Eye 89
John Lang's *Wanderings in India*
Rick Hosking

Up the Hooghly with James Hingston 105
David Walker and Roderic Campbell

Critics, Crucibles, and a Literary Career. 126
Inez Baranay and Her Indian Novel, *Neem Dreams*
Alison Bartlett

Connecting with India 138
Australian Journeys
Susan Cowan

Through an Australian Lens. 149
Explorations of India in Jane Campion's *Holy Smoke!*
Lisa French

Section II: Personal Journeys

Mad in India. 167
Sophie Cunningham

Jackal Eyes. 175
Richard Barz

Bahut Achhaa in Bharatpur 181
Linda Neil

Larry in Pondicherry. 189
Inez Baranay

Pandora 198
A Guided Tour of Various (Non) Fictions
Jayne Fenton Keane

Road to Bangalore. 208
Bernard Whimpress

Contributors 215

Index 221

Preface

Who was John Lang?

Rick Hosking

Grandson of a Jewish convict and stepson of a wealthy Sydney trader, John George Lang was the first writer to be born in Australia and spent his life in Australia, Britain and India.[1] He was born in Parramatta near Sydney, New South Wales, in 1816. His father was a Scots sea-captain and landowner and his mother was born on Norfolk Island. Her father, John Harris, a Jewish convict transported for stealing eight silver spoons, arrived in Australia in the First Fleet in 1788. In 1789 Harris proposed and became a principal member of a night watch, which was the predecessor of a police force in Sydney, before he was transferred to Norfolk Island in 1793. In 1819 Lang's mother married the Sydney merchant and sealing master Joseph Underwood, with the result that the boy grew up in a wealthy household that had strong connections with India and in particular with Calcutta. Lang was educated in William Cape's School in Sydney, later Sydney College, where he demonstrated his abilities as a classics student and linguist by completing in 1835 a translation of *Horace's First Satire*, his first published work; he won the school's Classics Medal twice.

In March 1837 Lang left for England, where he was admitted to Trinity College, Cambridge, as a pensioner (a fee-paying student), where he intended to study law. He was threatened with rustication and left Cambridge under a cloud, asked to leave for his flash style, or, as one source puts it, for his 'Botany Bay tricks, not gentlemanly tricks' (Crittenden 2005:38). His obituary records that he 'distinguished himself in his own peculiar way by writing a quaint litany which was condemned as blasphemous and for which he was rusticated for a time' (Crittenden 2005:58). There are also stories of a midnight session in which Lang climbed onto the roof of Trinity College to place a chamber pot on the weather vane, teaching the undergraduates assembled below the Australian 'coo-ee'.

---

[1] Biographical details are mostly taken from Victor Crittenden's indispensable study (Crittenden 2005).

Lang completed his legal studies at the Middle Temple in London, proceeding to the bar in May 1841. His associate James Sheen Dowling wrote to his father, Sir James Dowling, then Chief Justice of the Supreme Court of New South Wales, that 'Lang ... [is] a clever fellow but somewhat troublesome. His family connections will somewhat mar his fortune, they *will* be stumbling blocks in his path; he has married a lady of very good connections and she may help him out of the mess' (Earnshaw 1974:58). Dowling also recorded the view that Lang had left 'by no means a good character in England either for gentlemanly conduct or sobriety' (Crittenden 2005:45). In his last months in Britain he may have begun writing *Legends of Australia*.

Lang returned to Australia in October 1841 with his wife Lucy (née Peterson) and daughter; he was admitted as a barrister to the Sydney Supreme Court and tried to make his way in law. His brief stay back in Sydney was marked by his enthusiastic involvement in local politics and by further literary activity. His emancipist, 'flash' or currency lad (and Jewish?) background, no doubt fuelled by his ratbag spirit, made it difficult for him to find acceptance among the exclusives, sterling, or 'pure merinos', the wealthy free settlers untainted by the convict system. Lang was, as Crittenden rightly calls him a larrikin; his position in Sydney society became difficult. His behaviour before the courts in Sydney earned him a rebuke from the Chief Justice and he became known as the author of some highly embellished estimations of some of his fellow lawyers. Even though he was a supporter of William Charles Wentworth, Lang gave an unpopular and 'maladroit' speech in which he spoke against representative government (Crittenden 2005:38). It was time to find fresh fields.

Lang moved his family to Calcutta in India in 1842, where his wife's brother, barrister Andrew Turton Peterson, joined them a year later. For several years Lang practised law in Calcutta, with little success at first. His family life did not prosper; his wife left him probably sometime between 1843 and 1845, returning to England with their children and leaving Lang free to live the life of the peripatetic bachelor-barrister and writer. Significantly, he refers to his domestic life and 'home' only once in *Wanderings in India* (Lang 1859:359). Free to pursue his interests, he decided to set up a newspaper in Calcutta, the first issue of which appeared in August 1845. He called it *The Mofussilite* and aimed it at the English-speaking military and civil employees of the various British enterprises in India and at those especially living up-country.[2] The

---

[2] 'Mofussil' is defined in *Hobson-Jobson* (Yule and Burnell 1903:570) as '"The Provinces [in British India],"—the country stations and districts, as contra-distinguished from "the Presidency"; or, relatively, the rural localities of a district as contra-distinguished from the *sudder* or chief station, which is the residence of the district authorities ... The word

first number of the paper, incidentally, includes another version of his 'Fisher's Ghost' story, which Lang had written nearly a decade before.

In 1846 Lang moved to Meerut, a centre of British trade and administration in Uttar Pradesh northeast of Delhi, taking *The Mofussilite* with him. In 1849 he became editor and later proprietor of the paper, which he described in 1858, together with the *Delhi Gazette*, as 'With the exception of the Friend of India, when under the control of its original proprietor, these journals of the north-west that were by far the most remunerative of any newspapers in the East' (Lang 1858:114).[3] He had learned to speak Hindustani and Persian, his skill in the latter being apparent in his translations into English of the Persian poet, Sadi of Shiraz, which first appeared in *The Mofussilite* and has been republished more recently (Lang 1992). Lang also published many of his own stories and poems in the pages of *The Mofussilite*, some of his novels later appearing as books. (Crittenden (2005:223) gives a full account of Lang's literary output.)

It is clear from reminiscences by old India hands that Lang was widely regarded as a gadfly, a thorn in the side of 'John Company' and the British administration. The wonderfully named Lieutenant-Colonel Balcarres D Wardlaw Ramsay tells the story of Henry Hardinge, First Viscount Hardinge of Lahore, Governor-General of India from 1844 to 1848, responding angrily to 'more than ordinary abuse' in the pages of *The Mofussilite* in squibs written by 'Mr Lang, an extremely talented man' (Ramsay 1882:124–125). Hardinge first considered horse-whipping or shooting Lang, but then, on a visit to Meerut, called Lang in for an interview. Lang is urged to speak without reserve, so he does. He asked Hardinge if he came to India to make money. Hardinge responded in the affirmative, to which Lang responded:

> I came to India for the same reason; and I found I could not make money faster than by abusing your lordship's policy. If I could have made as much by praising it, it would have given me greater pleasure. It

---

(Hind. from Ar.) *mufassal* means properly "separate, detailed, particular," and hence "provincial," as *mufassal "adalat*, a provincial court of justice ... About 1845 a clever, free-and-easy newspaper, under the name of *The Mofussilite*, was started at Meerut, by Mr John Lang, author of *Too Clever by Half*, &c., and endured for many years"'.

[3] Lang refers to his newspaper in *Wanderings in India* (Lang 1859:113,233ff). He speaks approvingly of editors with whom he had worked, many of whom were Indians, and praised one Muslim editor in particular for the squibs (anti-Government pieces) he had written (Lang 1859:240–241).

is a simple question, not of principle, but of 'L.s.d.' Lord Hardinge was delighted with this frank avowal (Ramsay 1882:124–125).[4]

During the late 1840s and early 1850s Lang continued his legal practice, winning two important and lucrative cases that spread his fame through India, the first for Ajoodia (or Jyotee) Pershâd against the East India Company in 1851, and the second a case for the Rani of Jhansi. A reminiscence by William Forbes-Mitchell of the trial of Ajoodia Pershâd gives a fascinating insight into Lang's character; the man who emerges is a partying, witty, flash, quicksilver-tongued larrikin who feeds on the scraps from the 'John Company' table, making his way on the proceeds of successful court cases, his newspaper proprietorship, his journalism and his fiction. He was drinking and living hard. Forbes-Mitchell gives a lively account of a drinking bet Lang made with officers present during the Pershâd case, that he would describe prosecution witnesses as 'd—d *soors* [pigs]' to their faces in open court. The following morning he did so describe the various court officials without being held in contempt (Forbes-Mitchell 1893:153–159). The East India Company eventually had its revenge, however, and Lang went to jail in Calcutta for three months for libel, as a consequence of publishing libellous remarks about prosecution witnesses in the Pershâd case in *The Mofussilite* (Crittenden 2005:xxx).

Between 1853 and 1859 Lang lived in London, where he moved in literary and theatrical circles, travelled in Europe and published (and republished) a number of his plays, sketches and short stories, many of the latter in Charles Dickens' magazine *Household Words*. He may have known the famous writer, but the acquaintance was slight. The only reference to Lang in Dickens' letters is in one he wrote to WH Wills on 10 March 1853, describing Lang's piece 'Starting a Paper in India', which appeared in *Household Words*, 26 March 1853 as

> very droll—to us. But it is full of references that the public don't understand, and don't in the least care for. Bourgeois, brevier, minion, and nonpareil, long primer, turn-ups, dummy advertisements and reprints, back form, imposing stone, and locking up, are all quite out of their way and a sort of slang that they have no interest in (Storey, Tillotson & Easson 1993:48).

---

[4] Ramsay (1882:125) notes that Lord Dalhousie, who followed Hardinge as Governor-General, 'made much of Mr Lang, and invited him very often to stay at Government House'.

Most of these printer's terms were edited out from Lang's piece.

Lang returned to India in 1859, remarried in 1861 (possibly bigamously and possibly to a mixed-race woman, Margaret Wetter). He spent his last years at Landour, Mussoorie, in the Himalayas, where he died in 1864 at the age of 47 from the effects of an 'insatiable craving for champagne', according to one source (Lohrli 1973:337). An obituary in *The Madras Times* records that Lang:

> fell into the worst of habits and is a melancholy example of wasted talents and degraded abilities. Mr Lang might have lived many years an ornament to the society in which he might have shone as a literary man, but he chose otherwise (Routh 1964:207).

Lang is buried in the Camel's Back cemetery in Mussoorie, high on a ridge among the deodars, looking out on the snow-covered Srikanta peak and the Banderpunch massif. His gravestone reads 'John Lang: Barrister at Law'. These days several families run their goats in the old Christian cemetery, draping their washing on the headstones that still stand. We owe our knowledge of the location of Lang's grave to the Indian writer Ruskin Bond who rediscovered it in 1964 (Bond 1972, 1980). In August 2005 Lang was remembered when a plaque in his honour was installed in Christ Church, the little Anglican church in Mussoorie, thanks in no small part to the efforts of diplomat Rory Medcalf and Victor Crittenden (Mahapatra 2005).

Works cited

Bond, Ruskin 1972, 'Looking for John Lang's grave'. *Blackwood's Magazine* CCCXI.

— 1980, 'Coda to Nancy Keesing', *Hemisphere* 24(2).

Crittenden, Victor 2005, *John Lang: Australia's larrikin writer barrister, novelist, journalist and gentleman*, Mulini Press, Canberra.

Earnshaw, John 1974, 'Lang, John (1816–1864)', in *Australian dictionary of biography* vol. 5, Melbourne University Press, Carlton.

Forbes-Mitchell, William 1893, *Reminiscences of the Great Mutiny 1857–1859, Including the relief, siege, and the capture of Lucknow, and the campaigns in Rohilcund and Oude*, Macmillan, London.

Lang, John 1835, *Horace's First Satire*, JG Austin, Sydney.

— 1836, 'Fisher's ghost: a legend of Campbelltown', in *Margin* 70 (November 2006).

— 1836, *Violet, or, The danseuse: a portraiture of human passions and character*, Henry Colburn, London.

— 1842, *Legends of Australia*, James Tegg, Sydney.
— 1853, 'Starting a paper in India', *Household Words*, 26 March.
— 1853, *Too clever by half, or, The Harroways*. Nathaniel Cooke, London. (Previously serialised in *The Mofussilite*, 1847–1848.)
— 1858, 'Wanderings in India', *Household Words*, 16 January
— 1859, *Wanderings in India and other sketches of life in Hindostan*, Routledge, Warne and Routledge, London.
— 1992, *The rose garden: translations from the Persian of Sadi of Shiraz*, Mulini Press, Canberra. (First published in *The Mofussilite* 1845.)

Lohrli, Anne 1973, Household Words: *a weekly journal 1850–1859, conducted by Charles Dickens*, University of Toronto Press, Toronto.

Mahapatra, Anirban Das 2005, 'Remembrances of things past', *The Telegraph* 21 August, www.telegraphindia.com/1050821/asp/look/story_5131869.asp, viewed 21.2.2012.

The Mofussilite (Newspaper), 1845–1876, PS D'Rozario, Calcutta.

Ramsay, Balcarres D Wardlaw 1882, *Rough recollections of military service and Society* vol. I, William Blackwood and Sons, Edinburgh.

Routh, SJ 1964, 'The Australian career of John Lang, novelist', *Australian Literary Studies* 1(3).

Storey, Graham, Kathleen Tillotson and Angus Easson (eds) 1993, *The letters of Charles Dickens* vol. 7, 1853–1855, Clarendon Press, Oxford.

Yule, Henry and AC Burnell 1903, *Hobson-Jobson: a glossary of colloquial Anglo-Indian words and phrases, and the kindred terms, etymological, historical, geographical and discursive*, new ed, edited by William Crooke, John Murray, London. (First edition published by John Murray in London in 1886.)

Acknowledgments

We gratefully acknowledge the support of Professor Marika Vicziany, Monash University, for her interest in this edition. We would also like to thank all our contributors for their insightful, critical, creative pieces and patience. And a very special thanks to Sue Hosking and Reema Sarwal for their support and advice.

We are grateful to Nathan Hollier, Sarah Cannon, Kathryn Hatch, Les Thomas and other members of Monash University Publishing team in helping to bring out this volume.

Some of the pieces in this collection have been published previously and are revised here to update them. The editors and publisher of this collection are grateful to the following authors for permission to reprint their articles:

Alison Bartlett 2010, 'Critics, crucibles, and a literary career: Inez Baranay and her Indian novel, *Neem dreams*', in Mycak, Sonia and Amit Sarwal (eds), *Australian made: a multicultural reader*, Sydney University Press, Sydney. (First published in *Antipodes* December 2007.)

Bernard Whimpress 2005, 'Road to Bangalore', *Baggy Green* 7(2).

Bruce Bennett 2005, 'India through Australian Eyes, 1850–1950', in Kenneally, Michael et al (eds), *From 'English literature' to 'literatures in English': international perspectives – festschrift in honour of Wolfgang Zach*, Winter House, Heidelberg

David Walker 1999, 'The antique Orient', in *Anxious nation: Australia and the rise of Asia, 1850–1939*, University of Queensland Press, St Lucia.

Inez Baranay 2008, 'Larry in Pondicherry', in *With the Tiger*, HarperCollins India, New Delhi.

Linda Neil 2008, '*Bahut Achhaa* in Bharatpur', *M/C Reviews* 25 May, http://reviews.media-culture.org.au/modules.php?name=News&file=article&sid=2584; also *Extempore* 5 (November 2010).

Margaret Allen 2000, '"White already to harvest": South Australian women missionaries in India' in *Reconstructing femininities: colonial intersections of gender, race, religion and class*, special issue of *Feminist Review* 65.

Sophie Cunningham 2004, 'Mad in India', *AustralAsian*, special issue of *Meanjin* 63(2).

Susan Cowan 2006, 'Glimpses of India: a military dekko', in Sarangi, Jaydeep and Binod Mishra (eds), *Explorations in Australian literature*, Sarup & Sons, New Delhi.

– Rick Hosking and Amit Sarwal

Introduction

India is chaotic. India is aesthetic. India is cheap. India has good food. India is confusing. India wears its history for all to see like so many colourful, dusty, and sometimes shiny bangles. (Sophie Cunningham)

This collection of essays about diverse encounters between Australians and Indians in South Asia and the Antipodes shares its title with a curious and entertaining travel book written by the first Australian-born writer John Lang (1816–1864). He moved to Calcutta in 1842 to work as a lawyer and went on to become a gadfly writer and larrikin newspaperman, publishing pieces about his travels and travails, first in his paper *The Mofussilite* and later in Charles Dickens' magazine *Household Words*. The title of Lang's novel, *Wanderings in India*, suggests immediately one idea about India that still shapes how we think of it, as a sprawling place with room to wander, with much to see and experience.

The book contains some chapters written especially for it and some reprinted from other publications. The first section deals with the cultural history of Australia–India encounters and interactions; the second contains more personal accounts: memoirs, reminiscences, travel pieces. Taken as a whole they represent a range of responses, ideas and experiences that chart the course of the ongoing engagement between Australia and India, between Australians and Indians. Perhaps we need reminding that, while our two nations remain part of the Indo-Australian plate, once the ancient landmass of Gondwana, recent research suggests that the plate might be fracturing as South Asia continues its voyage northwards into Eurasia.

David Walker's opening chapter makes the case for immediate, extended and ongoing encounters between India and the Australian colonies after British settlement in 1788. As a reading of Australian colonial newspapers will reveal, comings and goings between the British colonies were commonplace, with many individuals, such as Charles Sturt and Caroline Chisholm, arriving in Australia after stints in India. Trading links were crucially important; Australia's first exports—seal skins—were shipped to Calcutta for sale and processing, and in states like South Australia the horse trade with India was for many years very significant, even if the horses came to be known as 'walers' after Australia's senior colony. The chapter reminds us that in recent times, since the 1960s in particular, the depth of Australian knowledge and understanding of India has been declining.

Kama Maclean's chapter charts the shifting cultural history of the fascination with Indian aestheticism and the picturesque at the Kumbh Mela, noting how stories about the gathering feature in the front pages of the Australian print media, which suggests that Australia is ill-prepared for a future in which India has a determining role in the world, and noting the decline in Indian studies in the Australian educational system.

Margaret Allen's chapter looks at the history of missionary encounters, noting in particular the South Australian Baptist Church's endeavours in Bengal and reminding us not only of the strong connections forged as a consequence of empire but also of the remarkable story of enterprising and energetic young women who contributed to the work of empire.

Christopher Vernon's chapter will help us all understand more about something that those of us who have travelled in India will have realised—that cityscapes in Australia and India often share some fascinating history. Vernon's emphasis is on Walter Burley Griffin and his wife Marion Mahony Griffin, especially on their architectural work in Lucknow, Agra, Varanasi and Kolkata.

Cricket is a recurring subject in a number of chapters. In several it is noted that the cricket relationship between Australia and India has been anything but smooth. Both Kama Maclean and Bernard Whimpress examine these links. While we are reminded of Shane Warne packing his tins of baked beans to help him through a tour of the Indian subcontinent, we also discover something of Steve Waugh's involvement with a children's leprosy home in Udayan. If cricket is to remain a bridge between Australia and India, Whimpress notes it has to be a robust one.

Bruce Bennett's chapter surveys the range of literary representations of India in Australian writing, noting that, while Australians may have shared with the British the idea of an exotic, exciting, extravagant India, many Australian writers have written with distinction about India. Bennett gives prominence to the writings of women and notes that India has challenged Australian writers' understanding of the imperial connection and the racial and social hierarchies upon which the British Empire was constructed.

There are several chapters on colonial travel writing about India and John Lang. Rick Hosking's chapter looks at Lang, the first Australian-born writer to represent Indian life and manners, noting how the clear generic distinctions we now draw between creative nonfiction and fiction were not so readily recognised in the mid-19th century. While many of Lang's pieces should be seen as fiction, they are still of considerable historical importance for their representation of the tensions between 'John Company' and many Indians, which culminated in the Sepoy Rebellion of 1857. David Walker's second chapter, with Roderic Campbell, deals with another travel writer, James Hingston, author of one of the liveliest books about Indian wanderings. The country challenged and charmed Hingston.

Alison Bartlett's is the first of a number of chapters examining the works of more recent Australian writers who have either travelled or lived in India, some following that hippy trail. Inez Baranay is an Australian writer often described as 'multicultural' (or 'global citizen') who has often written about India. Bartlett describes a 'prodding and stretching' relationship that links her with the writer, the academy and with postcolonial theory, bringing these 'crucibles' together in an analysis of Baranay's novel *Neem Dreams*, which was published in India in 2003 to considerable critical acclaim.

Susan Cowan's chapter is another survey of half a dozen of the more significant Australian writers who have written about India. She offers a further perspective on John Lang's work, setting his writings against those of Mollie Skinner and Ethel Anderson. All three writers lived and worked rather than travelled in India. Skinner worked there as a nurse, and Anderson accompanied her soldier husband in a decade-long sojourn. Cowan also writes of mid-20th occasional visitors, Manning Clark, Christopher Koch and Dal Stivens. In passing she quotes Sunil Badami's description of 'mango novels', such as those of Salman Rushdie, Vikram Seth and Rohinton Mistry: 'exotic-looking fruits of the imagination that conjure up colourful mirages of magical-realist wonders (or thrilling terrors) in faraway places' (Badami 2004: 200). On Cowan's evidence, it seems that ironic self-awareness and rueful satire save the Australian writers from the accusation that they too have written mango novels. Cowan mentions Dal Stivens' cricket story 'The Strange Business at Bombay and Madras' (1979); it's a piece that should be much better known.

Lisa French's chapter considers one Australian representation of India in film, Jane Campion's *Holy Smoke!* (1999), which uses India as a metaphor for different ways of thinking, encouraging us to reflect on the West's orientalist obsession with the exotic and mysticism.

Sophie Cunningham's chapter begins the second section and is a reflective and wide-ranging essay that spins out of Indian travels and travails, ranging over autorickshaws to clothing made in India, leading into a discussion of her novel *Geography* (2004), which is about a woman travelling in India. Richard Barz describes an encounter with jackals near Bharatpur in eastern

Rajasthan—an encounter that inspired a number of poems ranging across a series of Indian wanderings. Linda Neil's piece is also set in Bharatpur and is a traveller's tale about hotel rooms, wolfing down dhal, cricket, music, exoticism, mystical India and the idea of zero.

Inez Baranay offers an extract from her novel *With the Tiger* published in 2008 by HarperCollins in India, which swings between Sydney and Pondicherry and reflects on encounters, Sri Aurobindo's ashram, and sexuality. Her focus is on Indian spirituality, rewriting Somerset Maugham's *The Razor's Edge* (1942), the novel that is often seen as responsible for fixing that Western stereotype in the 20th-century imagination. Drawing on Baranay's *Neem Dreams* (2003), Jayne Fenton Keane's Indian experience is a meditation on how our reading can shape our expectations about a place like India, on food and cookbooks, and on how the tourist creates the experience that creates the tourist. Keane tells us how India taught her to distinguish between the smell of one spice from that of another in body odour and how to respond to the sound of frogs in deep wells. Bernard Whimpress' light-hearted chapter on a cricket test between Australia and India concludes the volume.

Finally, *Wanderings in India* is about the relationship between India and Australia 'on the cusp of something good, deep, long-standing and mutually beneficial—genuine substance', as noted by Professor Robin Jeffrey (2009) in the wake of a spate of opportunist attacks on Indian students in Australia. The chapters—creative, reflective and academic—have been selected over a period of two years to meet the objectives of a volume that provides snapshots of the wide range of interests and issues that Australians have shown towards India. While there is something of an emphasis on literary responses, charting the ebb and flow of writers' reactions to India from the 1850s, when John Lang published *Wanderings in India*, this volume also includes historical, political, sporting and other writings about the complex 'magnetic amalgams' (to use Alison Broinowski's phrase) that link Australia and India. The basic idea is to encourage ongoing research and other kinds of writing about cross-cultural engagements between India and Australia, and to help continue the dialogue about Australia–India relations in the rest of this century and beyond.

– Rick Hosking and Amit Sarwal

Works cited

Badami, Sunil 2004, 'Last mango in Pondicherry', *Meanjin* 63(2).

Jeffrey, Robin 2009, 'The good, the bad and the Section 420s', *Inside Story*, 4 June, http://inside.org.au/good-bad-section-420s/, viewed 22.2.2012.

Section I

Encounters and Interactions

Chapter 1

India

The Antique Orient[1]

David Walker

From the earliest days of the British settlement of Australia, India and the crown colony of Ceylon were a familiar part of the colonists' world. As Margaret Steven (1965:26) has noted 'the first links made by the new colony were with India'. When supplies ran short, as they often did, ships from Calcutta brought grain, foodstuffs, spirits, clothing and live animals. India provided a lifeline for the new settlement. Many trading and shipping connections then developed, creating an increasing flow of administrators, merchants, army personnel, clergy and tourists between the Indian subcontinent and Australia. Australians constantly heard about the conditions of life in India, along with its scenic marvels, architecture, philosophies, mysteries and climate. Australia's Indian connection was to remain strong for much of the 19th century.

From the beginnings of settlement, the diverse traffic in people, ideas and products between Australia and India was largely supported by the imperial connection. Robert Campbell, the first independent merchant operating in Sydney Cove provides an excellent illustration (Steven 1965:26). He was born in Scotland in 1769 and went to India at the age of 27 to join his elder brother in the family export business, which by the 1790s had become a regular supplier to the new colony in New South Wales. Robert later emigrated to Australia, where he built Campbell's wharf, an agency house to facilitate the

---

[1] This chapter was first published with the title 'The Antique Orient' in David Walker 1999, *Anxious Nation: Australia and the Rise of Asia, 1850–1939*, University of Queensland Press, St Lucia.

Indian trade and a private home that was the first Australian house built in the 'whole-hearted Indian bungalow form', a building style that was to become something of a fashion in colonial Australia (Irving 1985:46). Campbell went on to become a leading public figure and a wealthy pastoralist. Many other early colonists had Indian experience. At the highest level of early colonial society there is the example of Lachlan Macquarie who served in India before arriving at Sydney Cove late in 1809 to become Governor of New South Wales. He brought with him an Indian slave who worked as his manservant. There were regional identities like Foster Fyans, who spent some years with the British army in India before becoming first police magistrate in Geelong in the 1830s, or the medical practitioner, John Coverdale, who was born in Bengal in 1814 and practised in India before moving in the 1830s to Tasmania's more manageable climate. There are household names, like Caroline Chisholm, the famous philanthropist, who founded the Female School of Industry for the Daughters of European Soldiers in Madras, where she lived for six years before moving to Australia in 1838. Such links nourished an awareness of India in colonial society from the beginnings of European settlement.[2]

What motivated these various Anglo-Indians to come to Australia? Land grants to ex-army personnel and growing commercial opportunities made a new beginning in the Australian colonies an attractive proposition. There were, no doubt, less flattering reasons for thinking that Australia might be the place to go after India: legal trouble, money trouble, family trouble, drink trouble. Many early settlement choices were influenced by considerations of climate and health. In the 19th century, when the sources of disease were poorly understood, climate was thought to have a much greater impact on health than is now considered to be the case. Firm distinctions were drawn between demanding and healthy climates. Australia, it was hoped, offered a compromise between the extremes of cold in Britain and the tropical heat and associated diseases of India. Tropical heat was thought to coarsen white men and to ruin the health of white women and children. Writing as an intending settler in 1828, James Henty contrasted temperate New South Wales with India's 'pestilential climate under a burning sun' (Bassett 1962:35). Climate was one factor which influenced Henty to emigrate to Australia and by 1830, when he had taken up land on the Swan River in Western Australia, he believed his settlement might serve as a health resort for British officers and their families serving in India (Bassett 1962:138).

---

[2] For more on Chisholm, Coverdale, Fyans and Macquarie, see their entries in the *Australian Dictionary of Biography* (Iltis 1966; Sorell 1966; Brown 1966; McLachlan 1967).

Later in the 19th century, the effects of climate became the subject of serious medical study. Terms like 'tropical neurasthenia' were coined to characterise the state of settlers in tropical climates who appeared nervous and fearful, yet incapable of action or effort. The growing linkage between tropical climates and debilitating disease states in turn raised difficult questions about whether Europeans could ever successfully settle in tropical countries. In contrast to India Anglo-Saxons were expected to flourish in Australia. This certainly was the opinion of Phillip Muskett, the respected author of *The Illustrated Australian Medical Guide*, an influential text that appeared around 1899. Muskett based many of his reflections upon the relationship between climate and health on the British experience in India with particular reference to Sir William Moore's earlier work, *A Manual of Family Medicine for India* (1874).

Once having chosen to settle in Australia, colonists would be given chances to reflect on the benefits of their choice. All too often in the 19th century Australians read in their newspapers dreadful accounts of outbreaks of disease or famine in India. In October 1877, *The Town and Country Journal* publicised a call from the Lord Mayor of London for aid from cities throughout the Empire for a major famine in India. The paper, noting how 'wisely directed beneficence is better than artillery', urged its readers to give generously and so strengthen imperial ties (Famine in India 1877). By November, at least £6,000 had been collected for the Indian Famine Relief Fund. At a meeting in the Town Hall in Sydney, donors were to see an exhibition of photographs from the famine areas and to hear disturbing accounts read from a letter by a Madras Native Infantry Captain of how 'children were being killed and eaten by their parents' (Indian Famine Relief Fund 1877). After such searing tales, Australian life seemed rather benign.

Trade provided even stronger links with India than did charitable aid. As early as the mid-1820s trade with the 'East', the idea of eastern and particularly Indian trade formed one important reason for Lieutenant-Governor James Stirling's settlement of the Swan River district in Western Australia. Stirling anticipated that the export of horses and wheat to India would prove especially profitable. In the case of horses, these predictions proved correct as the export of Australian horses for use by the British in India expanded into a promising colonial trade from the 1830s. Remounts and sporting horses, soon called 'walers' by reference to New South Wales, were sent in increasing numbers until the 1870s when the once flourishing trade fell into some disrepute after dealers allegedly supplied too many animals 'of wretched sorts' (Australian Horses for India 1870; there was also discussion and correspondence in the *Sydney Morning Herald*, January to March 1870). By the 1890s most of these problems appeared to have been resolved and the Australian colonies were able to export 50,000 horses to India over the decade (Yarwood 1989:198).[3] Many were sent from Victoria, particularly from the Western District where the squatter, Francis Henty, one of James Henty's younger brothers, was one of the more successful exporters.

Australia also imported many goods from India. From the 18th century, India supplied the West with a range of new textiles, textile designs and loosely fitting garments, which were quickly appropriated into European style. The Indian *banyan* gave rise to the male lounging robe and dressing gown while the Kashmir shawl with its vivid patterns became an important item of fashionable dress for 19th-century women (Martin and Koda 1994:11). In addition, there were a wide range of culinary links traceable to India. Beverley Kingston (1990) has provided an extensive list of these items which included many herbs and spices, pickles, chutneys, curry powders and, not least, tea.

The habit of tea drinking, which colonial Australians seized upon with particular avidity, generated substantial imports. For decades, tea was routinely included in the staple provisions meted out to Australian shearers. Yet tea drinking was also a habit that had always been closely associated with British life in the tropics, particularly in India. That fortunes were there to be made in the Indian tea trade can be seen in the commercial success of James 'Rajah' Inglis, creator of 'Billy Tea'. Inglis, rather a colourful character who liked to sport an Indian turban, was an active member of the New South Wales Legislative Assembly and an outspoken advocate of free trade. He gave public lectures in Australia on Indian subjects and also wrote books on India with rousing titles, including the alliterative *Tent Life in Tigerland* (1888). In the early 1880s James Inglis and Co. won the lucrative Sydney agency of the Indian Tea Association of Calcutta. Inglis consistently promoted Indian and Ceylonese teas, which he insisted were ahead of the rival Chinese product because they were made under British supervision. By 1897 Ceylon and India had come to dominate the Australian tea market.[4]

---

[3] For more on early Australian trading links with Asia, see Tweedie (1994:12–21)

[4] After spending ten years in India, Inglis came to Australia in 1877 where he prospered as a tea merchant. He was a prolific and popular author and prominent politician. For an account of his period in India, see his *Our Australian Cousins* (Inglis 1880:Chapter 1). For his involvement in the tea trade, see *How a Great Firm Grew: The Story of the Tea Trade* (Inglis 1901). His books on India, *Tent Life in Tigerland* and *Sport and Work on the Nepaul Frontier*, were published in a single volume (Inglis 1888). Inglis's papers are in the Mitchell Library, Sydney (MSS6239, ML 1217/65). For the erosion of the Chinese tea market in Australia in the 1880s, see Sandra Tweedie (1994:26).

Even for Australian settlers without direct family or trading links, India was a country of great interest. India was seen as the glittering jewel in the imperial crown, a country of great strategic importance and one that also magnificently exhibited the benefits of British rule. In the 1830s the leading British historian, Thomas Macauley, marvelled how Britain managed to govern this distant country, whose people differed from us 'in race, colour, language, manners, morals, religion'. He concluded that these were 'prodigies' without precedent in world history (Sharpe 1993:63). Most 19th-century accounts of the Empire propounded the belief that the British exhibited a unique capacity for governance. To these writers, the British presence in India only confirmed the overwhelming importance of the British. No other race seemed able to retain so much territory and rule over such huge populations. Australian colonists, however, had another satisfaction from secure British rule in India. They perceived it as a substantial barrier to Russian imperial ambitions. For many years, Russia was believed to be the major enemy to British and therefore Australian interests in the Indian and Pacific Oceans.

But it soon became apparent that the British presence in India was under threat. Between May 1857 and late 1858 a series of Sepoy uprisings, collectively known at this time as the Indian Mutiny, although now interpreted by Indian historians as the early stirrings of the Independence Movement, challenged British rule. In response to the rebellion of native Sepoy troops in the Indian army, British troops and their families and dependents were driven into fortified positions at Agra, Cawnpore and the British residency at Lucknow. After fierce fighting, many British positions were eventually captured with heavy casualties. Women and children were prominent among the casualties. These actions swiftly generated severe retaliatory massacres of both Indian troops and Indian civilians by British units sent in to relieve the conditions of siege, which in turn sparked further Indian retribution (Hibbert 1978).[5] News of these events soon reached Australia where most newspapers covered the Mutiny in considerable detail and an Indian Mutiny Relief Fund to aid the British survivors was quickly established.

At the time, imperialist accounts saw the Mutiny as an event where the heroic British male gallantly defended vulnerable women and children against murderous 'natives' guilty of 'unreclaimed barbarism'. One example is the response of the Melbourne *Argus* to the Cawnpore massacre:

---

[5] See also Chaudhuri (1979) and Brantlinger (1988:Chapter 7). For more recent Indian approaches to the subject, see Guha and Spivak (1988). For Australian responses to the Mutiny, see D'Cruz (1973).

> Fiendish malignity and ferocious cruelty could not well devise any forms of torture more ingeniously horrible, repulsive, and appalling, than have been resorted to by the brutal ruffians of the Bengal Native army for the maiming, mangling, and murdering of the inoffensive women and innocent children who have fallen into the hands of these remorseless wretches (Crowley 1980:357–358).

Although there has been no detailed study of Australian responses to the Indian Mutiny, the evidence of the major newspapers suggests strong contemporary support for British policies.

The tale of the Indian Mutiny quickly entered the complex mythology of the Empire. Its story was to be told many times over in histories, popular fiction and biography and its resonances reached deep into the British psyche. There was a prolific flow of stories about the events of 1857, usually featuring the genus, 'Mutinous Native'. Stories about frontier life on the borders of empire also become popular, since the Empire had now burgeoned into a strident, red occupation of the globe. There were moves to ensure that children learnt correct Imperial sentiments. The history of the British Empire became an important school subject and from 1905 the celebration of Empire Day was an annual ritual in all Australian schools (Firth & Hoorn 1979).

India, with its wealth, size and diversity, its architectural splendours and mighty traditions was the great collector's piece of empire. Given the maritime links between Australia and India in the 19th century, India attracted many curious and enthusiastic Australian travellers. India was a natural stopping point for British immigrants on their way out to Australia and for Australians returning for a visit to the Old Country. For help in planning their tour, these travellers could consult James Hingston's *The Australian Abroad on Branches From the Main Routes Round the World* (1879). When Hingston's book first appeared in two handsome volumes, it quickly attracted enthusiastic reviews. Hingston was acclaimed as a travel writer and compared to Mark Twain, often to the latter's disadvantage. In 1885, *The Australian Abroad* was made more affordable and convenient, when it was reissued in a single volume by the Melbourne publisher, William Inglis and Company.[6] It was one of the major travel books to emerge from Australia before the First World War and remains one of the most comprehensive and engaging accounts of travel through Asia to have appeared in our literature.

---

[6] For bibliographical information on Hingston and other Australian travellers abroad, see Pesman, Walker & White (1996)

Already well-known for his journalism, James Hingston became something of a literary celebrity. His tone and jaunty manner marked him out as a distinctive voice. Hingston was a philosopher at large, for whom travel provided an opportunity to reflect upon human diversity. While not as circular and digressive as Laurence Sterne's famous creation, Tristram Shandy, Hingston nevertheless displayed a Shandean wit and a gift for storytelling. He was drawn to the strangeness and intractable difference of the mysterious East. He saw India as 'the land of the wonderful', home of 'all that is imaginative, fantastic, sensuous, and extravagant' (Hingston 1879:291). Like many of his contemporaries, he found in India the appeal of the Arabian Nights, that 'famous entertainer of our youth'. Hingston was fascinated by India's sharp contrasts, by all the glory and shame, splendour and decay, grandeur and ruins, to be found in 'this gorgeous Eastern Land!' (Hingston 1879:291). India was a site for cultural feasting. Hingston was keen to see Delhi, the setting for *Lalla Rookh* (Moore 1817), Thomas Moore's series of Oriental tales in verse. Here he found fascinating historical remains indicating how successive invasions had shaped this ancient city. It was a vivid reminder of that considerable 19th-century theme, the mutability of civilisations, captured in Shelley's 'Ozymandias' by the description of the ancient tyrant's statue, broken and abandoned in the desert sand.

Admittedly, Hingston travelled through India as a confirmed imperialist. He retained his robust enthusiasm for British rule. Like Macauley, he marvelled at the way little Britain had come to 'own' a country with a population of 250 million people (Hingston 1879:265). He recognised the importance of British trade and the vitality of the great 'producing powers' of India (Hingston 1879:334). But he was also aware that at times Britain had been guilty of commercial excess, particularly in relation to the opium trade, a commerce which he believed to be as sinister in its impact as slavery. Hingston believed that the greed of the East India Company had been a major precipitating cause of the Indian Mutiny. He blamed the annexation of the Kingdom of Oudh in 1856, of which Lucknow was the capital, for quickening the tempo of resentment towards the British. While acknowledging that the British were not beyond criticism, Hingston supported their rule, believing the loss of India would quickly reduce Britain to a second-rate power.

In Delhi, Lucknow and Cawnpore, Hingston was presented with potent reminders of the comparatively recent Indian Mutiny. As he visited massacre sites and memorials, he copied inscriptions into his notebook and recorded his impressions as an Australian who felt himself still very much a member of the British family. As he noted in Cawnpore, 'The dark blue sky of India has been terribly clouded for humanity, at many times, ancient and modern; but, for Great Britain and her family, never more so than in '57' (Hingston 1879:282). Characteristically, Hingston used European literary associations when describing events. 'We go to see Cawnpore', he wrote, 'as we would see Hamlet or Macbeth'. He found Cawnpore one of the great tragedies of the British Empire, as integral to the story of the British people as Shakespeare's greatest dramas. He knew that the names he read on the monuments at Lucknow would be 'familiar to all readers'—even those who read 'nothing beyond the daily press' (Hingston 1879:282). Yet as an Australian democrat he noted that, although the monuments listed the names of fallen officers, the rank and file were 'lumped together in death' with only a number (Hingston 1879:282).

Hingston took a keen interest in many aspects of Indian culture and threw himself into the life of the Indian cities, making a point of visiting and describing the bazaars and living conditions of ordinary Indians. In Benares he bathed in the Ganges and drank from the Well of Knowledge and the Well of Purification. He attended a cremation, which he described as one of the most moving and memorable things he had ever seen (Hingston 1879:277). Yet he honestly admitted there were some times when he would have gladly sacrificed time amidst the 'gilded' grandeur around him for a cold beer. Travel through India was thirsty work.

As he left India, Hingston was conscious of how much still remained for him to see and reflect on; 'it would take years' to thoroughly explore this vast country and a lifetime then to fully understand what had been seen (Hingston 1879:335). He was convinced that India was a profoundly important culture from 'the oldest of peopled countries' (Hingston 1879:334). No-one, he argued, was really fully educated without a knowledge of India. To see India was to learn 'there is an object in life' (Hingston 1879:265). Hingston was also deeply interested in India's great religions and the spiritual links between India and the West. He often alluded to the common Aryan origins linking the British Anglo-Saxon and the Hindu. At the same time, he had little difficulty in reconciling his interest in India's glorious past with a robust enthusiasm for British rule. He welcomed the British presence in India on defence and security grounds and also appreciated the potential cultural enrichment that might flow from a continued interaction between these two countries.

In later years, the antiquity and spiritual wealth of India noted by Hingston were to become regular themes in Western travel writing and an attraction for those fascinated by the ancient world and its treasures. But it is equally the case that many Australian visitors to India were powerfully struck by the specifically biblical nature of the scenes they encountered in Indian village life. The South Australian parliamentarian, Thomas Playford, sent by his government to investigate the suitability of Indian labour to develop the 'Empty North', was reminded of the Bible when he saw two women grinding corn not far from Delhi (Playford 1907:52). Others felt similarly when they saw women gathering water at wells. In the 1870s *The Town and Country Journal* identified the theme of 'Women at the Well' as a sign of the 'unchanging' nature of 'Asiatic peoples'. It noted that the well formed a focal point for many biblical stories: Jacob first met Rachel at the well, Christ talked with the woman of Samaria at the well; the Scriptures were full of references to wells and the drawing of water (Women at the Well 1875). Later, TB Fischer, an Australian missionary visiting India in 1912, found the sight of oxen in the fields and women grinding corn or drawing water from wells was a constant reminder of the people 'among whom our Saviour walked' (Fischer 1914:118).

Fischer travelled with a camera in one hand and his Bible in the other. Like many Australians of the time, he was convinced that in India there was missionary work to be done. The 'millions of India' had to be saved from the 'darkness of heathenism and the blackness of sin'. Fischer appealed to young Australians to help him in this grand Christian endeavour:

> God's word is a lamp—it guides in difficult places—it marks the rocks and shoals of the ocean—it is the lamp to light us through the valley of the shadow of death…Will you do your best to send that light to brighten dark India? (Fischer 1914:125).

Readers could follow the progress of missionary work in India in papers like the *Murray Independent*, including extracts from letters sent home by Eleanor Rivett, the first Australian to join the London Missionary Society in North India (Rivett 1965:10).

Alfred Deakin, one of the towering figures of Australian public life, was another to be struck by the biblical nature of Indian rural life. Born in Melbourne in 1856, Deakin grew to be an avid reader, fascinated by India. He quickly rose in public office, attaining the office of Prime Minister in 1903 when he was still an energetic figure in his forties. By his own assessment, India had been an enormous influence. He wrote:

> Some words are enriched with historic memories and the reflection of early enthusiasms so that they present themselves before us with a glamour

greater than that of romance. Such a magic name is *India*, before which the throng of unimpressive words falls back as if outshone by a regal presence, clothed 'with barbaric pearl and gold' (Deakin 1893b:5).

Deakin was first drawn to India for its inexhaustible stories, legends and mythologies. He then began to appreciate its human knowledge and spiritual depth and he began to study the great religions of Islam, Hinduism and Buddhism. During the 1870s and 1880s, he found in India many answers to pressing questions of his day, particularly on the origins of humanity and the nature of religious belief. It was only from the 1890s, when his interest turned towards nation building, that he became less concerned with India. Fascination with India then seemed somewhat beside the point, a little disreputable, even a forbidden luxury. India now seemed to demand a sensibility hardly permitted in modern, early 20th-century Australian public life. Although the older Deakin wrote of India as a powerful, but awkward memory, India always remained one of the 'impressive' words in his vocabulary.

Deakin's chance to visit India had come in 1890 when the proprietor of *The Age*, David Syme, invited him on a visit to inspect India's irrigation program. Deakin accepted with alacrity; irrigation was one of his many enthusiasms. Walter Murdoch, Deakin's friend and first biographer, described the trip as only a 'two month dash', but noted: 'the preparation for it had been spread over many years of study; he knew the history of the country as few Englishmen knew it' (Murdoch 1923:170). Deakin's two books on India, *Irrigated India* and *Temple and Tomb in India* were published in 1893 and confirmed his reputation as a keen student both of Indian religions and the British Raj, interests that have sometimes been overlooked. Murdoch had stressed Deakin's Indian enthusiasms, but his next biographer, JA La Nauze, researching his subject in the 1960s, clearly considered Deakin's religious interests and his fascination with India subjects best passed over as briskly as possible (La Nauze 1979:480–482). These seemed regrettable lapses in an otherwise impressive career. In a more recent study, Al Gabay (1992) has given Deakin's religious quests the centrality they deserve.

For his part Deakin wrote of India, its architecture, history, religions and stories without any sense that these were inappropriate subjects for an Australian politician. Interestingly, Deakin also could readily blur the boundaries between northern Australia and southern India to locate Australia firmly within an Indian sphere of influence. Deakin was convinced that Australian developments would be directly influenced by the course of events in India and that distances between the countries would soon decrease with rapidly improving transport and communications. He liked to describe Australians as a new people of Western background 'settled under the shadow of an antique Orient' (Deakin 1893b:151). Moreover, Deakin reminded his readers that people of Hindu background 'were not without kinship' to people in Australia. This was an acknowledgment of shared Aryan origins, the appreciation of which was sharpened by the new scholarship then emerging which marked Sanskrit as the source of all Indo-European languages. 'The study of Sanscrit', Deakin believed, has 'given a new tone and turn to 19th century thought' (Deakin 1893b:2).

This is not the place to test Murdoch's assertion that Deakin knew the history of India as few 'Englishmen knew it', though the claim, an interesting one, merits closer scrutiny. But what is clear is that Deakin had looked to India to furnish answers to some of the great questions of his day. He understood the growth of civilisation as an 'unceasing struggle for supremacy between East and West'. He felt Indian history confirmed this proposition, just as the British presence in India would help determine the outcome of the struggle. Deakin believed that anyone wanting to understand the modern world must understand the struggle for supremacy between East and West and so had a responsibility to learn about India. In *Temple and Tomb* he predicted that India and Australia would show a growing convergence of interests, arguing that the two countries were allied already 'politically and intellectually as well as geographically'. It was evident that Australia should be well informed also about other nearby 'Asiatic empires' whose future, Deakin believed, would be bound up with the future of 'our own tropical lands' (Deakin 1893b:151).

Deakin returned to the theme of the close community of interests between Australia and India in *Irrigated India*, citing shared concerns over 'trade and invasion, peace and war' (Deakin 1893a:11). He saw considerable mutual benefit in closer trading links and believed that free trade policies created export opportunities for Australian products in India, while Indian products were likely to find a growing market in Australia. These trade links would then draw the two countries closer 'year by year'. In addition, although Deakin was cautious about the future labour needs of northern Australia, he was prepared to make a case for the importation of Hindu workers, if 'coloured' labour should prove indispensable to northern development.

Deakin also turned briefly and rather tantalisingly to the intellectual implications of Australia's proximity to India. He anticipated growing occasions for cultural interaction. 'That intellectual give and take', he wrote, 'which is everywhere a stimulus to thought should be especially quick and prolific between Australasia, or Southern Asia, and its northern continent [India]' (Deakin 1893a:13). Since travellers already flowed freely between the two countries, Deakin thought it reasonable to suppose that Indian students might be attracted to Australian universities and that Australian intellectuals might become authorities on India and its people. Since geography had brought Australia and India 'face to face' Deakin supposed that it might yet 'bring them hand to hand, and mind to mind. They have much to teach each other'. Yet at the same time Deakin noted that many Australian colonists:

> in their pride of descent and haughtiness of national feeling, seem apt to forget that they have made their homes neither in Europe nor America, but in Austral-Asia–Southern Asia–and that their fortunes may by this means be linked in the closest manner, in trade and in strife (Deakin 1893a:13).

Deakin's use of the term 'Southern Asia' is of particular interest here, for it was a coinage that he hoped would encourage Australians to develop a more systematic awareness of how close they were to India. While Deakin acknowledged that Australians had made their homes on the edge of Asia, from his vantage point in 1890 this provided a golden opportunity to get to know India. He was ready to predict that India would have a growing and increasingly positive impact upon the cultural, spiritual and economic development of 20th-century Australia. Events, however, proved him wrong.

Deakin always remained deeply interested in Indian religions. He quoted the views of Sanskrit scholar and Oxford Professor, Max Müller, on how ancient India had been fundamental to the development of Western thought:

> we know that all the most vital elements of our knowledge and civilization, our languages, our alphabets, our figures, our weights and measures, our art, our religion, our traditions, our very nursery stories, come to us from the East (Deakin 1893b:2).

But Deakin drew a sharp distinction between ancient thought and the 'motley mass of degenerate and degraded beliefs' which he believed constituted modern Hinduism (Deakin 1893b:51). In this, he also followed Müller's opinions since Müller venerated the India of village communities

2000 years earlier but could argue in his private correspondence that degenerate modern India should best become Christianised (Müller 1892:7). Ancient India was readily celebrated while modern India and Indians were routinely disparaged (see Chaudhuri 1974; Rothermund 1986).

Deakin also subscribed to Müller's view that ancient Indian literature could assist Europeans to develop a fuller, more perfectly realised inner life. At this time, Deakin was hardly alone in drawing a sharp contrast between the spiritual wisdom of the East and the material wealth of the West; between other-worldly and this-worldly approaches to life and its meaning. He pictured an ideally balanced civilisation as one that displayed Anglo-Saxon energies, which he greatly valued, but which could be deepened and enriched by the spiritual traditions of India. A century later this distinction between the spiritual East and the material West has been repeated to the point of cliché.

India not only had its own great religions, it also provided a fertile environment in which Western people in search of spiritual truths could develop new religious beliefs. One of the most important of these, emerging in the 19th century, was Theosophy. Jill Roe has shown how closely the rise of Theosophy in Australia can be related to the growing interest in Eastern religions in the late 19th century. Edwin Arnold's celebration of Buddhism, *The Light of Asia*, first published in 1879, enjoyed great popularity. Its Australian readership is difficult to establish, though a character in Joseph Furphy's *Rigby's Romance* (1921) cites Arnold's book as an indispensable spiritual guide (Kingston 1990; see also Godwin 1994). Deakin soon noted how Theosophy, the 'latest doctrine' from India was finding converts among 'modern-minded men and women' (Deakin 1893b:2). He joined the movement himself, albeit briefly, in February 1895. The imperial connection, which guaranteed a regular shipping service, aided those seeking this type of spiritual connection with India. A stopover on the way to England in 1882 allowed Professor John Smith of Sydney University to visit Bombay where he joined the Indian chapter of the Theosophical Society (Hoare & Radford 1976).

Those attracted to Theosophy were typically dissatisfied with the teachings and practices of institutional Christianity, yet were unable to do without some form of religious faith. The appeal of Theosophical thought to Australians at this time can be evidenced by an unpublished sketch of Wilton Hack, written for his children in 1907 to record his life and spiritual struggles. He outlines how his search for spiritual wisdom led him from

Christianity to Freethought to Spiritualism and then to Theosophy. 'I went through the most terrible misery when I gave up the Xtian platform', he wrote. 'I saw that the old dogmas were bad & untrue, but I had nothing to put in its place; & that state of mind is wretched indeed'. Hack journeyed to India and Ceylon 'in search of wisdom & spiritual knowledge'. In the East he was sure he would find men of 'great intellectual power' with a 'wonderful knowledge of Philosophy' (Hack 1907:108). He visited Adyar, the Theosophical headquarters in India, where he worked as a librarian (Cross 1960). Returning to Ceylon, his attempt to initiate a mining venture ended in betrayal and bitterness. Only Theosophy, with its emphasis upon Brotherhood, could provide a stable point in his life. In the depths of despair and racked by illness, Hack turned to the Masters, the Mahatmas, the spiritually perfected ones, asking them to grant him a new beginning or put a swift end to his miserable existence. 'During that night', he wrote, 'I awoke & there was a bright golden light about me' (Hack 1907:83). Signs and occult messages persuaded him that the Masters had cured his physical and mental afflictions. On his return to Australia, Hack enjoyed the company of the 'ladies and gentlemen of intellectual & mental prominence' at the Adelaide branch of the Theosophical Society (Hack 1907:109). Yet, as will be seen later, for some others in the community, these small gatherings signalled the growth of a troubling pro-Eastern presence in Australia, a force to be counteracted.

As Roe (1986) reminds us, Theosophy spoke to its moment in history, to the 'collapse of old prescriptions' in the 1880s and the social turmoil that came with increasing industrialisation and urbanisation, both in Britain and her Australian colonies. It was one of a number of movements that 'promised a new unity amid the bewildering changes of modern life' (Roe 1986:54). The aim was to create a bridge between East and West. Using teachings from ancient Indian texts, Theosophy stressed the perfected inner life and the pursuit of a radiant spirituality. Its adherents believed Australia provided the ideal setting for spiritual awakening. They hoped the 'light of Asia' would shine brightly on Australia, a land whose providential purpose seemed to be to create a new race of beings of great spiritual sensitivity. Bernard O'Dowd, Melbourne poet, intellectual and parliamentary draughtsman, hoped for a new beginning in the Antipodes, among a race of 'sun gods' (Kennedy & Palmer 1954:105–106). He had studied Eastern wisdom throughout the 1880s.

Climatic affinities between tropical Queensland and India particularly encouraged the belief that Theosophy would flourish in Australia's tropical regions. Indeed, by 1896 the Theosophical Society in Queensland had 80 members, a promising beginning for a new colony. Theosophists' interest in Queensland stemmed from the belief that it provided the conditions suitable for the emergence of a new race. Madam Blavatsky, in her great tome *The Secret Doctrine* (1888), held that Mankind was divided into a number of root-races, each made up of various sub-races. Higher races supplanted lower races in an evolutionary cycle. She predicted that the Aryans, the fifth root-race, were at the end of the 19th century poised to evolve into a more spiritually perfected sixth root-race. The great event was expected to occur in California. But it quite possibly might also take place in Queensland which, Theosophists argued, had the right climate and a very promising population mix of British peoples augmented by Germans, Italians and Chinese. This was exactly the racial combination predicted for the emerging sixth root-race (Roe 1986:115). In these ideas, supported by its pursuit of spiritual truth and universal brotherhood, Theosophy challenged many concepts of racial exclusivity that had become so pervasive as themes in the intellectual debate at the end of the 19th century. Mainstream Australian opinion exhibited no enthusiasm for racial mixing under any pretext and was much more inclined to the view that Queensland's future lay in the development of a climatically adapted white race, protected against tropical diseases and alert to the dangers of a tropical climate.

While Australians learned about India through many different channels, the most persistent conception of India was of an ancient land which had long been a source of deep spiritual truths. Fakirs, bearded prophets and philosophers seemed to spring from the soil. In 1924 *The Pacific* saluted antique India:

> India is old. Before Egypt flourished India was. She saw Babylon rise and fall. Greece and Rome were but fragments of a passing dream beside the misty antiquity of this ancient Aryan land. That wisdom which she treasured through the ages she would give to the world were she but free and happy. She knows wonderful secrets of life (Girard 1924:4).

While the appeal of antique India persisted, the relevance of turbulent modern India as a guide to human conduct, with its complexities of caste, its crowded cities, dreadful diseases and awful poverty, was to fade for Australians as the 20th century wore on, not to be revived until the 1960s.

Works cited

'Australian horses for India' 1870, *Town and Country Journal* 5 February.
Bassett, Marnie 1962, *The Hentys: An Australian colonial tapestry*, Oxford University Press. (First published by Oxford University Press in1954.)
Blavatsky, Helena 1888, *The secret doctrine: the synthesis of science, religion and philosophy* (3 volumes), Theosophical Publishing Company, London.
Brantlinger, Patrick 1988, *Rule of darkness: British literature and imperialism, 1830–1914*, Cornell University Press, Ithaca.
Bright, Mrs Charles [Annie Bright] 1896, 'Mr James Inglis', *The Cosmos Magazine* 2(6).
Brown, PL, 1966 'Fyans, Foster (1790–1870)', in *Australian dictionary of biography* vol 1, Melbourne University Press, Melbourne.
Chaudhuri, Nirad C 1974, *Scholar extraordinary: the life of Professor the Rt Hon. Friedrich Max Müller, P.C.*, Chatto & Windus, London.
Chaudhuri, Sashi Bhusan 1979, *English historical writings on the Indian Mutiny, 1857–1859*, The World Press, Calcutta.
Cross, J 1960, 'Wilton Hack and Japanese immigration into North Australia', *Proceedings of Geographical Society of Australasia (South Australia Branch)* 61:55–59.
Crowley, FK (ed) 1980, *A documentary history of Australia* vol 2, Nelson, Sydney.
D'Cruz, JV 1973, 'White Australia and the Indian Mutiny', in *The Asian image in Australia: episodes in Australian history*, Hawthorn Press, Melbourne.
Deakin, Alfred, 1893a, *Irrigated India: an Australian view of India and Ceylon, their irrigation and agriculture*, W Thacker & Co., London.
— 1893b, *Temple and tomb in India*, Melville, Mullen & Slade, Melbourne.
'The Famine in India' 1877, *Town and Country Journal* 6 October.
Firth, Stewart and Jeanette Hoorn 1979, 'From Empire Day to Cracker Night', in Spearritt, Peter and David Walker (eds), *Australian popular culture*, Allen & Unwin, Sydney.
Fischer, TB 1914, *A month in India: the collected writings of T. B. Fischer*, Austral Publishing Company, Melbourne.
Furphy, Joseph 1921, *Rigby's romance: a 'made in Australia' Novel*, De Garis, Melbourne.
Gabay, Al 1992, *The mystic life of Alfred Deakin*, Cambridge University Press, Melbourne.
Girard, Louis E 1924, 'The genius of an empire', *The Pacific* 18 September.
Godwin, Joscelyn 1994, *The Theosophical enlightenment*, SUNY Press, Albany.
Guha, Ranajit and Gayatri Chakravorty Spivak (eds) 1988, *Selected subaltern studies*, Oxford University Press, New York.
Hack, Wilton 1907, 'Sketch of my life: for the instruction and amusement of my beloved children', 30 July (State Records of South Australia PRG 456/59).
Hibbert, Christopher 1978, *The Great Mutiny: India, 1857*, Allen Lane, New York.
Hingston, James 1879, *The Australian abroad on branches from main routes round the world*, Sampson Low, Marston, Searle & Rivington, London.
Hoare, Michael and Joan T Radford 1976, 'Smith, John (1821–1885)', in *Australian dictionary of biography* vol 6, Melbourne University Press, Melbourne.
Iltis, Judith 1966, 'Chisholm, Caroline (1808–1877)', in *Australian dictionary of biography* vol 1, Melbourne University Press, Melbourne.
'Indian Famine Relief Fund' 1877, *The Town and Country Journal* 10 November.
Inglis, James 1880, *Our Australian cousins*, Macmillan and Co., Sydney.
— 1888, *Tent life in Tigerland (1888) with which is incorporated Sport and work on the Nepaul Frontier (1878). Being twelve years' sporting reminiscences of a pioneer planter in an Indian frontier district*, A Hutchison & Son, Sydney.
— 1901, *How a great firm grew: the story of the tea trade*, William Brooks & Co., Sydney.

Irving, Robert (ed) 1985, *The History and Design of the Australian House*, Oxford University Press, Melbourne.
Kennedy, Victor and Nettie Palmer 1954, *Bernard O'Dowd*, Melbourne University Press, Carlton, Vic.
Kingston, Beverley 1990, 'The taste of India', in Walker, David (ed), *Australian perceptions of Asia* (Australian Cultural History 9), School of History, University of New South Wales, Sydney.
La Nauze, JA 1979, *Alfred Deakin: a biography*, Angus & Robertson, Sydney.
Martin, R and H Koda 1994, *Orientalism: visions of the East in Western dress*, Metropolitan Museum of Art, New York.
McLachlan, ND 1967, 'Macquarie, Lachlan (1762–1824)', in *Australian dictionary of biography* vol 2, Melbourne University Press, Melbourne.
Moore, Thomas 1817, *Lalla Rookh: an oriental romance*, Longman, Hurst, Rees, Orme, & Brown, London.
Moore, William 1874, *A manual of family medicine for India*, Churchill, London.
Müller, Max 1892, *India: what can it teach us?*, Longman Green, Calcutta.
Murdoch, Walter 1923, *Alfred Deakin: a sketch*, Constable, London.
Muskett, Philip 1899, *The illustrated Australian medical guide* (2 vols), William Brooks & Co., Sydney.
Pesman, Ros, David Walker and Richard White (eds) 1996, *Annotated bibliography of Australian overseas travel writing, 1830 to 1970*, compiled by Terri McCormack, ALIA Press, Canberra.
Playford, Thomas 1907, *Notes of travel in India, China and Japan*, JL Bonython, Adelaide.
Rivett, Eleanor 1965, *Memory plays a tune, being recollections of India 1907–1947*, The Author, Sydney.
Roe, Jill 1986, *Beyond belief: Theosophy in Australia, 1879–1939*, University of New South Wales Press, Sydney.
Rothermund, Dietmar 1986, *The German intellectual quest for India*, Manohar, New Delhi.
Sharpe, Jenny 1993, *Allegories of empire: the figure of woman in the colonial text*, University of Minnesota Press, Minneapolis.
Sorell, GF 1966, 'Coverdale, John (1814–1896)', in *Australian dictionary of biography* vol 1, University of Melbourne Press, Melbourne.
Steven, Margaret 1965, *Merchant Campbell, 1769–1846: a study of colonial trade*, Oxford University Press.
Tweedie, Sandra 1994, *Trading partners: Australia & Asia 1870–1993*, University of New South Wales Press.
'Women at the well' 1875, *Town and Country Journal* 2 January.
Yarwood, AT 1989, *Walers: Australian horses abroad*, Miegunyah, Melbourne.

Chapter 2

India in Australia

A Recent History of a Very Long Engagement[1]

Kama Maclean

While observing the media reportage of the 2001 Maha Kumbh Mela as it was being relayed into Australia, I noted a pattern in the 'idea' of India that underpinned the pages of newsprint that reproduced, in colour, fantastic images of crowds assembling to bathe in the sacred *sangam*, the confluence of the Yamuna and Ganga. Of course, the Kumbh Mela is eminently newsworthy. *Guinness World Records*, that compilation of the amazing and the bizarre, credits it as being 'the greatest recorded number of people assembled with a common purpose' (Glenday 2007:125), with an estimated 20 million pilgrims present in Allahabad on 30 January 2001.[2] Many like to think that the assembled crowd represents a microcosm of India–'a miniature nation bristling with paradoxes' (This Kumbh's a Confluence 2001)–in all of its linguistic, regional, and sectarian diversity.[3] The Kumbh Mela is all the more incredible given the limitations on the land available for the purpose of the *mela* and the enormity of the Uttar Pradesh state government's task in overseeing the arrangements (with some central-government funding). This

---

[1] This chapter was initially written in 2008, in the aftermath of the Indian cricket tour of Australia, but prior to the attacks on Indian students in Australia in 2009. I thank Amit Sarwal, who urged me to write this piece, and Michael Milne for his comments and ideas.

[2] For all of the record book's concern for accuracy, this is a mistake; the biggest bathing day in the 2001 *mela*, Mauni Amawasya, fell on 24 January. The figures, however, are consistent with other estimates of the number of people present on that day.

[3] During the Kumbh in 2001, the English-language media reported several vignettes about Muslims bathing in the *sangam* (Roy 2001; Tewari 2001; Kumbh Turns into a 'Sangam' 2001; Who'll Man My Rickshaw 2001).

Figure 1: 'Ganges Gathering Tests Political Water'
A serious news story about the politicisation of religion is juxtaposed with unrelated images which posit tradition against technology.
Photograph taken by Luke Harding

includes providing effective crowd control at all times, medical provisions, all-India transport arrangements, reuniting people separated in the crowd and overseeing that food and shelter is clean and affordable. In the interests of public health and safety the state has a duty of care to the pilgrims to achieve all of this and, in addition, it has to contend with the demands and needs of the 'kings of the *mela*', the *sadhu*s. The impressive administrative achievement of managing an influx of millions of people onto a small tongue of land over the course of a month without catastrophe, in the face of overwhelming challenges such as terrorist threats, deserved media coverage. But this is not what earned the Kumbh Mela a place in the Australian media.

In all of the Australian coverage, the emphasis lay on the *naga sadhus*, the colourful congregation of Hindu holy men who parade naked or nearly so to bathe at the *sangam* on three grand occasions during the *mela* and hold court in their camps for the remainder of the period (approximately 180,000 *sadhu*s attended the 2001 Kumbh Mela). The most widely circulated photograph (see image below) presented the ultimate anachronism: a holy man cradling a super-slim mobile phone to his dreadlocked head (Harding

2001).⁴ At the same time, he holds a *kamandal* (a pot), indicating a high state of withdrawal from the material world. So why does the holy man, who has abandoned all else, still cling to his mobile? To many in the West, Indian asceticism is logically incompatible with expensive, high-tech conveniences. This concept reveals a poor understanding of Hinduism in general and the modern history of Indian asceticism in particular, which reveals that Indian *sadhu*s have always been politically and materially engaged with the world.⁵

The *naga sadhu*s themselves had objected to the determination of media contingents to represent the Kumbh Mela internationally as an erotic, exotic show of the Mystical East. In an effort to regulate photographers' access to the *ghat*s, the *mela* authorities had allocated passes to the media, which prescribed the limits within which they could photograph or video pilgrims and *sadhu*s while bathing. This was in accordance with legislation framed in 1940, which explicitly banned photography at the bathing *ghat*s in Allahabad during a *mela*. Ever since the introduction of photography in India, local authorities had contested the right of photographers to capture sensational images of women bathing, their *sari*s clinging to their bodies, and of the *naga sadhu*s. Many colonial travellers had been attracted to the *mela* with the promise (advertised in early travel guides) of encountering the picturesque: a pre-industrial landscape, peopled with romantic figures engaged in 'ancient rituals' and peppered with statuesque, or perhaps ruined, buildings (Ghose 1998:41). The appeal of the picturesque lay in its raw, 'natural state', which was implicitly contrasted with the busy streets of the European metropolis. One such traveller, Constance Cumming remarked upon the curious fact that so many Indian women, when seen in public, would briskly draw a cloth over their heads and faces, but apparently had no reservation in bathing in sheer, clinging cloth at the *mela*'s *ghat*s (Cumming 1884:89). It did not occur to Cumming that these devotions were deemed private and were not intentioned for her gaze.

The ban on photography enshrined in the Mela Rules of 1940 aimed to protect the privacy of bathers, that they might perform their religious rituals unmolested by the gaze of photographers.⁶ Enforcing such a ban,

---

[4] The same image was published in Canada with the caption: 'Hello, Vishnu?' (Boisvert 2002).

[5] New research by William Pinch has revealed that militant ascetics might have triumphed over the East India Company in the 18th century, had they lent their significant support as mercenaries to the Marathas, instead of making an alliance with Lord Wellesley (Pinch 2006:256).

[6] One Australian photographer, Stephen Dupont, sells the images of pilgrims at the *mela* for astronomical prices, having established them as 'fine art'. It is highly doubtful that the

however, has never been easy, particularly when the administration is distracted by vital issues such as public safety and crowd regulation on the main bathing days, when dreadful accidents have been known to happen. In 1954, arrangements fell short of what was required and, when on 3 February crowds exceeded expectations, the result was the death of hundreds of pilgrims in a crowd crush.[7]

On the first main bathing day at the Kumbh in 2001, 14 January, photographers positioned themselves along the banks and in the water in front of the *akhara*'s processions, or *shahi snan*s, in order to get the best shots possible. The administration, distracted by the demands of organising the holy men's processions, had not anticipated this and were unable to remove the photographers before the *akhara*s charged towards the holy waters (Nandan 2002:87). The photographers had entered the sacred waters *before* the holy men whose right to enter the waters first is a well-enshrined custom, with the order of precedence still hotly contested among *akhara*s today. The *akhara*s objected to this and the Mela Authority responded by backing a Public Interest Litigation in the Allahabad High Court, seeking a strict ban on photography at the *ghat*s in accordance with the Mela Rules of 1940. This moderated media coverage somewhat, although the issue remained contested for the remainder of the *mela*.

Of course, the Australian press was not alone in this voyeuristic preoccupation with naked *sadhu*s and wet *sari*s at the *mela*. The Australian media relied upon images taken by international press agencies and, indeed, those taken by Indian freelancers, many of whom protested at the limits imposed upon them and faced the *lathi*s of police for their trouble (Kazmi 2001). There was considerable objection to the blithe broadcasting of such images in the Indian media, where the English-language press in particular portrayed the *mela* with a cosmopolitan sensibility that was interpreted by some as deeply disrespectful (An Uncultured Media 2001; Dutt 2001). In the United Kingdom complaints from Britain's Indian community at Channel 4's coverage of the first bathing day reached the *mela* management and the Commissioner of Allahabad, Sada Kant, responded, accusing the channel of taking a lewd, 'titillating' and immoral view of the *mela* (Lewd Charge 2001). This media interpretation of the *mela* as an esoteric, exotic and erotic festival raised the ire of Hindus who argued that the sentiments of the devout

---

    pilgrims who constitute his subject gave their permission or share in the profits, which must be considerable given advice that his art is collectable and a desirable thing to add to one's investment portfolio (Jenkins 2007).

7   For an extended discussion on the Kumbh Tragedy of 1954, see Maclean (2008:Chapter 6).

pilgrims were being treated with disregard. In Australia, with its relatively small Indian diaspora drawn from diverse regions and communities, there was no such response.

In 2001 the Kumbh Mela was the only Indian news story to reach the front pages of major broadsheets in Australia. In fact, India had scarcely occupied space on Australian front pages since the outraged coverage of the 1998 nuclear tests. (I am not counting cricket coverage here—on which, more later.) Why was the Kumbh Mela so newsworthy? How did it affect the lives of Australians that it justified prime position in the newspapers and large colour photographs on several occasions?

To newspaper editors, the Kumbh Mela justified such coverage because it was an 'entertaining' human-interest story. The Australian public consuming this news was one that believed that the world was gradually becoming more secular as modernity continued to advance. (The events of 9/11 had yet to force a public reconsideration of the secularisation thesis—that societies secularise as they modernise.) By contrast, here was India, still mired in rituals carried out regardless of the degree of inconvenience to the pious. Many Australians were unable to relate to the deep religiosity that drew such immense numbers to the *sangam* to bathe in 'water unfit for humans' (Kremmer 2001b:11). This was perhaps best critiqued by sardonic cartoonist Michael Leunig's sketch of three Aussie couch potatoes, eyes agog, in front of a television, with one viewer reflecting that 'we call our television "Ganges" because we immerse ourselves in it and are saved' (Leunig 2001). Leunig's cartoon suggested that in late Western modernity television had been substituted for religion as an opiate of the masses and that any civilisational smugness was premature.

* * *

Mass-mediated photographic representations of the Kumbh Mela as a quaint religious observance performed by 'unmodern, superstitious and irrational' Indians serve only to reinforce global relationships and of cultural dominance. And that is gratifying to a Western audience. If this sounds far-fetched, compare this with media coverage that reveals a sense of discomfort with India's rising economic and military power: 'India Jumps Queue' (2004) in a large, angry font, on the Indo-US nuclear deal; and the indignant front-pager in the *Daily Telegraph*, 'Where Our Jobs Went: The Indian Call Centres Undercutting Our Workers' (McIlveen 2006). Former Prime Minister John Howard repeatedly framed his refusal to sign the

Kyoto protocol in terms that it was 'unfair', because it would not 'impose the obligations it would have imposed on Australia on countries like China and India' (PM: Kyoto Won't Work 2006).[8] Such headlines reveal a sense that India is transgressing its 'rightful' place in the global economy and in geo-strategic politics, or rather, the subordinate place it has occupied since the early modern era. This is what Thomas Friedman (2005) meant when he declared that the world was becoming 'flat', after centuries of Western hegemony and exploitation of underdeveloped regions.

While I share many of the concerns of Friedman's critics, including that global equality is likely to remain elusive for some time, media coverage such as this would suggest that Australia is ill-prepared for a future in which India has a determining role in the world. The breadth of India-knowledge for the average Australian is lamentably narrow, despite a very long history of linkages and connections. There were Indians on the First Fleet in 1788 and small numbers of Indian indentured workers came to Australia in the early 1800s (Raj 2006:383). While it is true that we have a shared history through joint membership in the British Empire, the fact remains that this membership was held under very different terms—a 'white dominion' and a 'tropical dependency' respectively.[9] This point is most spectacularly demonstrated by the fact that India went through a protracted and sometimes violent struggle for independence in the early part of the 20th century, whereas Australians in a 1999 referendum still maintained the role of the British monarch as their Head of State.

Nor were postcolonial politics and global currents particularly conducive to close bilateral relations in the latter half of the 20th century, leading to a protracted period of relative disengagement and missed opportunity (Gurry 1996). The White Australia policy's infamous European language test was partially devised with English-speaking Indians in mind.[10] Cold War politics in the latter half of the 20th century saw India, while technically

---

[8] In fact, greenhouse gas emissions *per capita* are much higher in Australia; in terms of tonnes per capita, Australia is fourth highest in the world, whereas India ranks as 140th. This is not to deny that India faces an environmental challenge, but it does point out problems with Howard's argument; it is an argument that no India-savvy Australian would accept.

[9] An exhibition held at the Museum of Sydney in 2003 drew public attention to some of these forgotten linkages (see its catalogue (Broadbent, Rickard & Steven 2003)). Historians are beginning to explore these connections in more depth, for example Devleena Ghosh and Stephen Muecke (2007).

[10] Immigration officials policing the boundaries of White Australia could test applicants on their proficiency in any European language and thereby exclude people who had acquired fluency in English as a result of colonial connections. One of the greatest challenges to

non-aligned, sidle towards the USSR, putting it at odds with Australian alliances (Gurry 1992/93:511–512). Both India and Australia maintained degrees of economic protectionism during this period, which kept bilateral engagement to low levels.

In fact, India's relatively undeveloped, internationally disengaged economy allowed it to secure a unique place in the Western imagination as a spiritual contrast to the capitalised, globalised West. 'India was undoubtedly "consumed" by the sixties counterculture', writes social historian Julie Stephens; 'Here consumption refers to certain practices which take a cultural and social form, like travelling, participating in rituals, reading, imbibing drugs, chanting and buying artefacts' (Stephens 1998:49–50). India became a haven for 'alternative tourists', who imagined India in affirmative Orientalist terms and used it to mount a critique of Western society, which they perceived as spiritless and materialistic.[11] Other tourists, seduced by skilful marketing campaigns that capitalised on the romance of the Taj Mahal, went to India and struggled with the harsh contradictions that only a rich culture constrained within a developing economy can produce. I have personally been upbraided for the difficulties and trials faced by more than one India-returned Western tourist, who had expected spiritualism and exoticism on their sojourns and were horrified to have that fantasy interrupted by frequent interactions with those who are desperately poor, as though their single-minded concern with poverty is indicative of a flaw in Indian theologies.

Addressing stereotypes such as this in Australia can best be done through education from the earliest levels. Currently, the Australian school system is more likely to introduce students to French language, culture and history, than it is to Indian—a striking anomaly given that 'in the twenty-first century every sixth human being will be an Indian' (Varma 2004:1). Explaining in historical terms India's late development is vital if Australians are to understand and appreciate the South Asian region, with its diverse peoples and cultures. Nobody who had any knowledge of India would have supported former PM John Howard's Kyoto excuse (that Australia should not sign the Kyoto protocol, because it would place limits on Australian emissions, but not on India and China's, and that this would be 'unfair'), which suggested that Australians and Indians were on an equal economic footing. Equally prevalent ideas of 'mystical India' are partially a product

---

these racist immigration laws was the dramatic case concerning a young Indian–Fijian girl, Nancy Prasad (Tavan 2005:147–153).

[11] Two excellent unpublished Australian theses investigate this (Phipps 1990 and Matthiesson 1999).

of the fact that educational institutions, starting from schools, have been constrained from offering engaging courses on the subcontinent. Funding cuts to the humanities in particular in universities have hit South Asia specialists hard, paradoxically at a time when Australian universities have come to heavily rely on the seemingly inexhaustible market of international students to make up for funding shortfalls. With few academic specialists to draw upon (and the available academics too snowed-under with administration, teaching and research demands to intervene consistently and effectively in the public sphere), the public is susceptible to media stereotypes and wild inaccuracies.

This was not always so, at least not in the tertiary sector. The Ingleson Report into the state of Asian Studies in 1988 identified 15 out of Australia's then 19 universities which offered intensive teaching on subcontinental topics (Ingleson 1989). Most of the courses offered were focused on India, reflecting its dominance in the South Asian region. In the recent past, a student might choose from a range of what would now be derisively styled 'boutique courses' (classes with small but committed enrolments focusing on a fairly specialised area), a format of study which favoured topics of 'lesser demand'. In 1992, for example, the University of Sydney offered a large and rich program of 'Indian Subcontinent Studies', in which it was possible to study Indian languages such as Hindi, Urdu, Sanskrit or Bengali, and courses offered in the departments of History, Studies in Religion and Government gave students the contextual knowledge in which to position their language skills (see University of Sydney 1991:93–95, 193, 196, 236). The University of Melbourne had comparable offerings. Australia was a place in which research on Indian history had attained international attention; much of the early work of the Subaltern Studies Collective was based at Australian National University in Canberra, and researchers such as AL Bascham, Ravinder Kumar, DA Low, Robin Moore, Robin Jeffrey, Tom Weber and Peter Reeves achieved global recognition for their scholarship (see the Jeffrey Report (Jeffrey et al 2002:22)).

Several factors contributed to the decline of subcontinental studies in Australia from the 1990s. The end of the Cold War led to the fall in concern with, and funding to, 'Area Studies', where students had more often than not encountered Indian subjects in a range of disciplines. The so-called Dawkins Revolution, which among other things favoured faculties whose degrees were vocational and could be directly related to economic growth, was followed by over a decade of Howard government funding cuts to education. This decimated the capacity of Australian universities to teach and research in an internationally comparable or competitive fashion and it had a particularly detrimental effect on the humanities, for which alternative funding is harder to secure. The current model of tertiary education has become known by colleagues as the 'Marsupial Model'—cute, fluffy and unable to survive outside of Australia. This model favoured research over teaching, in theory, but still required intensive, primarily large class instruction of broad, generic survey-style courses. Such subjects did not favour Indian topics, which had been attracting steady enrolments since the 1960s and 1970s. As a result of these changes, in conjunction with the retirement of academics who, given the funding constraints, were not replaced with fresh scholars, the study of India in Australia contracted; even the key Go8 institutions[12] have been unable to maintain their Indian history, culture or language programs.

Then there was the 'brain drain'. Many academics, tired of endless, fruitless funding rounds and increasing administrative incursions into their research time, found the terms offered overseas much more conducive to their careers. In universities in the United States, in particular, the academic culture is more clearly focused on research, undergraduate classes focus on discrete topics and are capped at relatively low numbers, the opportunities for postgraduates are less constrained, the conference scene is vibrant and funding comparatively abundant. By 2001 only five universities taught subjects related to India and the Jeffrey Report noted in 2002 that 'if trends continue, there is a strong possibility that in five years no Australian institution will teach undergraduates specifically about South Asia' (Jeffrey 2002:23). Indian specialists are still employed in the academy, but have been appointed in and therefore teach (and feel the pressure to research in) other, broader fields.

To be sure, global economic trends have always informed demand for subjects and, given the increasingly strained funding environment, they always will. The opportunistic nature of such demands creates problems of its own as it pegs learning (and, by extension, productive relations with other countries) to the mercy of the market. In the 1990s, Japan was Australia's leading trading partner and students saw a secure future in studying Japanese. Lecturers of Japanese, while in demand, were less enthusiastic about the money-minded focus of the students they taught. This, in the past, was rarely an issue for academics teaching Indian languages, history,

---

[12] The Go8 is an Australian consortium of eight universities (of approximately 40) who form an interest group of sorts and define themselves as the nation's elite universities, primarily on the basis of research intensiveness and, to a lesser degree, comprehensiveness.

religions and culture. These lecturers faced a small but committed band of students, hippies, ashramites, the occasional missionary, but scarcely the business-minded. This also reflected the influence of Indian religions on New Age interpretations of spirituality, which had a considerable impact on the religious landscapes of the West in the closing decades of the 20th century. In 1980s and 1990s Australia, one did not study Sanskrit for three years on the basis of any sound financial calculation or on any reasonable expectation that there was a guaranteed career path as a Sanskritist, as I was told on several occasions by well-meaning friends.

In the late 1990s, in an attempt to boost falling Hindi language enrolments, advertisements were posted around the campus of my alma mater, La Trobe University.[13] The colourful poster pointed out that Hindi was the second-most spoken language in the world. This did not save it from virtual extinction at La Trobe or in other Australian universities.[14] The near extinction happened despite a 1998 government inquiry, which recommended that the Department of Employment, Education and Training 'increase funding to preserve the study of the Hindi language and eliminate the uncertainty surrounding the availability of Hindi courses in Australia' (Joint Standing Committee on Foreign Affairs, Defence and Trade 1998:Recommendation 7).

Expertise in Hindi–Urdu would have important consequences, not only for productive cultural, trade and diplomatic exchanges, but also for Australian intelligence and security. When Dr Mohammed Haneef was arrested in 2007 and run through the gauntlet of newly-created and randomly-applied Australian terrorism laws, La Trobe Hindi lecturer, Dr Peter Friedlander, was able to publicly question the Australian Federal Police's translations of Haneef's interview transcript (Friedlander 2007). This expertise added volume to the growing concerns in legal circles and, eventually, in the Australian public about the powers invested in Australian security laws as they were applied to the hapless doctor's case.

Not all of the blame for disengagement can be laid at the door of the Howard government. India was not at the forefront of the push to Asian engagement that was symptomatic of the Hawke–Keating era (1983–1996).

---

[13] The campus served as the backdrop for the graduation scene in the 2005 movie, *Salaam Namaste*. It is also worth mentioning that Indira Gandhi visited the university in 1968 on the first visit of an Indian Prime Minister to Australia.

[14] The teaching of Hindi at La Trobe University has been revived, although it remains one of only two Australian universities (the other is the Australian National University) teaching Hindi in the classroom.

At a time when India was undergoing post-liberalisation economic reform and beginning to re-enter the global economy, it was overshadowed by the spectacular economic growth of the Asian 'Tiger' economies. Commentators made snide comments about India's 'Hindu' rate of growth (based on an Orientalist understanding of what is an incredibly dynamic religion), or extended the wild animal metaphor by invoking the slow lumbering gait of the Elephant to contrast it with the voracious Tigers. Further, India was maligned internationally after the nuclear tests of 1998, in the aftermath of which the Howard government distinguished itself by exceeding the response of the United States, suspending all but humanitarian aid and breaking all ties (with the exception of trade) in a series of actions which have been justly described as 'extreme' (Vicziany 2000:163).[15] Australia continued to resist India's application to join the key regional economic forum, Asia-Pacific Economic Cooperation (APEC) and the Howard government response to the Pokhran II nuclear tests 'became an acute irritant in the relationship of the two countries' (Kaul 2002:230). The 1998 parliamentary report on the Australia–India relationship mused that 'relations were distant, but cordial and based on some shared experiences and national passions for cricket' (Joint Standing Committee on Foreign Affairs, Trade and Defence 1998).

While the cricket rationale has become a familiar refrain even in governmental circles, fans of the game know that the Australia–India cricketing relationship has been far from smooth. The 'common language' of cricket tends to be spoken in a dialect peppered with sledging and racial taunts, and this is not just one-way traffic as the controversy in the cricketing season of 2007–2008 showed, where truly sublime moments of cricket, such as Tendulkar's test century and standing ovation at the Sydney Cricket Ground on 4 January 2008, were overshadowed by ugly and shameful behaviour on the field, which led to a crisis of truly international proportions (Conn 2008; Lalor 2008).[16] India threatened to withdraw from the series; someone at the International Cricket Council did the maths, calculating that the Indian subcontinent generated about 70% the game's revenue. It was subsequently thought that it might be prudent to try to save the series from collapse by taking on board some of the Indian team's concerns. This led to yet another tabloid headline which indicates Australian unease with India's

---

[15] Vicziany further notes that it was academic intervention from a loose affiliation of Melbourne scholars that created meaningful security dialogues.

[16] For an amusing take on the cricket crisis of 2008, see Nicholson (2008).

rising clout, 'Indians hold world to ransom' (Wilson 2008), a phrase that was repeated in more in-depth reportage of the cricket crisis (Vincent 2008). In the past it was not uncommon to be stopped in the streets of India and, on discovery of one's national identity, be happily reminded of the greatness of Allan Border; not anymore.

Nor was this the first cricketing incident that has mired the relationship. Jubilant Australian cricketers committed a major faux pas in November 2006, when Damien Martyn nudged an Indian union minister and then President of the Board of Control for Cricket in India, Sharad Pawar, from the stage at the Champions Trophy award ceremony in Mumbai, leading to mass insult and a flurry of letters of apology from the Australian side. On the other hand, Brett Lee has performed exemplary work as a cultural ambassador, by singing a popular duet with Asha Bhosle, a famous Bollywood playback singer, in which he promises to 'even learn Hindi' if it will help develop their romance (Bhosle & Lee 2006). The song, 'Haan, Main Tumhara Hoon' (Yes, I'm Yours) made number 2 on Indian pop charts. Steve Waugh is also widely respected in India for his support of orphanages and charities and is known as *bhaiyya* (big brother) by those he supports in the Udayan home for children affected with leprosy (Bose 1998). Despite these great examples, the highly competitive and ultra-nationalistic nature of our cricket relationship is far too volatile to be the basis of India–Australia co-operation.

Delhi-based scholar Shanta Nedungadi Varma identifies two factors that need emphasis in the building of stronger bilateral ties: 'One is the need for positive image projection of each other by the print and audio-visual media; second, for more people to people contact through a much greater promotion of academic and cultural exchanges' (Varma 2002:265). The creation of the Australia–India Council in 1992, as a result of a Senate Committee Report on Australia–India Relations in 1990, has significantly broadened the scope for bilateral educational linkages and many distinguished Indian professors and younger scholars have come to Australia for periods of study and research. The Indian Association for the Study of Australia (IASA) has proven to be a vibrant body which hosts a biennial conference attracting scholars from all over India and Australia, supported by the Australia–India Council and the Australian High Commission in New Delhi. Importantly, Australian organisations, such as the Asia Education Foundation (AEF) and Asialink, have been working consistently at finding ways in which Indian history, culture and society can be incorporated into Australian school curricula. In late September 2007 the AEF organised a superb teachers' conference, Linking Latitudes, which took 300 schoolteachers from Australia and New

Zealand to Delhi and Agra for a series of lectures, tours and visits to a range of Indian schools (Sheridan 2007a). This is beginning to bear fruit as Australian teachers begin to apply their India experience to their practice; already there are inspiring pedagogical projects being developed which aim to educate the coming generations in India-literacy.

The Indian diaspora in Australia is growing at an incredible rate; between 1996 and 2001 the population of Indians in Australia increased by 23% and a high percentage of Indian immigrants seek citizenship (Lakha 2006:387).[17] The number of Indians living in Australia in 2004 was put at 200,000 and, in addition to this, Australia receives 40,000 Indian students into its higher education sector every year (Hugo 2004)—the numbers in 2009 were greater still. Just a few years ago, for Indians with an eye to international tertiary offerings, Australia was the second choice, behind the United States, as an education destination, because the cost of living and the exchange rate against the rupee made it relatively more affordable. However, the Great Financial Crisis has turned this around, although this factor is secondary to the crisis and controversy following the attacks on Indian students in Victoria.

On his return from Delhi in October 2007, respected foreign affairs editor of *The Australian*, Greg Sheridan, predicted, 'Like the US [does now], India will eventually shape the world we live in' (Sheridan 2007b). Of course, in the past there have been several short-lived bursts of India-enthusiasm in areas of trade, security and diplomacy; Mark Thirlwell notes that 'it has been a rule of thumb among Australian diplomats that every Australian government will "discover" India at least once in its term of office' (Thirlwell 2004:112). We need to cultivate, through education in schools and universities, an India-literate population that appreciates India's history, society and culture. Such a project will not be realised quickly or cheaply, but will minimise the chance of the next burst of India-enthusiasm faltering and Australia missing out on the opportunity to understand (and engage with) this rising world power. This is not simply about taking economic advantage of India's rise. The interconnected nature of Australia in the 21st century is such that knowledge about India has the capacity to inform issues that we should all be concerned about, from international environmental policy, the politics of nuclear weapons, and framing reasonable and effective terrorism laws.

---

[17] Salim Lakha writes that 79% of Indian residents in Australia take up citizenship, against a figure of 75% for those born elsewhere.

Works cited

Bhosle, Asha and Brett Lee 2006, 'Haan main tuhara hoon', *Asha and Friends* vol I, YouTube, www.youtube.com/watch?v=6pZuGJW08Uw, viewed 25.2.2012.

Boisvert, Mathieu 2002, Personal communication 3 July.

Bose, Saibal 1998, 'A good sport: Steve Waugh pitches for kids of leprosy patients', *Indian Express* 22 July.

Broadbent, James, Suzanne Rickard and Margaret Steven 2003, *India, China, Australia: trade and society 1788–1850*, Historic Houses Trust of NSW, Glebe, NSW.

Conn, Malcolm 2008, 'Kumble's bodyline bouncer', *The Australian* 7 January, www.theaustralian.com.au/news/sport/kumbles-bodyline-bouncer/story-e6frg7rx-1111115261499, viewed 25.2.2012.

Cumming, CF Gordon 1884, *In the Himalayas and on the Indian plains*, Chatto & Windus, London.

Dutt, Anuradha 2001, 'Greatest simulated show', *The Pioneer* 25 January.

Friedlander, Peter 2007, Interview with Jon Faine, ABC Radio 774, 1 August.

Friedman, Thomas 2005, *The world is flat: a brief history of the twenty-first century*. Farrar, Straus & Giroux, New York.

Ghose, Indira 1998, *Women travellers in colonial India: the power of the female gaze*, Oxford University Press, Delhi.

Ghosh, Devleena and Stephen Muecke 2007, *Cultures of trade: Indian Ocean exchanges*, Cambridge Scholars, Newcastle.

Glenday, Craig (ed) 2007, *Guinness world records 2008*, HiT Entertainment, Barcelona.

Gurry, Meg 1992/93, 'Leadership and bilateral relations: Menzies and Nehru, Australia and India, 1949–1964', *Pacific Affairs* 65(4).

— 1996, *India: Australia's neglected neighbour? 1947–1996*, Nathan, Centre for the Advanced Study of Australia-Asia Relations, Griffith University.

Harding, Luke 2001, 'Ganges gathering tests political water', *The Age* 13 January.

Hugo, Graeme 2004, 'Recent population movements between India and Australia: trends and implications', in Gopal, D and Dennis Rumley (eds), *India and Australia: issues and opportunities*, Authorspress, New Delhi.

'India jumps queue' 2004, *The Weekend Australian* 23–24 July.

Ingleson, John 1989, *Asia in Australian higher education: report of the Inquiry into the Teaching of Asian Studies and Languages in Higher Education*, Asian Studies Council, Canberra.

Jeffrey, Robin, John FitzGerald, Kama MacLean and Tessa Morris-Suzuki 2002, *Maximising Australia's Asia knowledge: repositioning and renewal of a national asset*, ASAA, Melbourne.

Jenkins, Diana 2007, 'The smart art' *The Australian* (Smart Money Special Section) 2 June.

Joint Standing Committee on Foreign Affairs, Trade and Defence 1998, *Australia's trade relationship with India*, The Committee, Canberra, www.aph.gov.au/Parliamentary_ Business/Committees/House_of_Representatives_Committees?url=jfadt/india/reptindx.htm, viewed 25.2.2012.

Kaul, Man Mohini 2002, 'Australia–India relations: a critical survey', in Gopal, D (ed.), *Australia in the emerging global order*, Shipra, Delhi.

Kazmi, M Nikhat 2001, 'Battle lines drawn: it's media vs cops at the Kumbh', *Times of India* 21 January.

Kremmer, Christopher 2001a, 'Pilgrims progress', *The Age/SMH Good Weekend Magazine* 3 March.

— 2001b, 'Tempting fate or testing faith?', *The Age* 24 January.

'Kumbh turns into a "sangam" of Hindus, Muslims' 2001, *Times of India* 12 January.

Lakha, Salim 2006, 'Indian cultural identity in Australia', in Lal, Brij V, Peter Reeves and Rajesh Rai (eds), *The encyclopaedia of the Indian diaspora*, University of Hawaii Press, Honolulu.

Lalor, Peter 2008, 'Ugliness of racism will not go away quietly', *The Australian* 7 January, www.theaustralian.com.au/news/ugliness-of-racism-will-not-go-away-quietly/story-e6frg7mo-1111115260196, viewed 25.2.2012.

Leunig, Michael 2001, [Cartoon], *The Age* 12 January.

'Lewd charge causes a splash in the Ganges' 2001, *The Age* (Green Guide) 17 January.

Maclean, Kama 2008, *Pilgrimage and power: the Kumbh Mela in Allahabad*, Oxford University Press, New York.

Matthiesson, Josephine 1999, 'Doing the India trip: myths and paradoxes of a travel culture', MA dissertation–Department of History, University of Melbourne.

McIlveen, Luke 2006, 'Where our jobs went', *Daily Telegraph* 10 October.

Nandan, Jiwesh 2002, *Mahakumbha: a spiritual journey*, Rupa, New Delhi.

Nicholson, Peter 2008, 'It's not cricket: India v Australia', 18 January, http://media.theaustralian.news.com.au/nich/20080118_not_cricket.htm, viewed 21.1.2008.

Phipps, Peter 1990, 'The budget traveller in India: a deconstructive analysis and cultural critique', BA(Hons) dissertation–Department of History, University of Melbourne.

Pinch, William R 2006, *Warrior ascetics and Indian empires*, Cambridge University Press, London.

'PM: Kyoto won't work' 2006, SBS News Service, 31 October.

Raj, Sushma 2006, 'Australia', in Lal, Brij V, Peter Reeves and Rajesh Rai (eds), *The encyclopaedia of the Indian diaspora*, University of Hawaii Press, Honolulu.

Roy, Arindam 2001, 'Salim's holy dip', *Hindustan Times* 12 January.

Sheridan, Greg, 2007a, 'Cricket aside, the indians are coming', *The Australian* blog posting 4 October, http://blogs.theaustralian.news.com.au:80/gregsheridan/index.php/theaustralian/comments/cricket_aside_the_indians_are_coming, viewed 25.2.2012.

— 2007b, 'Powerful dash of new spice', *The Australian* blog posting 6 October, http://

blogs.theaustralian.news.com.au/gregsheridan/index.php/theaustralian/comments/powerful_dash_of_new_spice, viewed 25.2.2012.

Stephens, Julie 1998, *Anti-disciplinary protest: sixties radicalism and postmodernism*, Cambridge University Press, Melbourne.

Tavan, Gwenda 2005, *The long, slow death of White Australia*, Scribe, Carlton North, Vic.

Tewari, Vinay 2001, 'A progressive pilgrim breaks communal barriers', *Times of India* 12 January, http://timesofindia.indiatimes.com/articleshow/29562138.cms, viewed 24.2.2012.

Thirlwell, Mark 2004, *India: the next economic giant*, Lowy Institute, Sydney.

'This Kumbh's a confluence of two worlds' 2001, *Indian Express* 11 January.

'An uncultured media' [Editorial] 2001, *The NavHind Times* 2 February.

University of Sydney 1991, *Faculty of Arts handbook 1992*, Sydney.

Varma, Pavan K 2004, *Being Indian: the truth about why the 21st century will be India's*, Penguin, New Delhi.

Varma, Shanta Nedungadi 2002, 'India and Australia: towards forging a dynamic relationship', in Gopal, D (ed.), *Australia in the emerging global order*, Shipra, Delhi.

Vicziany, Marika 2000, 'Australia–India security dialogues: academic leadership in a diplomatic vacuum', in Weigold, Auriol (ed.), *Midnight to millennium: Australia–India interconnections*, published as *South Asia* 23(1).

Vincent, Michael 2008, 'Cricket tour remains in limbo', transcript of 7.30 Report. ABC TV, 8 January. www.abc.net.au/7.30/content/2007/s2134310.htm, viewed 25.2.2012.

'Who'll man my rickshaw when i take a dip?' 2001, *Times of India* 16 January.

Wilson, Rebecca 2008, 'Indians hold world to ransom', *Sunday Telegraph* 13 January.

Chapter 3

'White Already to Harvest'

South Australian Women Missionaries in India[1]

Margaret Allen

In rethinking histories of empire, scholars have turned to explore the interrelationships between the metropole and the colony. Thus Catherine Hall has written of the need to understand the ways in which 'the histories of Britain and empire have been mutually dependent'. She comments,

> It was the colonial encounter that made both colonisers and colonised, all of whom are subjects of the erstwhile British empire, sharing a common history, all post-colonial subjects, made by the relations of empire, with identities constituted through different relations to colonial and imperial hierarchies of power (Hall 1995:49).

While colonisers and colonised might be seen as subjects of the erstwhile British Empire, it is important to note differences among the ranks of the colonised. With regard to the Australian colonies, the settlers cannot be seen as being in the same relation to the metropole as Britain's colonial subjects in, for example, the Indian subcontinent. The settlers were very

---

[1] Previously published in 2000 in *Reconstructing Femininities: Colonial Intersections of Gender, Race, Religion and Class*, a special issue of *Feminist Review* 65. 'White Already to Harvest' was the name of a missionary publication associated with the Poona and India Village Mission, where some of the South Australian women missionaries were located. The title is derived from the New Testament: 'They are white ready to harvest', (John 4, v35). I play with its meaning to allow an allusion to 'whiteness'. I would like to thank Rosalind Gooden for discussing her work with me and Deane Fergie, Jane Haggis, Glenda Mather and Robin Secomb who read and commented upon an earlier version of this chapter and the anonymous reviewers for *Feminist Review* for their comments.

aware of their whiteness and of the cultural heritage they shared with the metropole.

Accordingly, Leela Gandhi has criticised the tendency of some postcolonial critics to construct an all-inclusive category of 'colonialism' which claims that

> settler societies stand in the same relationship to colonialism as those societies which have experienced the full force and violence of colonial domination...Equally, they confer a seamless and undiscriminating postcoloniality on both white settler cultures and on those indigenous peoples displaced through their encounter with these cultures...[D]isparate societies such as Bangladesh and Australia, are unified upon the somewhat dubious premise that 'their subjectivity has been constituted in part by the subordinating power of European colonialism' (Gandhi 1998:169).

While allowing for the different positions of the settlers in Australia and of Indians in British India, it is also important to note that the Australian settlers, who in some ways were colonised, must also must be seen as colonisers. As Susan Sheridan (1995:166) proposed, 'Non-Aboriginal Australia's role as coloniser as well as colonised outpost of Empire demand[s] recognition'. All these peoples within the Empire, the Indians, the British, the Aboriginal Australians and the Australian settlers can be seen as relating to one another within racialised and gendered hierarchies. While historians have focused upon relationships between some people within these hierarchies, other aspects have been ignored.

The highly privileged relationship between the Australian settlers and Britain has been the subject of innumerable works. The attempt to elaborate a separate Australian identity in relation to Britain during the later 19th century and into the 20th century has attracted the interest of scholars in a wide field of cultural and political studies. Feminist literary scholars, in particular, have explored the writing of 'the Australian girl' as she was delineated against the outline of her British cousin (Kingston 1986; Sheridan 1995; Giles 1998).

Recently, a considerable amount of work has re-visioned relationships between Aboriginal and settler women and has recognised the complicity of the latter 'in an imperialist civilising project that saw the near destruction of Australia's indigenous peoples and their language and culture' (Grimshaw et al 1994:1). Increasingly Aboriginal writers and others have researched white settler women's part in the controlling and disciplining of Aboriginal women (Huggins 1987/88; Goodall 1995). Other recent work has identified some settler women who recognised a responsibility to protect the Aboriginal people (Grimshaw 1998; Paisley 1998). A number of researchers have explored the work of settler women such as Mary Montgomery Bennett, who worked in the 1920s and 1930s to bring the exploitation of Aboriginal women to wider notice through imperial organisations such as the British Commonwealth League and the Association for the Protection of the Coloured Races (Lake 1994; Holland 1995; Paisley 1998).

However, discussions around 'the Australian girl' and settler women's relations with indigenous women have rarely extended to include relationships between the Australian settlers and other British subjects within the wider British Empire. Indeed, the relationships that existed between many in the Australian colonies of the 19th century and other extra-metropolitan parts of the British Empire have attracted little attention from historians. Exceptions to this can be found in work by Angela Woollacott (1997) and Ros Pesman (1998) who, in exploring the experiences of white Australian women travelling to Europe, discuss their encounters with non-white British subjects. As Woollacott (1997:1005) puts it, they 'participated in the racial structures of colonialism', generally by way of a fleeting encounter in a port of call, at Colombo or Bombay.

In fact, a number of Australian men and women had an enduring relationship with the peoples of the subcontinent. A web of kin networks linked officials of the British army and administration in India with many in the Australian colonies. Trade in a diverse range of goods, from tea to horses, linked Australia and the subcontinent (Kingston 1990). One interesting strand of relationships emerges from the growth of Theosophy in Australia, which saw its adherents travelling to India and Sri Lanka (formerly Ceylon) to work and study. Jill Roe (1986:27, 275ff) has commented on how these links fostered an 'historically rich Indian perspective' in Australian awareness until the 1960s.

Strong ties were also developed from the work of Australian missionaries across India. These involved not only those who went as missionaries, but also large numbers of Australian Christians who financially supported these missionaries, read of their exploits in church and missionary society publications, heard them speaking when they returned on furlough, and prayed for them and for those they sought to convert. Although it may often be assumed that Australians of the late 19th and early 20th centuries had little contact with India, it could be argued that the scores of missionary-supporting associations in Australia's towns and suburbs attest to a strong and ongoing involvement.

While there has been some research into the women's organisations that supported the missionaries (Godden 1997), there has been surprisingly little new work on the missionaries themselves (Gooden 1998). This chapter sets out to situate some Australian women missionaries to India of the late 19th and early 20th centuries within gendered and racialised hierarchies of the contemporary imperial setting. It examines some relationships between the Australian women missionaries and Indian women, before turning to an exploration of Australian colonial womanhood, largely it is as constructed in the domestic and religious novels of the South Australian writer, Matilda Evans.

'We met with real Australian hospitality in this jungly place'

In 1894, Ellen Arnold, a missionary of the South Australian Baptist Missionary Society (SABMS) left the mission station at Pubna in Bengal to go on a missionising trip in the region, accompanied by an Indian Christian woman described only as 'Nunda Lall's wife'. Taking the boat down the Itchamuti River they sought to put 'the Gospel plainly' before whomever they met. On one of these afternoons, they spent three hours in 'continual preaching and singing to a houseful of women and a verandahful of men' This was a co-operative effort: 'I sat by the door so that all could hear, and Nunda Lall's wife sat amongst the women, quietly giving explanations, by the way, to those who did not quite understand' (Arnold 1894:3). At sundown most of the people left. After a meal Ellen Arnold and her companion settled down for the night and she wrote, 'We met with real Australian hospitality in this jungly place, the people of the house turning out of their own bed to give us a chance of sleeping' (Arnold 1894:3).

This notion of 'real Australian hospitality' is curious. The house at which they were staying and receiving this hospitality was that of an Indian woman, described only as one of the first patients of Dr Laura Hope, the South Australian Baptist medical missionary. The way the hospitality was described can be seen as invoking its opposite—a cold English reserve, lacking in hospitality. This opposition would have been clearly understood by colonial readers.

The phrase occurs in a letter Arnold wrote in *Our Bond*, a missionary publication for Australian supporters of the mission. While it is necessary to read the women missionaries' home letters with their intended audience in mind, 'a consciousness of their audience clearly affected the interpretation and presentation of their work' (Rowbotham 1998:254), here is the suggestion, nevertheless, that the colonial women, the Indian and the Australian women might have developed links and understandings in opposition to the British imperial power—that they might have a shared colonial understanding of the superiority of warm hospitality.

This raises a number of fascinating questions about Australian identity in relation to the metropole, about relationships between the Indian and Australian women and about the place of Australian women as overseas missionaries. Might the colonials, the Indians and the Australians, have shared views in relation to the metropole? Would racial divisions make impossible the development of such a common identification as colonials? How might the common Christian faith of the Indian converts and the missionaries cut across racial hierarchies and intersect with the metropolitan-colonial axis? While this brief chapter cannot pursue all these issues, it will explore the Australian women's missionary vocation in the contemporary imperial setting.

Much of the recent rethinking of imperial history has focused upon relationships between the metropole and the colony and, apart from Catherine Hall's work tracing 'imperial identities' (Hall 1996a:72; 1996b) in the imperial careers of individuals like Edward John Eyre, as they moved across different imperial sites, there has been relatively little work on relations between different parts of the periphery. While missionary activity is often thought of as being carried out by missionaries from the metropole, working within its own colony, here the missionaries came from South Australia, a small colony on the edge of Empire, to intervene within another different colonial site. The South Australian colony was begun in 1836 when British settlers invaded the lands of the Kaurna people and the adjacent lands of other indigenous peoples. In the colony, often described as a 'Paradise of Dissent' because there was no established church, the Baptists were a small denomination amounting to 2.9% of the white population in 1860 and 6% in 1901 (Hilliard & Hunt 1986:145). Their smallness did not deter them from branching out into foreign missionary work.

In 1864 the South Australian Baptist Missionary Society was formed at a meeting held at the Flinders Street Baptist Church in the colony's capital city, Adelaide. Initially these supporters of missionaries confined themselves to providing financial support to 'native' preachers in Bengal, but in 1882 it was decided to send out two young women as the Society's first missionaries to East Bengal. They were to be neither connected nor auxiliary to the London-based Baptist Missionary Society (BMS); rather they were to be independent and responsible to the SABMS. Ellen Arnold and Marie Gilbert were the first two missionaries and were to undertake *zenana* work. They would seek access to the women's quarters (*zenana*) in order to convert the women secluded there.

The two young women spent their first year learning Bengali, while living in the house of George Kerry, agent for the SABMS who supervised the building of a residence for them. Once the South Australian mission house was completed at Faridpur in East Bengal, the two women moved into their missionary district. Here they worked with Indian bible-women and with the 'native' preachers, the most prominent of whom was Punchanon Biswas whose visit to South Australia in 1881 had been instrumental in Ellen Arnold's discovery of her vocation as a missionary (Arnold 1882:145).

Shortly after they were settled in their new home, Ellen Arnold had to go home for health reasons. As she recuperated, she went on a speaking tour thoughout South Australia and neighbouring colonies, recruiting more women missionaries. When she returned to Bengal in 1885, she brought four more women with her. One, Alice Pappin, was to work with the SABMS, while the other three were to establish missions in other regions of East Bengal on behalf of Baptists in other Australian colonies, (Gooden 1998:132–133). In the lore of Australian Baptist Missionary history these five women are known as the 'five barley loaves' (Redman 1982:14; Gooden 1998:134), which is a reference to Christ's miracle of feeding a multitude of people with only two fishes and five barley loaves (John 6 v9–14). The five young Christian women were seen as going forth to provide spiritual food to the multitudes in India.

The South Australian Baptist mission at Faridpur was staffed only by women missionaries until 1887, establishing a pattern of dominance by women which was repeated in the early years of the Baptist missions of other Australian colonies. Rosalind Gooden notes that, at their first missionary convention in 1888 there were 11 women and one man (Gooden, 1998:133). Between 1882 and 1913, Australian Baptist mission societies sent 54 women and only 16 men to the field. A number of Baptist women also joined faith missions, inspired by the model of the China Inland Mission. Thus Amy Parsons from Nairne in the Adelaide Hills, who spent one six-year term with the SABMS at Faridpur from 1888, later joined the Poona and Indian Village Mission (Dover 1964). Ethel Ambrose, an early medical graduate from the University of Adelaide, with her sister Lily, a nurse, joined the Poona mission in the first decade of the 20th century (Hinton 1936).

Hall's contention that 'cultural identities are always a construction, are never fixed and essential' seems particularly apt for these women who might identify themselves variously as British, English, South Australian, colonial, Australian, white, Christian and Baptist (Hall 1996a:70). A number of these Baptist women missionaries were recent immigrants to Australia from Britain. Ellen Arnold was born in Warwickshire, emigrating to South Australia only three years before she went to Bengal (Ball 1994:13). Less is known of Marie Gilbert, but she had also immigrated to Australia some years before

Arnold (Gooden 1997; Redman 1982). A number of others were born in the Australian colonies; Alice Pappin, Amy Parsons and Bertha Tuck were all South Australian born (Dover 1964; Collins 1953).

Wild colonial girls?

The category of colonial or Australian woman was contested in the late 19th and early 20th centuries. Through much Australian literature written of the period, we can read a concern about the colonial girl and woman. In comparison with her English and at times British sisters, the question was asked whether she was too forward, too precocious and too well-developed. There were anxieties, to which some writers responded that in the warmer climes young girls matured sexually too early.

The South Australian Baptist writer, Matilda Jane Evans, writing under the pseudonym Maud Jeanne Franc, published 14 novels between 1859 and 1885 set in South Australia. These domestic, religious and temperance novels, the first substantial body of fiction written in the young colony, promoted the view that it was possible to live a worthy and religious life in the colony and contested the notion that colonials were necessarily rough and degenerate. Women were represented as being particularly influential in relation to raising the religious life and morals of the community. The Baptist women missionaries would have known Evans' works, which were often given as Sunday School prizes. Evans had strong associations with the Baptist tradition. Her parents had both been members of the Rye Lane Baptist Chapel in Peckham, Surrey, where her father had been a deacon. In South Australia, she had married a Baptist minister and was later a deaconess in the North Adelaide Baptist Church.

In Evans' first and best-known novel, *Marian; Or The Light of Someone's Home* (1859), we meet the young, wild colonial girl, Bessie Burton 'flying through the room with a garland of scarlet pea-flowers wreathed around her slender little figure' (Evans ca 1925:3). It is the task of her new immigrant governess, Marian Herbert, to tame her and to mould her into a respectable young woman. But this colonial girl cannot easily be drawn to gentle pursuits. When her governess goes away, Bessie reverts to her wild life:

> Bessie was too much the romp, too wild to have the least sympathy for quiet pursuits. In her own little heart she had the greatest contempt for both work and books. It grieved her not at all to throw these on one side; she could now race Rover and Hector at her own sweet will...Or she

could go and dabble barefooted in the creek for hours together, fishing for crawfish, with morsels of meat tied to a string, and feel certain of but little rebuke (Evans ca 1925:200–201)

Here a little girl could become what is now known as a tomboy and, if unchecked, could grow up wild and unwomanly. The image of Bessie wreathed in the bright red flowers of a native plant suggests the dangers of early sexual maturity and of a lack of proper modesty.

In Evans' novels there is a fear that proper social standards will be abandoned in the colonial setting. The proper gender training of colonial girlhood is crucial. Young colonial women had to be demure and feminine and not too competent at vigorous, 'masculine' activities. In this first novel, *Marian*, it is the young governess from England, Marian Herbert, who brings respectable domesticity and Christianity to Bessie Burton and her family. But in the process, she herself becomes colonial, by her commitment to the settler colony, by her ability to do practical work and by her willingness to adapt to her circumstances. But in Evans' later novels, the peerless Christian heroines are generally colonial-born.[2] It is curious to note, however, that, while the colonial girl is represented as having a responsibility for the moral and religious tone of the young community, it is not suggested that her responsibility extend to the moral, religious and physical wellbeing of the indigenous inhabitants.

Matilda Evans' novels were deeply implicated in the colonial environment. They cannot be understood as mere colonial exotica written for the British market. Evans' works can be seen as part of a struggle to define the meaning of 'colonial' and to develop a commitment to the colony among her readers. Her loyalties were with the young colony, with the settlers and their descendants (Allen 1984).

In the picture Evans draws of colonial society, the Aboriginal people of Australia are firmly excluded. While her novels survey many aspects of pioneering life in the colony, including the establishment of farms and the building of houses and chapels, the Aboriginal people are almost never mentioned. These texts do not address the destruction of the Aboriginal people and their dispossession of the land that settlers were putting under the plough. In her representation of colonial life, discussion of the idea of prior Aboriginal ownership of the land, their cruel fate and the harsh

---

[2] In another of Evans' novels, *Golden Gifts* (1867/68), Winnie Aland is also a tomboy. Raised by her father after her mother's early death, she can ride and run like a boy and lacks any feminine skills and graces. In the course of the novel, Winnie becomes a feminine young lady.

relationships between black and white in South Australia is absent. She wrote at a time when the occupation of the land by white settlers was contested by the Aboriginal people, so the avoidance of any discussion of it must be seen as strategic (Allen 1995).

Indeed, there is only one discussion of the Aboriginal people in her writing. This appears in the novel *Golden Gifts, an Australian Tale* (1867/68). It appears that this discussion was included at the prompting of a local reviewer of an earlier work *Vermont Vale* (1863/64).[3] *Golden Gifts* is, in part, a celebration of what God has given the white settlers—their talents and the rich earth—and an entreaty for them to make the most of these gifts. Settlers are shown busily establishing farms and gardens, tilling the earth. The narrative is framed as an account of the settlers being unjustly thrust out of the Old World, but gaining their rewards in the new land. Nowhere is there any discussion of the rightfulness of their taking the land of the Aboriginal people.

In the novel there is an encounter between a settler family, the Wallaces, and a group of Aboriginal people. The Aboriginal people are represented as alien curiosities, beggars and thieves. Their humanity is questioned when the young heroine, Edith Wallace says, 'And then to think that these beings are really of one blood with us!...Does it not seem strange? They have souls; and yet how near they seem to approach the lowest order of animals' (Evans ca 1912:61). The possibility of working with the Aboriginal people is raised by Edith ('I wonder whether there is really any effort made to do them good?'), but it is quickly dismissed by her brother Harry ('I should think by their appearance that it would not be easy to make an impression on them') (Evans ca 1912:61).

There is little sense of a shared humanity with the Aboriginal people. There is no suggestion that efforts should be made to bring them to Christianity. The Aboriginal people are represented as strange creatures who wore dirty ill-kempt clothes and blankets and lived in the open, sleeping under rough bough shelters known as 'wurlies'. They stood across a great gulf from Evans' other characters, who were devoted to making warm, secure and pleasant homes, secure from the elements. The glimpse of Aboriginal life in *Golden Gifts* is revealing. It uncovers a disorder very much in contrast to the order of Evans' novels. The destitution of the Aboriginal people stands against the modest security of virtually all of her white characters. The domestic

---

[3] The anonymous reviewer wrote that 'She should put a blacky [sic] or two in her next work, and describe them as they really are' (*The South Australian Register* 17 September 1866:2). I thank Barbara Wall for sharing this reference with me.

arrangements of the Aboriginal people she describes amount to an offence against the domesticity nourished in the novels as a symbol of personal and social worth.

The Aboriginal woman in the group is represented as being inappropriately gendered and, therefore, particularly repulsive. Edith reacts with a mixture of disgust and pity. She is visibly shocked when the woman approaches her: '"A woman! can it really be?" she exclaimed, in a low tone of disgust. It was a woman, wrapped in the customary blanket' (Evans ca 1912:61). Neither Edith nor any of the other female characters in these novels think of dedicating themselves to helping the Aboriginal people or bringing them to Christianity.

This representation of Aboriginal people draws upon powerful contemporary discursive construction of Aboriginal people as an inferior race doomed to destruction (McGregor 1993). It also shows them as irrelevant to the developing settler society. However, the reasons for the South Australian Baptists turning their gaze to India rather than to mission fields closer to home also need to be understood in the context of the traditions of the BMS.

South Australian Baptist missionaries

Some accounts of the South Australian Baptist mission have emphasised how separate and independent its activities were from the BMS. Nevertheless, its conception and, indeed, its location owed much to the traditions of British Baptists' work in India. Manley (1993:17) notes, 'Australian Baptists revealed their essential "Britishness" in following Carey to India'. The Reverend Silas Mead, minister of Flinders Street Baptist Church in Adelaide can be seen as particularly central in the transmission of the Baptist missionary traditions. Called the 'father of Australian Baptist missions', he studied at the Baptist training institution, Stepney College in London, under Dr Joseph Angus, secretary of the BMS (Gooden 1994:69–70). Here he learned to revere the work of William Carey and his colleagues, who had begun the work of the BMS in Bengal in 1792. As well as beginning 'a heroic tradition' of missionary work in Bengal, Carey, who never saw any Australian Aboriginal people, denounced them as the epitome of ignorance and savagery. He wrote that they were 'poor barbarous, naked pagans as destitute of civilisation as they are of true religion' (quoted in Harris 1998:180).

Inspired by his studies to offer himself for missionary service, Silas Mead was instead appointed to the Flinders Street church in 1861, but, as he recalled later, 'really in those days it seemed very much like foreign mission work, to settle in a place so distant and unknown. It took me three months to get there'. From his first days in South Australia, Mead held prayer meetings 'seeking God's blessing on missionary efforts' (Gooden 1994:72–73). When the SABMS began its work in India, it operated in a part of Bengal adjacent to the region in which the BMS operated.

The young women missionaries were well-versed in the BMS tradition. In one of their first letters back to the South Australian Baptist Sunday Schools, Ellen Arnold and Marie Gilbert wrote:

> On Saturday last we went to Serampore, where those devoted missionaries, Cary [sic], Marshman, and Ward, lived and laboured. Perhaps you may remember that they were the first Baptist missionaries who came to India, and were amongst the very first to bring the glorious Gospel to these poor people. Although the last of them has been dead more than 45 years, their memories and work still live, and everywhere one finds traces of them (Arnold & Gilbert 1883:30).

Here it is instructive to note that Mead did not work with Aboriginal people in Australia; nor did he inspire others to work with the Aboriginal people, but rather facilitated the development of new mission fields in India and the translation there of women such as Ellen Arnold and Marie Gilbert. While the congregation at Flinders Street church gave money each year to Aboriginal missions at Point McLeay and Point Pearce, both within 90 miles of Adelaide, it appears to have has no closer involvement (Gooden 1994:729). Missions to Aboriginal people were set up throughout Australia, but it seems that Baptists did not attempt much Aboriginal work. John Harris, who has written extensively on Christian missions to Aboriginal people in Australia, has noted: 'By the middle of the nineteenth century, Australia was generally believed to be the most difficult mission field on earth, perhaps even an impossible mission field'(Harris 1998:180). He attributes this in part, to the notion of the hopelessness and inferiority of the Australian Aboriginal people. He also quotes contemporary observers who concluded that 'the gospel message was drastically counteracted by the awful example of a corrupt and brutal white society' (Harris 1998:186). These discourses of Aboriginal inferiority, which were highly apposite for those taking Aboriginal land, were pervasive and, as has been shown, were circulated by writers who were accessible to the women missionaries.

Like Edith Wallace in *Golden Gifts*, the young Baptist women missionaries appear not to have concerned themselves with the Aboriginal people, who were so close at hand. Rather they were much more able to perceive Indian women as women with souls that needed to be saved and as oppressed women who needed uplifting. In this venture they joined a great movement of British and American women, feminists and other reformers to save the women of India (Burton 1994; Jayawardena 1995). The missionary women wrote back to the South Australian Baptist community regularly about their Indian mission. Although their letters were often addressed to the Sunday School children of South Australia, they appeared in the South Australian Baptist publication *Truth and Progress*, where they could also be read by adult members of the Baptist congregations. In some of their first letters, Marie Gilbert and Ellen Arnold sought to entertain their readers with descriptions of the exotic others they encountered in Bengal. Marie Gilbert wrote of visiting a girls' school:

> I think you would be greatly amused to see the quantity of gold and silver jewelry these little girls wear, most of it being very heavy. Some had their ears pierced in five or six places round the ear, and a large gold ring in each, many had nose rings, which looked very awkward, falling down over the mouth...I must tell you how the Bengali women and girls dress. They have a long strip of white muslin, about 1 1/4 yards wide, and edged with a coloured border. This garment, called, a sarree, they wrap gracefully around themselves, so as to form a skirt. One end is brought across the chest and over the head, forming a substitute for a hood and shawl (Gilbert 1883:56).

These accounts were shaped liked a travel commentary, implicit in which was the notion of normality at home and the difference of India. The homes and domestic arrangements, such as those in the *zenana*, were represented as strange and amounting to incarceration (Grewal 1996:5).

> Each lady has her own little cell, where she and her children live, never going outside of the court, except under close cover, and only then to visit a relation, which is very seldom. They do not know what a street in Calcutta is like. Their only occupations are to prepare their husbands' food and mind the children; still, they seem very contented (Gilbert 1883:56).

Despite the strangeness, the women were usually represented in a relatively positive, albeit patronising manner: 'After a few minutes a young interesting lady about fifteen came in. She looked very contented and cheerful. She had been married five years' (Gilbert 1883:56).

It is interesting to note the lack of condemnation of child marriage here. This may have been because the letters were addressed to Sunday School children and it may have been thought improper to raise the evils of child marriage with that audience. In any case, the avoidance of the subject was in marked contrast to the strong denunciations of the practice by British feminists and other reformers (Burton 1992: 145–148).

Marie Gilbert expressed a loving concern for 'our dear Bengali sisters'. In one of her early letters, Ellen Arnold writes similarly of an 'affectionate girl', 'a lively, active individual', and of one of the native *zenana* teachers as 'a pleasant little body' (Arnold 1883:67). The Indian women were not necessarily seen as equal to white women, but were represented in a more positive manner than indigenous women of Australia were.

Conclusion

These missionaries' greater interest in the souls of Indian women, rather than those of indigenous Australian women can be understood in the light of contemporary Darwinian discourses and racist hierarchies, which placed Australian Aboriginal people in a position infinitely inferior to that occupied by the Indians, who were recognised as being in possession of a civilisation. In engaging in the missionary field in India, however, the missionary women may also be seen as negotiating their own positioning within imperial hierarchies. Angela Woollacott has commented on the position of Australian settler women in the imperial hierarchy of the later 19th and early 20th centuries: 'Occupying an in-between ranking in imperial hierarchy, Australian women sought to elide the inferiority inherent in their colonialness by emphasizing their whiteness and their economic and cultural privileging' (Woollacott 1997:1006).

The woman missionaries were particularly influenced by the broader Baptist tradition, which defined missionary activity as activity carried on in places like India. It might be asked how much their missionary activity was related to the desire to show themselves worthy in the larger imperial framework? While Evans sought to write of the colonial settler woman as a worthy Christian woman, the women missionaries were enacting that on a larger stage, that of the British Empire. There is no evidence that the Australian and Indian women drew together as colonials; rather the Australian women missionaries' desire to bring India's women to Christ may be implicated in a wish to constitute Australian women as 'big sisters' and 'mothers', in much the same way as Indian women were 'little sisters' or young children for the English missionaries (Tinkler 1998:221). Through their missionary work the Australian women were affirming the gender and race hierarchies of the British Empire.

Works cited

Allen, Margaret 1984, 'Domestic ideology and Maud Jeanne Franc', in Women and Labour Publications Collective, *All her labours* vol 1, Hale & Iremonger, Sydney.

— 1995, 'The ideological work of "terra nullius": the work of Matilda Evans', unpublished paper.

Arnold, Ellen 1882, *Truth and Progress* 1 December.

— 1883, *Truth and Progress* 1 June.

— 1894, *Our Bond* 10 September.

Arnold, Ellen and Marie Gilbert 1883, Letter, *Truth and Progress* 1 March.

Ball, Gerald, 1994, 'Arnold, Ellen', in Dickey, Brian (ed), *Australian dictionary of evangelical biography*, Evangelical History Association, Sydney.

Burton, Antoinette 1992, 'The white woman's burden: British feminists and "the Indian woman", 1865–1915', in Chaudhuri, Nupur and Margaret Strobel (eds), *Western Women and Imperialism: Complicity and Resistance*, Indiana University Press, Bloomington.

— 1994, *The burdens of history. British feminists, Indian women, and imperial culture, 1865–1915*, University of North Carolina Press, Chapel Hill.

Collins, GE 1953, *Christ's ambassador: India's friend*, Australian Baptist Foreign Mission, Melbourne.

Dover, Irene 1964, *Pathway through India: the life of Amy Parsons, pioneer*, Poona and India Village Mission, Bombay.

Evans, Matilda Jane ca 1912, *Golden gifts, an Australian tale*, Sampson Low, Marston & Co., London. (Originally published in the *Kapunda Herald*, May 1867–March 1868.)

— ca 1914, *Vermont Vale, or, home pictures in Australia*, Sampson Low, Marston & Co., London. (Originally published in *The Australian Evangelist*, August 1863–July 1864.)

— ca 1925, *Marian, or, the light of some-one's home*, Sampson Low, Marston & Co., London. (Originally published in four parts by Alfred Waddy, Mt Barker, in 1859.)

Gandhi, Leela 1998, *Postcolonial theory: a critical introduction*, Allen & Unwin, Sydney.

Gilbert, Marie 1883, *Truth and Progress* 1 May.

Giles, Fiona 1998, *Too far everywhere: the romantic heroine in nineteenth-century Australia*, University of Queensland Press, St Lucia.

Godden, Judith 1997, 'Containment and control: Presbyterian Women and the missionary impulse in New South Wales', *Women's History Review* 6(1).

Goodall, Heather 1995, '"Assimilation begins in the home": the state and Aboriginal women's work as mothers in New South Wales, 1900s to 1960s', in McGrath, Ann, Kay Saunders and Jackie Huggins (eds), *Aboriginal workers*, special issue of *Labour History* 69.

Gooden, Rosalind 1994, 'Silas Mead, Baptist missions motivator', *Our Yesterdays* 2.

— 1997, 'Awakened women: initial formative influences on Australian Baptist Women in overseas mission, 1864–1913', MTheology thesis, Melbourne College of Divinity.

— 1998, '"We trust them to establish the work": significant roles of early Australian Baptist women in overseas mission, 1864–1913', in Hutchinson, Mark and Geoff Treloar (eds), *This gospel shall be preached: essays on the Australian contribution to world mission*, Centre for the Study of Australian Christianity, Sydney.

Grewal, Inderpal 1996, *Home and harem: nation, gender, empire, and the cultures of travel*, Duke University Press, Durham, NC.

Grimshaw, Patricia 1998, 'Gender, citizenship and race on the Woman's Christian Temperance Union of Australia, 1890–1930s', *Australian Feminist Studies* 13(28).

Grimshaw, Patricia, Marilyn Lake, Ann McGrath and Marian Quartly 1994, *Creating a nation*, Penguin, Melbourne.

Hall, Catherine 1995, 'Gender politics and imperial politics: rethinking the histories of empire', in Shepherd Verene, Bridget Brereton and Barbara Bailey (eds), *Engendering history: Caribbean women in historical perspective*, James Currey Publishers and Ian Randle Publishers, London.

— 1996a, 'Histories, empires and the post-colonial moment', in Chambers, Iain and Lidia Curti (eds), *The post-colonial question: common skies, divided horizons*, Routledge, London.

— 1996b, 'Imperial man: Edward Eyre in Australasia and the West Indies', in Schwarz, Bill (ed), *The expansion of England race, ethnicity and cultural history*, Routledge, London.

Harris, John 1998, 'No moving in the tops of the mulberry trees: Australia as a difficult place to do mission', in Hutchinson, Mark and Geoff Treloar (eds), *This gospel shall be preached: essays on the Australian contribution to world mission*, Centre for the Study of Australian Christianity, Sydney.

Hilliard, David and Arnold D Hunt 1986, 'Religion', in Richards, Eric (ed), *The Flinders history of South Australia social history*, Wakefield Press, Adelaide.

Hinton, Mrs WH 1936, *Ethel Ambrose: pioneer medical missionary*, Marshall, Morgan and Scott, London.

Holland, Alison 1995, 'Feminism, colonialism and Aboriginal workers: an anti-slavery crusade', in McGrath, Ann, Kay Saunders and Jackie Huggins (eds), *Aboriginal workers*, special issue of *Labour History* 69.

Huggins, Jackie 1987/88, '"Firing on in the mind": Aboriginal women domestic servants in the inter-war years', *Hecate* 13.2 (1987–1988): 5–23.

Jayawardena, Kumari 1995, *The white woman's other burden: western women and South Asia during British rule*, Routledge, New York.

Kingston, Beverley 1986, 'The lady and the Australian girl: some thoughts on nationalism and class', in Grieve, Norma and Ailsa Burns (eds), *Australian women: new feminist perspectives*, Oxford University Press, Melbourne.

Kingston, Beverley 1990, 'The taste of India', in Walker, David (ed), *Australian perceptions of Asia* (Australian Cultural History 9), School of History, University of New South Wales, Sydney.

Lake, Marilyn 1994, 'Between Old World "barbarism" and Stone Age "primitivism": the double difference of the White Australian feminist', in Grieve, Norma and Ailsa Burns (eds), *Australian women: contemporary feminist thought*, Oxford University Press, Melbourne.

Manley, Ken 1993, 'Our heroic Carey and Australian Baptists', *Our Yesterdays* 1.

McGregor, Russell 1993, 'The doomed race: a scientific axiom of the late nineteenth century', *Australian Journal of Politics and History* 39(1).

Paisley, Fiona 1998, 'Citizens of their world: Australian feminism and indigenous rights in the international context, 1920s and 1930s', *Feminist Review* 58.

Pesman, Ros 1998, 'Australian women encounter the East; the boat stops at Colombo', *Journal of the Royal Australian Historical Society* 84(1).

Redman, Jess 1982, *The lights shines on: a story of one hundred years of Australian Baptist mission work*, Australian Baptist Mission Society, Melbourne.

Roe, Jill 1986, *Beyond belief: Theosophy in Australia, 1879–1939*, University of New South Wales Press, Sydney.

Rowbotham, Judith 1998, '"Hear an Indian sister's plea": reporting the work of 19th-century British female missionaries', *Women's Studies International Forum* 21(3).

Sheridan, Susan 1995, *Along the faultlines: sex, race and nation in Australian women's writing, 1880s–1930s*, Allen & Unwin, Sydney.

Tinkler, Penny 1998, 'Introduction', *Women's Studies International Forum* 21(3).

Woollacott, Angela 1997, '"All this is the Empire, I told myself": Australian women's voyages "Home" and the articulation of colonial whitemess', *American Historical Review* 102(4)

Chapter 4

Almost Forgotten, if Not Unknown

Australian and Indian Capital Connections

Christopher Vernon

Australia has long recognised Walter Burley Griffin as the American who designed its federal capital city, Canberra. More recently, it has begun to acknowledge Marion Mahony Griffin as the capital's co-designer. Walter's wife and professional partner, Marion Griffin was an architect and graphic artist in her own right. Today they are popularly known by their first names and collectively as 'the Griffins'. Almost forgotten, if not unknown, is that the duo's remarkable careers culminated in the 1930s with a flourishing practice in India.[1] Even more surprising for some is to learn that one of Canberra's designers is buried there. How these former protégés of Frank Lloyd Wright came to practice in India is a saga that, as Rosie Llewellyn-Jones (2000:177) put it, 'began in hope, but ended in tragedy'. Today, as India's ever-burgeoning economy continues to transform the face of the subcontinent's landscape, it is timely to revisit the couple's little known Indian swansong—and its imperiled legacy.

The journey that led the Griffins to India began with their 1912 victory in the international design competition for Canberra. As a point-of-beginning then, an overview of their entry's symbolic content offers a contextual backdrop against which to consider these Americans' trans-hemispherical movements, first to Australia and then to India. It also reveals resonance between Canberra and its immediate successor—and to

---

[1] To date, Kruty and Sprague (1997) is the only study to focus exclusively upon Walter and Marion Griffin's practice in India. Information on the couple's Indian projects can also be found in Johnson (1977) and Turnbull and Navaretti (1998).

some degree, heir—New Delhi, and illustrates the unevenness of Great Britain's imperial project.

Canberra's origins can be traced to 1901, when six of Britain's antipodean colonies federated to form the Commonwealth of Australia. Unlike India's then imperial circumstance, Federation was initiated from within by Australians themselves. Though the new nation's forces were still serving the British Empire in the South African Anglo-Boer war, ambition to build a national capital quickly arose from this ethos of political reconfiguration. However, ongoing rivalry between the Commonwealth's two largest cities, Sydney and Melbourne, compelled it to construct a capital *de novo*. Having adopted American precedent, the Australian Constitution required the city be positioned within its own federal territory, not in one of the six states. Seven contested years later, in 1908, an inland district in the state of New South Wales was selected. Next, the Commonwealth surveyor was instructed to determine the city's specific site from a 'scenic standpoint, with a view to securing picturesqueness, and with the object of beautification' (Minister for Home Affairs 1908). As these qualifications suggest, the capital building enterprise was as much a landscape design proposition as it was an architectural or engineering concern. In 1909, the surveyor selected a largely pastoral site within the broad valley of the Molongolo River as meeting these criteria. With the future capital's site now fixed, the new nation was ready to contemplate the design of the city itself.

In April 1911 Australia idealistically launched a competition to secure a city plan. Controversy quickly followed. The government's decision that a layman—the Minister of Home Affairs—would have final adjudication authority sparked professional outcry and led the Royal Institute of British Architects to censure its members' participation. Despite the furore, and to the surprise of many, Australia self-confidently proceeded with the contest, a choice that also attracted professional ire. For instance, believing the competition 'antagonistic to imperialistic ideals', Britain's *Town Planning Review* complained:

> to ignore the advice of a Royal Society like the Institute of British Architects, which numbers amongst its members not only the more eminent of the Australian architects, but also the best brains of the mother country, was hardly what one would have expected (Abercrombie 1912:165).

By contrast, the decision to commission Herbert Baker and Edwin Lutyens to design New Delhi would be made autocratically.

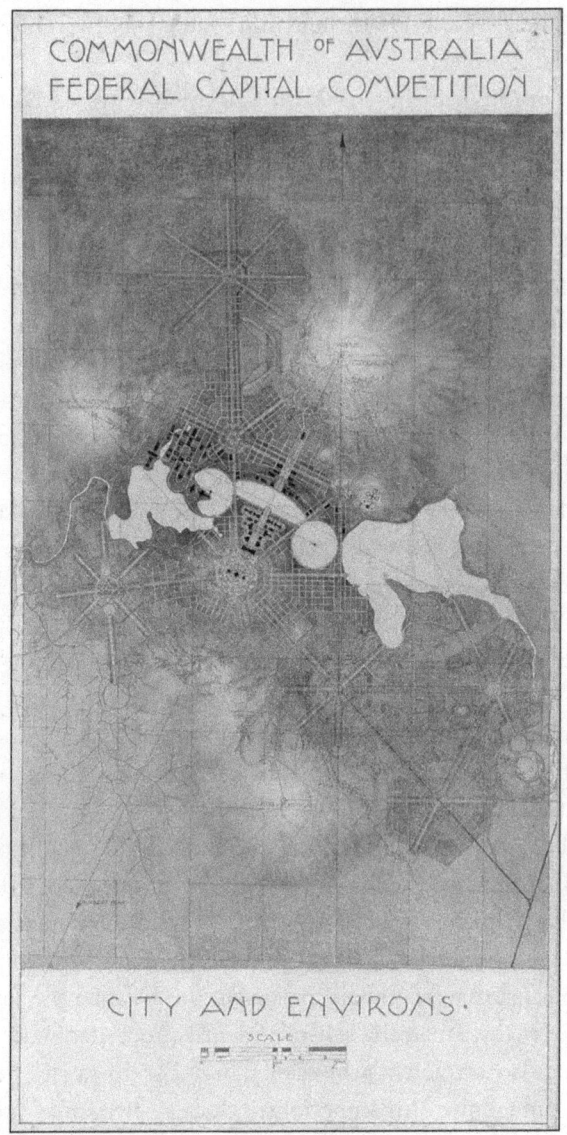

Figure 1. Walter and Marion Griffin's prize-winning Plan of Australia's Federal Capital City, Canberra, 1911
Courtesy: National Archives of Australia

In December 1911, a world away in the Griffins' native Chicago, Marion concentrated her creative energies to produce a remarkable ensemble of drawings representing the vision she and her husband shared for Australia's capital. That same month, further east across the globe, King

Emperor George V announced the transfer of India's seat of government from Calcutta (now Kolkata) to Delhi. For *The Chicago Tribune*, the newly-crowned Emperor's announcement was a 'wonderfully sagacious and totally unexpected proclamation' (Shift to Delhi 1911; see also George Crowned Emperor 1911).

Although designed collaboratively with Marion, the plan for Canberra was submitted in Walter's name, and in May 1912 Walter Burley Griffin was selected the winner. The Griffins' entry was distinguished by its sensitive response to the site's physical features, especially its rugged landforms and watercourse.[2] This attribute proved paramount to their design's success. Organised on a cross-axial scheme, the plan fused geometric reason with picturesque naturalism. When negotiating the fit of their geometric template with the actual site, the couple opted to venerate existing landforms. Hills, for instance, were not design impediments to be erased, but 'opportunities to be made the most of' (Griffin 1912: 9). Discerning a linear correspondence between the summits of four local mounts, the couple inscribed and accentuated the alignment with a 'land axis' (Griffin 1912:10). Anchored by Mount Ainslie at one end, the land axis extends some 25 kilometres to its other terminus, Mount Bimberi. By using its topographical features as axial determinants and visual foci, the Griffins sacralised the future city's site. The Molongolo River valley posed no less a design opportunity for the pair than did the site's landforms. Accordingly, they delineated a 'water axis' (Griffin 1912:10) across its land counterpart at a right angle, aligning it with the river course; in turn, the Griffins reconfigured the river to form a continuous chain of basins and lakes.

Enlarging their cross-axial geometry, the Griffins composed the city centre as a triangle, aligning its points with local summits. Concentrated within the triangle, public edifices are distributed in accordance with a systematic, topographically articulated political symbolism (Weirick 1988). Near the triangle's base, national cultural institutions line the northern margin of the central basin. At the triangle's northwest point, a hill became the nodal focus of the municipal centre. Another summit punctuates the triangle's northeast point, becoming the city's market centre. Collectively, the two centres and cultural institutions represent the people. Across the ornamental waters at the basin's southern edge, an area gently rising to the triangle's apex becomes the government centre. The judiciary, legislative and other departmental buildings are positioned at the foot of the hill,

---

[2] For more on the Griffins' Canberra plan, see Vernon (2006).

near the water's edge. Ascending towards the triangle's apex, one next encounters the Houses of Parliament midway up the hill. The summit is symbolically occupied not by the government but by the people. Here, at the highest elevation within the city's centre, the Griffins positioned a monolithic Capitol. Unlike its American namesake, however, this one was envisaged as a commemorative building to enshrine the achievements of Australian citizens.

Within the capital's ceremonial centre, a network of avenues radiate from the triangle's Capitol Hill apex. The hill itself is circumscribed by four concentric boulevards, named respectively Capital Circle and National, State and Australasia Circuits—physically and symbolically accentuating Capitol Hill as the epicentre of the federated nation. From this hub, the Griffins projected radial avenues or spokes named for and geographically aligned with the actual locations of each outlying state capital. Two other radials, Commonwealth and Federal Avenues, delineate the triangle's sides, and Constitution Avenue its base. Through this street configuration the Griffins spatially represented Australia's Federation. In a symbolism made legible by their names, the radial avenues gather in power from the sub-centre state capitals throughout the country and concentrate it within the national capital.

Although it occupied a geologically ancient continent, the new Australian nation lacked the cultural artefacts and other monuments typical of Old World and, by this time, even New World capitals. In compensation, the Griffins fashioned Australia's new national cultural history from its natural history, as demonstrated by the design significance they awarded the site's physical features. This approach was born of their American fascination with the natural world, if not wilderness, and the desire to conserve it within urban environments.

In excess of the competition's requirements, the Griffins also envisaged a notional architecture scheme—a palimpsest of global cultural references—for the city. Most remarkable was their unrealised Capitol. An organic extension of its hilltop setting, the building obscures the boundary between architecture and nature. Instead of the 'inevitable dome', the Capitol culminates in a stepped pinnacle or ziggurat (Griffin 1913: 68). For Walter this form expressed 'the last word of many long-lived civilizations heretofore' such as 'Egypt, Babylonia, Syria, Indo-China, East Indies, Mexico or Peru' (Griffin 1913: 68). This view reveals the role architecture was awarded within their broader symbolic program; if the city's layout monumentalised the local, then its buildings would reference the timeless global. Curiously, the couple excluded Australia's indigenous culture; the native landscape venerated in their design was *terra nullius*. Although this omission was not unusual for the times, the Griffins' silence is perplexing, given that they had a longstanding interest in indigenous cultures. It is perhaps explained by the fact that, unlike the Meso-Americans, the indigenous Australians did not make enduring monolithic architecture that could be readily adapted for the new capital's buildings. India, by contrast, would offer Baker and Lutyens indigenous traditions not only in architecture but also in garden design.

In 1913 Australia's federal capital gained a name, itself the outcome of another competition (Daley 1976). Those evocative of Britain, such as New London and Shakespeare and diverse others, were rejected in favour of Canberra. Apparently derived from an indigenous language, the new name was thought to mean 'meeting place'. This early and prominent appropriation was indicative of the new nation's self-confidence in the success of its imperial conquest. When dedicating Canberra's foundation stone that March, the Governor-General proudly revealed that the Viceroy of India had requested a reproduction of Canberra's plan; 'It is interesting to note', he continued, 'that those engaged in the building of the capital of one of the oldest of civilised countries are apparently not above accepting ideas from this, one of the youngest countries in the world' (Canberra, the New Capital 1913).

Taking up the official position of Federal Capital Director of Design and Construction, Walter, along with Marion, moved to Melbourne (then the temporary national capital) in 1914. He next began implementing the future capital's design, prioritising street layout and planting with local species. Buildings were to be constructed afterwards, carefully inserted within this template. However, Griffin's tenure proved short-lived. Political antagonisms and the financial restraints of the World War conspired against the complete realisation of the couple's design. In 1920, Walter's Canberra affiliation ended controversially with the abolition of his position. Afterwards, his singular role was usurped by a succession of advisory bodies (Reid 2002). A version of the Griffins' design was officially gazetted and enshrined in Commonwealth law in 1925, but this plan reproduced only the street layout and deleted the land-use allocations and symbolic content of the original design. Griffin's successors literally and metaphorically treated the couple's design as little more than a street map. Adding insult to injury, even the street names were mostly replaced.

These official acts of erasure, however, are of no less symbolic import than the architect's original conceptions. In his nomenclature scheme, Griffin projected an imagined Australian republic onto the Government Centre's street cartography. There, as we have seen, he ascribed thoroughfare appellations such as Federal, State and Australasia. In a dominion still closely tied to the empire, these were tellingly renamed Kings, Dominion and Empire. In another example, Griffin's Oceanic Circuit became Captain Cook Crescent. According to one government official, John Butters of the Federal Capital Advisory Committee, the new system redressed concerns that the American's names were 'not in keeping with Australian sentiment' (quoted in Roberts 1990:7). The government's alternatives evoked Australia's colonial past and powerfully asserted its imperial present and imagined future; Australia has yet to become a republic.

Despite the demoralising finish to their Canberra work, the Griffins chose to remain in Australia and by the 1930s had developed an extensive practice that included built works throughout the eastern seaboard (Turnbull & Navaretti 1998). New commissions, however, dwindled as the Great Depression escalated. In remedy, two mutual Australian friends, one then living in India, facilitated new work for the couple on the subcontinent in 1935. As an indirect result, and perhaps owing to his lingering prestige as an author of Australia's capital, the University of Lucknow solicited Walter Burley Griffin to design its new library. Earlier, around 1920, United Provinces Governor Harcourt Butler had commissioned none other than Edwin Lutyens to lay out the new university's campus and design its major buildings. For reasons that remain unclear, however, the English architect's plans were set aside. When later studying his predecessor's design, Griffin would dismiss Lutyens' plan as 'pure Roman from Letarouilly ("Edifices de Rome Moderne")' (Griffin, M 1939:44).

By September 1935, working remotely from Sydney, Griffin had dispatched a preliminary study for the library. Eschewing Lutyens' imperial aestheticism, Marion characterised Walter's scheme as 'one which looks and feels quite Indian and yet is the last word in modernism' (Griffin, M 1939:9). Impressed with the American's solution, the university cabled: 'Plans accepted, come on first boat' (Griffin, M 1939:9). Anticipating only a three-month absence, Walter took up the invitation and set sail for India that October, unaware that he would never return.

After briefly visiting Sri Lanka, Walter Burley Griffin arrived at Bombay (now Mumbai) in November 1935. Touring sites of architectural interest en route to Lucknow, he called at New Delhi and recorded his impressions of the new imperial capital in a letter home to Marion:

> 'New Delhi', which might better be called X Delhi for it is the tenth new Capital City of India in this same locality in as many centuries, two Hindu, six Muslim, two British, is the newest of the cities such as I have described, with more uniform and Roman character of buildings, and with roadways with great lawn parkways and handsome avenue trees of selected types of considerable variety, mostly unfamiliar to me. It is almost perfectly flat but planned with many monumental terminal vistas and has already attained completeness and finished elegance though there is of course much construction work going on in the business and residential sections. The long wide walk with reflecting canals and many fountains and the governmental terrace with vast stone buildings and several domes and extensive colonnades effectively massed is essentially roman even to the togas of the statues of the viceroys despite the efforts to supply local color in all the details. Except for the luxuriant verdure of the avenues however the pre-European capitals, the ruins of which extend continuously for some thirteen miles in each direction, must have been even more magnificent and certainly more imaginative and romantic, and the more ancient they are the more architecturally satisfying (Griffin, M 1939:33).

Only four circuitous sentences in extent, Griffin's account is astonishing in its brevity. Given Walter's awareness that the Viceroy and the Delhi town planning committee had studied Canberra's layout, one anticipates a lengthy rumination, if only for his absent partner's benefit. Envy of New Delhi's 'finished elegance' might explain his virtual silence. Although begun in advance of the Indian capital, Canberra remained more fully developed on paper than in reality and, as Griffin knew all too well, Australia's political commitment to its embryonic capital was tenuous. Earlier, in 1931, the *New York Times* had gone so far as to report that the 'Dream City' of Canberra might yet be 'abandoned' (Australia Likely to Abandon Capital 1931:31). Meanwhile, New Delhi was inaugurated in that very year.

In late November 1935, Walter reached Lucknow, which was then, as now, a destination far removed from the tourist path. Perhaps most notably, the city entered Western ken in 1857 as an epicentre of the First War of Indian Independence or, for the British, the Mutiny. The conflict's consequences were not exclusively political; the British victors physically and emphatically transformed Lucknow's urban fabric in the aftermath. Most prominently, the Nawabs' intricate garden palace complexes and other buildings were obliterated, replaced with deceptively bucolic parklands. Along with this new profusion of sylvan verdure, expansive axial thoroughfares were blasted through the dense, labyrinthine city. In Griffin's day and in ours, one might be tempted to appreciate Lucknow's parks and boulevards only aesthetically as benign civic 'improvements'. In reality, these vandalic urban interventions were palpable, spatial expressions of colonial power (Oldenburg 1984). In the opening decades in the 20th century, Harcourt Butler and his successors continued to remould Lucknow, faintly echoing the Empire's project to build New Delhi. By the 1930s, Butler's 'New' Lucknow had attracted provincial capital status and gained a new Legislative Assembly building emblazoned with fish heraldry usurped from the Nawabs. Griffin's arrival marked the beginning of a new chapter in Lucknow's urban evolution, although his impact would be at a far more diminutive scale.

Walter Burley Griffin grew quickly enchanted with this 'city of gardens'. In contrast to his British travel guidebook's dismissal of the city's remaining Nawabi architecture as 'degraded and barbarous' (Eastwick 1933:470), the American architect believed the buildings to be 'exquisite' and likened Lucknow's skyline to 'a perfect Arabian night's dream of white domes and minarets' (Griffin, M 1939:41–42).

Ethereally feeling 'at home', anthroposophist Walter mused to Marion, 'My physical appearance does not suggest much of the Indian, but I have a hunch that much of my architectural predilections must have come from Indian experience [in a previous life]' (Griffin, M 1939:43). Abandoning his plan for a brief stay, Walter decided instead to launch a new practice and, by June 1936, Marion had joined him to assist. After some 20 years living in the British Empire's Australian dominion, the pair now immersed themselves in an India on the road to independence.

When Walter was asked if he 'was going to follow the Indian style', Marion recounted, he laughingly answered that he was 'going to lead it' (Griffin, M 1939:18). Unlike the historicist stylism favoured by imperial architects, the couple's architecture featured bold, earth-pressing cubic masses; smooth, planar surfaces punctuated with sculptural ornament abstracted from indigenous sources. For the Griffins, such a localised modernism offered a means to distance India from its colonial past.

Figure 2. Narain Singh House, Varanasi, 1936
Courtesy: Art Institute of Chicago

Superficially resembling Art Deco, the couple's dwellings proved appealing to the emergent Muslim and Hindu elite.

Walter's work on the University of Lucknow library also led to his first private works; a number of professors commissioned him to design their own homes. Of these, the Bir Bhan Bhatia house (1936) is one of the finest dwellings the couple ever produced anywhere.

One of the very few architectural firms in Lucknow, the Griffins' new practice soon burgeoned. Surviving drawings, photographs and textual sources confirm that their Lucknow office produced more than 50 projects between November 1935 and February 1937. These ranged from private dwellings, gardens and public edifices to housing projects and suburban communities.

Perhaps most spectacularly, the Griffins also designed the layout and an extensive array of pavilions for the United Provinces Industrial and Agricultural Exhibition, hosted by Lucknow in 1937. Other important landscape architecture commissions included a new campus plan for the University of Lucknow and a garden for its library.

The latter composition featured more than 50 different tree species. Although their work was concentrated in Lucknow, they also made designs for projects in, for instance, Agra, Varanasi and Calcutta (Kolkata). Significantly, the couple employed and trained local assistants, although their identities and number remain uncertain. Nonetheless, these Indian apprentices may well have extended the Griffins' influence through their own work.

Ultimately, the Griffins' new Indian experiences, for them quite exotic, became a catalyst for professional renaissance. Tragedy, however, intervened. In February 1937, Walter succumbed to peritonitis and was buried locally in an unmarked grave. Having lingered only long enough to complete projects at hand, a bereaved Marion was back in Sydney within months, closing this remarkable episode in Lucknow's history. Soon finding life in Australia too difficult without Walter, she returned home to her family the next year. Once again in Chicago, Marion would lecture on her experiences in India, despite its grief-filled associations. Poignantly, *The Chicago Tribune* recollected in 1942, apparently erroneously, that, along with Canberra, Marion's late husband had 'contributed materially' to 'the building of New Delhi' (Wisner 1942:16).

Today in Lucknow and India more broadly, sadly, local knowledge of the Griffins is scant at best. Only in 1987 did an Australian living in Canberra relocate Walter's grave and spearhead an initiative to have it permanently marked. More broadly, as though the city's history ended in 1857, heritage esteem for Lucknow's architecture apparently does not include the 20th century within its temporal scope.

To date, most of the scholars who examined the Griffins' Indian projects did so working from Australia or America, relying primarily upon locally-held records. Collaboration with Indian scholars is the next vital step toward conclusively identifying the full extent of the Griffins' oeuvre. Local research expertise and on-site surveys, for instance, are required to determine which projects were actually built and what physical artefacts might remain. As well, a thorough investigation of Indian archival repositories may well yield documentation that not only enlarges our appreciation of known commissions but also reveals additional, heretofore unknown projects.

In the 21st century, like the 19th, Lucknow has again become a site of urban erasure. This time, however, the wounds are self-inflicted. India's accelerating economy fuels not only new construction but also demolition and clearance of the past. This phenomenon now poses an urgent, immediate threat to documenting and conserving the Griffins' built and landscape legacy. For instance, a new office and works for the Pioneer Press at Lucknow was the most substantial of the Griffins' Indian buildings to be constructed. Tragically, the Press was razed in the 1990s and replaced with a multistorey concrete tower. There is, however, a remarkable exception; astonishingly, the Bhatia house still stands—at least for the moment.

Works cited

Abercrombie, Patrick 1912, 'The federal capital for the Commonwealth of Australia', *Town Planning Review* 3(3).

'Australia likely to abandon capital; many leaders argue that the $66,000,000 "dream city" of Canberra is a failure' 1931, *New York Times* 15 March.

'Canberra, the new capital' 1913, *The Age* 13 March, http://150.theage.com.au/view_bestofarticle.asp?straction=update&inttype=1&intid=546, viewed 29.2.2012.

Daley, C 1976, 'Canberra nomenclature', in Selth, PA (ed), *Canberra collection*, Kilmore, Vic: Lowden Publishing.

Eastwick, EB 1933, *A handbook for travellers in India, Burma and Ceylon*...14th ed., John Murray, London.

'George crowned Emperor of India; Delhi is capital' 1911, *Chicago Tribune* 13 December.

Griffin, Marion Mahony 1939, *The magic of America*, Electronic ed, The Art Institute of Chicago and The New-York Historical Society, Chicago, 2007, www.artic.edu/magicofamerica/index.html, viewed 29.2.2012).

Griffin, Walter Burley 1912, 'The plans for Australia's new capital city', *American City* 7 (1).

— 1913, 'Canberra: II: the federal city site and its architectural possibilities', *Building* 13.

Johnson, Donald Leslie 1977, *The architecture of Walter Burley Griffin*, Macmillan, Melbourne.

Kruty, Paul and Paul E Sprague 1997, *Two American architects in India: Walter B Griffin and Marion M Griffin, 1935–1937*, University of Illinois School of Architecture, Urbana–Champaign, Ill.

Llewellyn-Jones, Rosie 2000, *Engaging scoundrels: true tales of old Lucknow*, Oxford University Press, New Delhi.

Minister for Home Affairs 1908, Instructions in 'Yass–Canberra Site for Federal Capital General (1908–1909) federal capital site: surrender of territory for seat of government of the Commonwealth', National Archives of Australia (NAA) (ACT): A110, FC1911/738 Part 1.

Oldenburg, V 1984, *The making of colonial Lucknow, 1856–1877*, Princeton University Press, Princeton, NJ.

Reid, P 2002, *Canberra following Griffin: a design history of Australia's national capital*, National Archives of Australia, Canberra.

Roberts, A 1990, 'Memorials in the national capital: developing a sense of national identity', *Canberra Historical Journal* 26.

'Shift to Delhi shrewd move' 1911, *Chicago Tribune* 17 December.

Turnbull, Jeff and Peter Y Navaretti 1998, *The Griffins in Australia and India: the complete works and projects of Walter Burley Griffin and Marion Mahony Griffin*, Melbourne University Press, Melbourne.

Vernon, Christopher 2006, 'Canberra: where landscape is pre-eminent', in Gordon, David (ed), *Planning twentieth century capital cities*, Routledge, London.

Weirick, J. 1988, 'The Griffins and modernism', *Transition* 24.

Wisner, Carl V 1942, 'Chicago's gift to Australia'. *Chicago Tribune* 23 April.

Chapter 5

Australia–India Cricket

A Bridge in Cultural Relations

Bernard Whimpress

There is little question that cricket in both India and Australia is the fruit of Empire. Yet, in both countries, it has become the national game. It is also a game that is playing an important bridging role between the cultures of these two nations. Australia's cricket roots are the backyard and the beach, where it is now often played with plastic bats and stumps, or with refuse containers serving as the wicket. In previous times it was the cobbled back lane or the macadamised road, the bat a piece of paling, the wickets made from half a fruit case or a kerosene tin. Six and out was an undisputed law of the game. India's cricket roots are the gully or the *maidan*. The gully could be a narrow walled lane in a big city, safe from traffic, the pitch being a road made of stone chips and coal tar; the wicket is three vertical lines painted on a wall. Mumbai's *maidan* is the most famous in the world, a parkland strip where the grass struggles to stay alive amid the constant clamour and bustle of a myriad of cricket matches which overlap each other in an atmosphere teeming with colour and excitement (Bose 1986:73–77). The cricketing cultures of the two nations are distinctive.

Australia's first main cricket contact with India in 1935–36 was shaped by the turbulence of cricket politics. The Maharaja of Patiala's Team of Australian Cricketers, an ageing side, was organised by the former Victorian and Middlesex all-rounder Frank Tarrant and led by former Australian captain Jack Ryder. The Australian Board of Control set severe conditions on the tour, the main ones being that the word 'Australia' should not be used and that no games should be designated as Test matches. The Board also insisted that Tarrant could only select players who had retired or were not required for selection in the Sheffield Shield competition.

Using who knows what authority, the Australian Board also banned Bill Woodfull, Bill Ponsford and Allan Kippax, even though they had all retired from first-class cricket so that Tarrant's selection task took six months. Mihir Bose in *A History of Indian Cricket* (2002:96) describes the process as having an element of comic opera about it, as, apart from Ryder who was 46, the team included Charlie Macartney, 49, Bert Ironmonger, 48, Ron Oxenham, 44, and Hammy Love and 'Stork' Hendry, who were both 40. Despite this the tour proved both a playing and social success with the team winning 11 and drawing nine of its 23 matches, 17 of which were first-class. Four 'Test'-style matches against All-India sides resulted in two wins apiece. At the end of the tour Ryder predicted that India would one day be a force in world cricket (Harte & Whimpress 2003:364–367; Williams 2007/8:13).

India was not a destination Lindsay Hassett's Services side desired to visit after playing five 'Victory Tests' in England in 1945. They were desperate and scheduled to return home. Instead, from late October to mid-December they were thrust into a ten-match tour of the subcontinent, under pressure from Australian External Affairs Minister Dr Bert Evatt. The tour included three unofficial Tests. Six games were drawn with the Australians winning two and losing two matches. There was more turbulence and team dissent. The tour was seen as a reward for India's war effort and aided the Red Cross and local hospitals (Harte & Whimpress 2003:389–390; Woodward 1994:74).

The Australian side included some excellent players besides Hassett himself, especially Keith Miller, Cec Pepper, Keith Carmody and Stan Sismey. Australia had the best of a drawn Test at Bombay, but the second Test at Calcutta was staged in a revolutionary atmosphere. In a provincial lead-up game between the Services side and East Zone, play took place amid a political riot with troops firing on students. The Calcutta match was drawn but the final Test in Madras saw centuries to Lala Armanath and a double century to Rusi Modi, which enabled India to win its first representative series (Bose 2002:146–147).

Armanath led India's first team to Australia in 1947–48, but the side suffered from the absence of two of its star batsmen, the original captain Vijay Merchant and Rusi Modi, as well as vice-captain Mushtaq Ali and talented fast-medium bowler Fazal Mahmood, who was based in Pakistan following Partition (Williams 2007/8:15). The Indian side opened solidly with three draws against state teams, but the rot set in after confronting

Ernie Toshack on a sticky wicket in Brisbane in the first Test. Toshack took 11/31 (5/2 and 6/29) in that game and the Australians had no difficulty in winning the series four nil with one draw. Without Merchant and Mushtaq Ali, India lacked a pair of opening batsmen. Mankad opened with Chandu Sarwate and in five Tests their partnerships were 0, 14, 2, 17, 124, 10, 6, 0, 3 and 0. They had no answer to Ray Lindwall, Miller and Bill Johnston, leaving aside Toshack.

The Indians were also in awe of Don Bradman and some players were said to be honoured if he made a century against them. He obliged with six, four in the Tests. He also reached important milestones. His 100th first-class century was posted for an Australian XI at the Sydney Cricket Ground in November 1947, and his only post-war double century (201) was made in the Adelaide Test of 1948. Bradman never played in India, but that did not prevent him attaining a god-like status. Perhaps his absence made the Indian heart grow fonder.

Tour schedules were irregular in the 1950s and 1960s. Australia's first tour to India came in October 1956 when three successive Tests were played after the English tour. The Australians also played one match on matting in Pakistan at Karachi. It was expected that India might have had the advantage after the Australians demoralising loss in England. Instead, Australia won the first match in Madras, drew the second in Bombay and won the third in Calcutta. The man who stood out for the first time as a bowler, with 23 wickets, was Richie Benaud. He would return as captain three years later.

Australia's first full tour in 1959–60 was arduous, combining five Indian Tests with three in Pakistan. India had its first win in the second Test at Kanpur where off-spinner Jasu Patel took 14/114, but Australia took the series two to one with two draws. Benaud and Alan Davidson were dominant with the ball. Overriding their success, however, was the emphasis given to the team casualties down the years. Fast bowler Gordon Rorke and opening batsman Gavin Stevens contracted hepatitis, which confirmed prejudices that India was a dangerous place to visit. Bose makes the point, however, that All India Radio brought a greater awareness of Australian cricket to India with broadcasts of the 1960–61 Australia–West Indies series running from 6 am until lunchtime (Bose 2002:233).

A third Australian tour in 1964 was again tacked on to an English tour and the matches were played at the worst time of year—in September and October. However, Indian perceptions were that Bobby Simpson's team had just won the Ashes and at least the Australians (unlike the English) always sent their strongest teams, with leading players like Miller, Lindwall, Neil

Harvey, Benaud, Davidson and Wally Grout having toured the country in the 1950s (Bose 2002:234). This three-Test series was drawn one all, Australia winning the first game at Madras, losing the second at Bombay, and drawing the third in Calcutta. India's captain, the Nawab of Pataudi, emulated his father by making a century in his first appearance against Australia in the first match.

Pataudi led India's second team to Australia 20 years after the first in 1967–68 and the result statistically was even worse, as the team lost all four matches. Simpson's retirement meant a captaincy handover to Bill Lawry midway through the series. Three of India's greatest spin bowlers, Bhagwat Chandrasekhar, Erapally Prasanna and Bishen Bedi, toured together for the first time but only Prasanna, with 25 wickets, made a real impact.

Two years later, on Lawry's Indian tour, Prasanna and Bedi were leading the home attack with 26 and 21 wickets although they were bested by Australian off-spinner Ashley Mallett who took 28 wickets. Australia won the series three to one with one draw, the last series victory for Australia on the subcontinent for 35 years, but controversies plagued the tour.

In the first Test in Bombay a riot occurred at the Brabourne Stadium. When a decision was given against all-rounder Srinivasaraghavan Venkataraghavan (Venkat) in the second innings, hessian surrounding the tennis courts behind the East Stand was set on fire, but skipper Lawry insisted that play go on. It did, with bottles and chairs being thrown onto the ground. On the fourth day at Calcutta in the fourth Test a riot occurred during the morning over a shortage of seats and six people were killed. The match ended in mayhem and stones were thrown as Lawry hit the winning runs the crowd threw stones. In running off the field Lawry was alleged to have beaten a photographer when, in fact, he pushed him away and he fell. Disturbances also continued late on the fourth day of the final Test in Madras, with broken bottles, chairs and bricks being thrown onto the field. Play ended with small fires raging around the ground as the home side collapsed (Bose 2002:246–247; Beecher 1970:45, 47).

Australia–India series bookended the Packer interregnum. Forty-one-year-old Simpson returned to Test cricket after a ten-year break, making over 500 runs and leading Australia to win by three matches to two in the 1977–78 home series. Sunil Gavaskar made three second-innings hundreds in the first three Tests, but Bedi and Chandrasekhar proved an even greater menace with 59 wickets between them. Kim Hughes took the last full tour to India in September and October 1979, but although he and Allan Border scored 500 runs, Australia lost the six-Test series in which India won two

Tests with other four drawn. Gundappa Viswanath also made 500 runs for India and Dilip Doshi took 27 wickets in his debut series.

India drew a series in Australia for the first time in 1980–81, ending the series with one win, one loss and a draw. After losing the first Test in Sydney by an innings, it fought hard to secure a draw in Adelaide and snatched victory in Melbourne where Kapil Dev's 5/28 bundled Australia out for 83, chasing 143. On this tour India competed for the first time in the triangular World Series Cup, which also involved New Zealand. Kapil, along with England's Ian Botham, Pakistan's Imran Khan and New Zealand's Richard Hadlee, was one of the four great all-rounders of the 1980s. He also captained India to its surprise win over the West Indies in the 1983 World Cup, which established India's place on the world cricket map more than any other match.

The proliferation of one-day cricket, in addition to Test matches, in the 1980s strengthened Australian ties with India. Australian Test cricket reached its nadir in the middle of the decade. Around this time, it contested two drawn series against India—three draws in Australia in 1985–86, and two draws and a second fabulous tied Test match at Madras the following summer. Dean Jones' heroic 210 in 503 minutes in the Madras Test match was one of the greatest Test innings ever and the game, which was not broadcast on Australian television, has grown in stature with the passing of time. Off-spinner Greg Matthews gained a leg-before-wicket (lbw) decision against Maninder Singh with the penultimate ball of the final over to emulate the result against the West Indies at Brisbane in 1960. Australia had reached its highest score in India of 7–574 declared in the first innings, with David Boon and captain Allan Border adding centuries to that by Jones. In reply, Indian captain Kapil Dev top-scored with 100 out of 397 before Australia declared for a second time at 5–170, setting India 348 runs to win at the start of the final day. An explosive start by Sunil Gavaskar saw India to 1–158 and, at 6–331, they appeared to be in control. However, the Australians fought back and Matthews with 10/249 (5/103 and 5/146) achieved the only five-wicket analysis of his career. Gavaskar also became the first player to make 100 consecutive Test appearances during the game.

The real boon to Australian appreciation of India came via television with the World Cup co-hosted with Pakistan in October and November 1987. Australia entered the competition with modest expectations but won an important opening match against India at Madras by one run. Victories against Zimbabwe and New Zealand followed, but Australia lost a return match to India before beating New Zealand and Zimbabwe a second time.

By this stage, the Australians had reached the semifinals, in which they downed Pakistan at Lahore. Australia's victory over England in the final at Calcutta by seven runs marked the team's resurgence. It was noteworthy that the Indians adopted the Australians as the home team and that India and Pakistan together organised an excellent World Cup.

Allan Border's team inflicted a heavy defeat on India in 1991–92. Mohammed Azharrudin's party lost four matches and drew one, although there were some bright spots. At Sydney the Australians selected Shane Warne for his first Test appearance, but he made heavy weather of it as Ravi Shastri made a double century and 18-year-old Sachin Tendulkar made 100 in the first of his many battles with Warne. Craig McDermott was the main match-winner for Australia, taking 31 wickets in the series.

India's fascination with the shorter form of the game meant that no Test matches were played until a single Test at Delhi in October 1997, although the main purpose of the tour was the Titan Cup, a triangular series with South Africa as the third participant. Twenty months before, India had co-hosted the sixth World Cup with Pakistan and Sri Lanka and the series was watched avidly in Australia as their side won five out of six games in India before losing the final to Sri Lanka in Lahore. The event was managed with commercial savvy that had no precedent, so that the two organisers who underwrote the costs, India and Pakistan, ended up making profits of near $US50 million.

Cricket contact with India came thick and fast for the rest of the decade. In 1998 Mark Taylor's Australian team lost Test matches at Chennai (Madras) and Kolkata (Calcutta) but won the final Test at Bangalore. The series provided a duel between Tendulkar and Warne, which was won by the batsman who scored over 400 runs at an average of 111. Two limited-over competitions for Pepsi and Coca-Cola Cups followed. Led by Steve Waugh, the Australians defeated India in the final of the first and lost the second final in Sharjah.

Either Waugh or Warne might have become Australian Test Captain in 1999. Both had strong leadership skills, but Waugh had greater cultural sensitivity and the contrast was perhaps best revealed with respect to India. Warne packed his bag with baked beans for the tour of the subcontinent in 1998; on the same tour a letter was placed under Waugh's door during a cricket Test in Calcutta asking for help with charities which had as its outcome Waugh's continual involvement with a children's leprosy home in Udayan. Warne had another Indian connection which the Australian Cricket Board (ACB) and the International Cricket Council (ICC) thought best to suppress. This concerned 'John' the bookmaker, who paid Warne $5,000 and Mark Waugh $6,000 for supposedly innocent information about weather reports and the state of the pitch for matches in Pakistan in 1994. Although Warne and Mark Waugh were fined by the ACB, this sleazy business was not exposed until December 1998 and it was not until then that a public apology by both players for being 'naïve and stupid' was made. Warne's card as captaincy material had been marked.

Steve Waugh was captain in 1999–2000 when Australia swept to a three to nil Test success and his team maintained the momentum by winning nine games in a row in the triangular series in which Pakistan was the third side. In February 2001 Waugh's team reached 16 consecutive Test wins at Mumbai, but were stopped in their tracks after a fantastic fightback by India at Kolkata. A record fifth-wicket partnership of 376 by VVS. Laxman and Rahul Dravid enabled Harbhajan Singh to spin India to victory. Harbhajan gathered 13 wickets in the game and a further 15 in the final Test at Chennai for a phenomenal 32 wickets in three games. For the losers, opening batsman Matthew Hayden re-established his Test career with over 500 runs at a century average.

Steve Waugh ended his Test career at Sydney in January 2004 with a drawn series against India. The first and last Tests at Brisbane and Sydney were drawn; India won in Adelaide after a second 300-run partnership between Laxman and Dravid, and Australia won in Melbourne. The home side was without Glenn McGrath and Warne and, as a result, bat dominated ball; Ricky Ponting and Dravid each averaged over 100.

Australia finally found fulfilment in India in October and November 2004. With captain Ponting at home nursing a broken thumb, the side broke through under Adam Gilchrist's leadership with wins at Bangalore and Nagpur and a draw at Chennai. Ponting then arrived to make victory speeches before losing on a spinner's wicket at Mumbai. Damien Martyn was instrumental in the result, with his century at Chennai denying India a win and that at Nagpur setting up the victory. Anil Kumble and Harbhajan Singh were the dominant spin bowlers with 48 wickets between them, while Jason Gillespie took 20 wickets for the visitors.

India's economic power began to grow in the 1990s, especially in the information technology industry, and there are strong educational links with Australian universities offering a wide range of courses for Indian postgraduate students. The 2007–8 Test tour of Australia was billed as the 'New Ashes' (Morrissey 2008), beyond which one can foresee thousands of India's middle class coming to support their teams in the future, as the

Barmy Army has supported England in the recent past. Ponting's team equalled the performance of Steve Waugh's Australian side of 16 successive wins following an easy victory at Melbourne and a controversial win in Sydney during the 2007–8 tour.

Disputes raised during the Sydney Test bore some resemblance to those in the Ashes series of 1932–33. By 1932 Australia had been an independent nation for 31 years and felt it had thrown off its colonial status. In the Adelaide Test of 1933 the Australian Board of Control for Cricket raised English ire by sending a telegram to the Marylebone Cricket Club describing the tourists' bodyline tactics as 'unsportsmanlike'. English captain Douglas Jardine threatened to end the tour unless an apology was made. The Sydney Test disputes of 2008 were twofold; they related first to poor decisions made by umpires Steve Bucknor and Mark Benson, and second to the conviction, and suspension for three Tests, of Harbhajan Singh on circumstantial evidence for racial abuse for calling Andrew Symonds a 'big monkey'.

The first issue brought to a head complaints about the Australians' persistent appealing of umpires' decisions over several years and the consequent mental disintegration of the umpires. India, an independent nation for 61 years, raised its protest against the Australian manner of winning. The second issue revealed the flaws in administrative law when match referee Mike Procter took the word of three Australian players (two white and one black) against three 'coloured' Indians. As one Bangalore blogger remarked, this was unsatisfactory given that the adjudicator was raised in apartheid South Africa. The common person's defence of Australia's on-field hegemony was to complain that Indian purse strings control the off-field world game, a reality that world cricket must increasingly deal with. In some respects it was ironic that the Australians laid a charge on racial grounds, because they had provided their opponents with the strongest verbal onslaughts during the previous decade. Overt on-field racism had not been evident in Australia–India encounters in the past, although Symonds became the target of off-field racism, including monkey chants, during one-day international matches at Vadodara and Mumbai in India in October 2007. ICC chief executive, Malcolm Speed, had then moved swiftly to urge member nations to follow a zero-tolerance policy towards racism.

The Indians bounced back with a strong win in Perth, a draw in Adelaide, and the best part of a win from Harbhajan's appeal to the ICC Appeals Commissioner, Justice John Hansen, the day after the end of the Adelaide Test. Harbhajan's charge was reduced from the more serious Level 3 offence to a Level 2 offence of abuse and insult, and the ban was turned into a fine.

In making his decision, Hansen pointed to the importance of context and of Harbhajan replying to a vulgarity (fuck) from Symonds. What he did not comment on was historical context. Three months earlier Harbhajan had claimed the Australians had targeted him with 'vulgar personal comments' and added, 'They think you cannot fight back and they do not like it when you do' (Aussies made vulgar comments 2007),

What led Symonds to use the offending word in Sydney is revealing. At the end of a Brett Lee over Harbhajan had patted Lee on his backside. The action was interpreted by some observers as friendly, even congratulatory, but not by Symonds. Under questioning from the advocate for Harbhajan and the Board for the Cricket Council of India (BCCI), Vasha Manohar, about whether he objected to that pat, Symonds replied, 'Did I have an objection to it—my objection was that a test match is no place to be friendly with an opposition player, is my objection'. Of that reply, Hansen observed, 'If that is his view I hope it is not one shared by all international cricketers. It would be a sad day for cricket if it is' (Text 2008).

Cricket, like many other sports and entertainments, has experienced, and is more likely to experience, sad days in the modern era. In his book, *Patrons, Players and the Crowd*, Richard Cashman relates a story of Services player Keith Carmody stepping away from the wicket several times in 1945 because the noise of the crowd at Brabourne Stadium made it difficult to concentrate on bowling. Perhaps this was an example of emerging Indian cricket nationalism, but home team captain Vijay Merchant gave good-mannered advice: 'If you show you are taking notice of the crowd they will carry on. Best to disregard the noise if you can' (Cashman 1980:119). In the same chapter, Cashman quotes Indian journalist KN Prabhu on the Brabourne Stadium's East Stand: 'In terms of cricket, Bombay's East Stand is as famous a landmark as the Hill at Sydney. To secure the approval of the East Stand is almost as good as securing a place in *Wisden*' (Cashman 1980:118). Prabhu, writing in 1973, was perhaps romanticising the East Stand as the place where the deepest cricket intelligence of the crowd lay. The fire in the vicinity of this stand in 1969 caused dismay because it was an assault on Indian cricket intelligence. The Hill has long gone from Sydney, but one suspects that among those who mourn its passing are those for whom it represents a loss of cricket romance as well as intelligence.

If Australia–India cricket is a bridge in cultural relations, it has to be a robust bridge because it carries an increased flow of Test, one-day and Twenty20 traffic. The likelihood of both contact and collision is great. Whether former cricketers make good ambassadors probably depends on the individuals concerned, but it is noteworthy that ex-Australian vice-captain Darren Lehmann has been pressed into service on South Australian Government trade missions to the subcontinent. Who knows where that will lead?

There have been some answers to these questions in the last few years, and there have been ironies. Andrew Symonds, the man whom Indian cricket followers had begun to hate has become the man some, at least, love to love, namely those followers of the Hyderabad Deccan Chargers, for whom he was initially contracted for $1.4 million per season to play in the Indian Premier League (IPL). Symonds now has had his contract cancelled with Cricket Australia, so it is likely that his first loyalty will now be to his Indian club. A lot of cricketers around the world, including a number of Australians, are viewing the huge rewards of playing in either the IPL or the Indian Cricket League (ICL) as being far more than they could ever hope to earn representing their countries. Whereas Australians once turned their back on Indian cricket connections, the lure of instant riches now means they are only too ready to embrace them.

Works cited

'Aussies made vulgar comments in Kochi: Harbhajan' 2007, *Times of India*, 4 October, articles.timesofindia.indiatimes.com/2007-10-04/top-stories/27969522_1_aussies-harbhajan-singh-andrew-symonds, viewed 3.3.2012.

Beecher, Eric (ed) 1970, *Australian cricket yearbook 1970*, Modern Magazines, Sydney.

Bose, Mihir 1986, *A maidan view: the magic of Indian cricket*, Allen & Unwin, London.

— 2002, *A history of Indian cricket*, Andre Deutsch, London.

Cashman, Richard 1980, *Patrons, players and the crowd*, Orient Longman, New Delhi.

Harte, Chris and Bernard Whimpress 2003, *A history of Australian cricket*, Andre Deutsch, London.

Morrissey, Tim 2008, 'India the "New Ashes"', *Daily Telegraph* 29 February, www.news.com.au/india-the-new-ashes/story-e6frf3ll-1111115670748, viewed 3.3.2012.

'Text: Harbhajan Singh appeal decision' 2008, *The Australian* 31 January, www.theaustralian.com.au/business/legal-affairs/text-harbhajan-singh-appeal-decision/story-e6frg97x-1111115435545, viewed 3.3.2012.

Williams, Ken 2007/8, 'The development of cricket in India and the first Indian tour of Australia in 1947/48', *The Yorker* 37.

Woodward, Ian 1994, *Cricket not war: the Australian Services XI and the 'Victory Tests' of 1945*, SMK Enterprises, Melbourne.

Chapter 6

India Through Australian Eyes, 1850–1950[1]

Bruce Bennett

The study of national images and stereotypes has slipped from fashion in some quarters since the rise of postcolonial theory in the 1980s followed by globalisation studies in the 1990s. But as Wolfgang Zach ably reminds us, opposition to the study of national images was also opposed by universalist theorists in the 1950s and 60s led by Rene Wellek (Zack & Kosok 1987:ix–xii). Despite such opposition, then and since, national studies have continued in a variety of forms ranging from the impressionistic to the systematic. Stereotypes and autostereotypes, as well as more in-depth, qualitative analyses recur as writers from one nation attempt to describe or typify another. This essay attempts to explore some of the ways in which India and Indian people were presented in prose narratives by Australians between 1850 and 1950. The approach is eclectic, taking into account historical context, genre and the use of national image-making of selves and others during a century of changing ideas of the nation.

Few Indians may be aware of the pervasive lexical effects of the noun 'India' on the Southern Hemisphere. In 1770, Captain James Cook's naturalist on the *Endeavour,* Joseph Banks, wrote: 'Our boat proceeded along shore, and the Indians followed her at a distance' (quoted in Ramson 1988:324). This early linkage of Indians with a people later to be called 'aborigines', 'aboriginals' or 'blacks' has its counterpart in early 21st- century scholarship as a number of scholars from India investigate psychological, social and environmental links between indigenous Australian people and similarly underprivileged

---

[1] A revised version of a lecture given at Jadavpur University, Calcutta, on 8 February 2005 and first published in Kenneally, Michael et al 2005, *From 'English Literature to Literatures in English': International Perspectives: Festschrift in Honour of Wolfgang Zach*, Winter House, Heidelberg.

Indians, especially Dalit people. And by one of those strange coincidences, 'India' is becoming a favourite name for European Australian girls. I have not yet heard of 'Australia' as a favourite name among people of the Indian subcontinent.

Thanks to, or curses upon, the British Empire, 21st-century Australians can reflect upon a sociocultural history of representations and misrepresentations of India and Indian people partially shared with certain opinion-makers in Britain, which represents a pattern that is quite different from Australia's historic relationship with our other great northern neighbour, China. Invasion-scare novels of the late 19th and early 20th century, for example, feature China and Japan as invaders of Australia, but never India (Walker, 1999:Chapter 8). By the 1960s, Australian novelist Christopher Koch (born 1932) could write his novel *Across the Sea Wall* (1965), which showed a certain rapport with India, while Greg Clark wrote his symptomatic analysis of a still current attitude, *In Fear of China* (1967).

By contrast with Clark's litany of perceived historical, political and psychological barriers to engagement with China, Koch shows his Australian protagonist travelling through India and recognising that he and his Indian friends are really 'brothers under the skin'. But it's an edgy, taut relationship between Robert O'Brien and Sunder Singh, which is exemplified in a stand-off between them on Marine Drive, Madras, when Sunder speaks out:

> 'You see, O'Brien', he said, 'you bloody Australians don't know what you are. You don't think much of colonialism, but then suddenly you're waving the Union Jack. It's disheartening.' They passed a statue of Queen Victoria, on a plinth beside the Drive, and he pointed up at her. 'There you are, why don't you salute her? You'd like her back, wouldn't you?' (Koch 1982:96).

The novelist does not let his character off this particular hook. Indeed, he reinforces the point:

> [T]o his own surprise, O'Brien found himself looking up at the pudding-faced queen with a certain wistfulness. Relic of the Raj, bereft in independent India, she grilled in the terrible heat, a figure of fun, her majesty a joke; and he felt sorry for her, Victoria Regina, Empress of India, perhaps simply because she was familiar, and he had a sudden thirst for anything familiar (Koch 1982:96).

Koch's Indian scene reverberates backwards into our real colonial history and forwards into the new reality of the American empire vying with Australia's still awkward and tentative, though developing, cultural relationship with the countries of Asia, including India. (I differentiate here between the notion of deeper *cultural* relations, which are my central interest, and the development of trade and commerce, though the two are clearly linked in some respects.)

In more visionary mode in 1987, Christopher Koch wrote a scenario wherein a greater 'family closeness' might be developed through spiritual and cultural links between Australia and the countries of what he called 'the Indo-European zone', especially Australia, Indonesia and India:

> Without myth, the spirit starves, and in postcolonial Australia, we are going to have to build a new myth out of old ones. And I would suggest that these old ones will not belong simply to the European zone, but to the Indo-European zone, of which India and Indonesia are both inheritors, as we are. Other great cultures, such as China, we may admire, we may gain from, but we will not find such family closeness with; the sense of common roots. (Koch 1987:15–16)[2]

We have been made aware recently of fundamental geological links between Australia and the countries of Asia through the earth's plate. We are told by seismologists that when the India plate, which is part of the Indo-Australian plate and is drifting north-east an average of 5cm a year, suddenly slipped 15 metres below the Burma plate in late December 2004 the seabed was thrust upwards by 10 metres. It would normally take three centuries for the India plate to move as much as it did in that instant. At any rate, the fourth largest earthquake recorded since 1900 unleashed what an Indian fisherman later called 'the angry sea' which devastated many coastal areas in the region (Lusetich 2005). It remains to be seen how the slow recovery from this catastrophic tsunami will be played out in terms of 'a family closeness' or otherwise. The early signs of international co-operation in this process are positive.

Against the background of such shattering events, the smaller human dramas of late 19th- and early 20th-century Australians' encounters with Indians and the idea of India may seem inconsequential. Yet these are the kinds of small but significant human interactions, played out under the

---

[2] I have considered the prospects for such development further in an essay, titled 'A Family Closeness? Australia, India, Indonesia' (Bennett 2003).

banners of different empires and geopolitical forces, that are proceeding all around our region today. Perhaps, in retrospect, we can even afford the ironic smiles that our forebears' represented behaviour, as displayed in short stories, novels and travel narratives, may evoke.

For in retrospect, it is clear that many white Australians who visited India or thought about inhabitants of the subcontinent saw themselves as proxy representatives of the British Empire, however lowly their status in Australia may have been. Behind this, of course, was a racism that saw 'white men' as superior to 'brown men' (men, rather than women taking the role of representatives of their race). This, we have seen, was a continuing tradition of thought and attitude since at least Captain Cook's voyages in the 1770s. But for the particulars of lived experience and their emotional tonalities we turn here to literature, in particular prose narratives.

The place to begin is perhaps in the mid-19th century in the figure of John Lang (1816–1864), accurately described by CD Narasimhaiah (1980:xxi) as 'the first Australian-born novelist on Indian soil'. The grandson of a Jewish convict at Botany Bay, Lang was educated in Australia and in England and moved to India in 1842, where he continued in his profession as a lawyer, wrote novels, stories and a travel book, and edited a newspaper—*The Mofussilite* (1845–1876) in Meerut. A recent essay by Rick Hosking (2003) has examined Lang's first novel set in India, which bears a typically long Victorian title: *The Wetherbys, Father and Son; Or, Sundry Chapters of Indian Experience* (1853). The book was first serialised in *Fraser's Magazine* (1853) in London before it was published in book form in 1853 by Chapman and Hall and was also serialised in *The Mofussilite* (1855). Hosking summarises his impressions of *The Wetherbys*, which contains

> no fine and solemn writing about Empire. Instead, Lang describes the sordid experience of cantonment life where rakish subalterns and ancient, incapable colonels are supposedly in charge of disorderly regiments, where 'the Titans of the Punjab' are seen as barely able to cope with disorderly marital situations and brittle domestic arrangements. India as a place has little impact on the colonizers, and India as a place of complex and ancient cultures simply does not exist. The few Indians who are represented are without exception subordinate and inferior, and typically nameless servants (Hosking 2003:49).

Nevertheless, Hosking suggests an Australian slant to Lang's writing of India as that of 'a larrikin outsider' and 'against the convention which found romance in empire' (Hosking 2003:53). An aspect of research that remains to be done is a full bibliographical record of Lang's short fiction and other writings about India; but the available record suggests a mid-nineteenth century perspective on British India that was as alert to the absurdities of expatriate life there as in Australia.

Many Australian narratives of India are stories of travel. As David Walker has shown, Australia's first major travel book about India is James Hingston's *The Australian Abroad* (1879), which is witty, informative and unrepentantly imperialist in outlook (Walker 1999:17–19). Hingston's enthusiasm for new places is infectious, if at times also bumptious. Walker remarks that Hingston was drawn to 'the strangeness and intractable difference of the mysterious East' and was influenced in this by the tales in *The Arabian Nights* (Walker 1999:17). According to Hingston, India had a special place in any educated man's imagination and was seen to have a spiritual dimension; to see India was to learn 'there is an object in life' (quoted in Walker 1999:19). Hingston's wit is his saving grace and perhaps a sign of an emergent 19th-century Australianness. Like Clive James (born 1939), Hingston places an image of himself at the forefront of his travel stories, where he is vulnerable to the charms of places and people, and he looks for philosophies of living behind appearances. In his short narrative about a visit to the Parsees' Towers of Silence at Bombay in *The Australian Abroad* (Hingston 1995:46–50), Hingston lightheartedly presents himself as a somewhat clumsy detective wanting to solve a mystery, who drops his new hat into an enclosure at the Towers and goes searching for it. He feels like 'Bluebeard's wife among the remains of her predecessors in the forbidden chamber' (Hingston 1995:49) and is swooped by the vultures who are there to pick the bones of the dead. Almost a century later, in the mid-1960s during a stopover at Bombay from the P&O liner *Himalaya*, on my way from Australia to study in Oxford, I visited the same tourist site, but with a greater readiness to accept its evocation of awe and horror rather than to see myself as a detective and travel guide. I noticed that some of my fellow travellers, though, viewed the Towers with the same jaunty insouciance that Hingston had shown 85 years earlier. Cross-cultural perspectives on religious observances often seem absurd to those steeped in a particular way of seeing things.

Military life provided one of the main avenues for Australian understanding of life in 19th- and early 20th-century India. Many narratives reflect this, ranging from journalistic sketches in magazines or newspapers, such as *The Australian Town and Country Journal* (January 1870–June 1919), the *Bulletin* (1888–present) and *The Lone Hand* (1907–1921), to the whimsical, historical romance tales of Ethel Anderson (1883–1958) and Molly Skinner's (1876–1955) novel *Tucker Sees India* (1937). I will return to both of these women writers shortly.

A theme that runs through much early Australian writing about India is the puzzle of masculinity. The 'manly' military virtues of courage, strength and solidarity are comically tested, for example, in an anonymous piece, 'A Strange Night-watchman: A Story of Northern India', in *The Australian Town and Country Journal* in 1889. The story features the fears of a tremulous English visitor, advisedly named Mr Tremmell, when he visits military and missionary friends at a hill station in northern India, who 'looked upon all India as one great menagerie with a "ravening tiger" crouching behind every tree, and a boa-constrictor, as long as a ship's cable, hidden in every thicket' (A Strange Night-watchman 1889: 28). His fears seem to be realised at the missionary's house, when he sees a six-foot black and yellow snake gliding along the floor towards him. He yells loud and long before he is told that this is Dickie, the 'house-snake' and a pet of the children. Like colonial tales of Englishmen lost in the Australian bush, this story purports to show the comical shortcomings of men who fail to live up to the *Boys' Own Annual* adventure-tale format of stoical courage in adversity. Such tales reinforce notions of wild and exotic other worlds where only 'true' men can be men. The men who retreat in fear provide a comic counterpoint to the many other action/adventure tales of tiger- or cheetah-hunting in India in which men *are* said to be men.

Women's fiction contains some illuminating comparisons. Both Ethel Anderson and Mollie Skinner experienced something of barracks life in India and used it as a point of departure in their fiction. Born in England of Australian parents in 1883, Anderson was educated in Sydney before, in 1904, she married a British officer who served for ten years with the Indian Army. Anderson's colourful *Indian Tales* (1948) and *Little Ghosts* (1959) range in their subject matter from the 16th century to the last days of the British Raj and show an appreciation of Indian legends and folklore.

The women of India especially fascinate Anderson and many of her tales deal with thwarted love or love triumphant in the face of military violence or racial difference and discrimination, past and present. In the long story 'Mrs. James Greene', the eponymous heroine survives uprisings, violence and threats to her virtue in Sitapur to become the adored mistress of Mirza Khan to whom she devotes the rest of her life (Anderson 1959:57–87).

Anderson takes an inquisitive and ironic stance towards the complexities of racial and cultural inheritance in India in her story 'The Eurasian'. In

Dinapore, where the story is set, Anderson notes a tendency towards isolation in the Eurasian community. Such households, she observes 'vary as their blood fluctuates between British, Spanish, Portuguese, French and Dutch origins on the paternal side and between the admixture of Mogul or Hindu strains on the maternal' (Anderson 1959:180). She also observes the extreme fascination of British men, especially for Eurasian women, and the ironies of fate that sometimes enable the crossing of racial lines. Her appreciation of India, past and present, shows a curiosity about exotic facts and details and is at times rhapsodic in its exuberant, peacock display of language. The following scene-setting paragraph from 'The Eurasian' shows something of the flavour of Anderson's prose:

> So these figures met, the servant Nedoo with his child, the jealous colonel, the young soldier, the Eurasian girl, the half-seen watcher by the wall. They stayed grouped among the immense trees, under a sickle moon, beside an unruly river. They had collected there by chances as fortuitous as those which assembled the butterflies in their dances above the red bouvardias, as casually gathered together, as carelessly dispersed. Yet forces which governed the human pattern—hate, greed, love—were perhaps deeper in origin than the love of sunlight, the joy of colour, that linked the dancing butterflies together above the red flowers. It may be so. For a moment the jealous colonel saw the young Eurasian girl in Hew's arms. For one moment Hew held her, a girl whose name was unknown to him (later, under tragic circumstances, he was to swear ignorance of it), and then the pattern made by those meeting figures dissolved. They parted and went their several ways (Anderson 1959:186).

Anderson's tale of mystery and romance ends ironically and unexpectedly with the 'jealous colonel' triumphantly defying racial barriers in the pursuit of true love—which may be truer for him than for his lover.

Mollie Skinner's novel, *Tucker Sees India*, is less subtle and insightful than Anderson's stories of India, but more definitively and self-consciously Australian. Skinner was the co-author with DH Lawrence of *The Boy in the Bush* (1924), a novel about the tribulations of English settlers in Western Australia in the 1880s which shows the passionate individuality of one settler, Jack Grant, in defiance of a conventional, colonial society and a sense of the threatening bush. *Tucker Sees India* draws on Skinner's time as a nurse during much of the First World War when she worked at hospitals for soldiers in Calcutta, near the frontier at Rawalpindi, at Peshawar at the end of the Indian railway, Bunnu, the Malakand Fort, Lahore, Baroda and elsewhere (Skinner 1992:14–15). As an Australian nurse in Lady Minto's private nursing service, Skinner was aware of the way Australians could be put down as mere 'colonials' by their British superiors and this insight informs her novel. Skinner's leading character, Tucker, is a member of the Australian Imperial Force sailing for Europe who is left behind in Bombay when he misses the boat after a hard night out. Tucker is a rough-and-ready Australian male of his generation who gets caught up in a number of Indian adventures en route to the 'real' war. At the end, he has 'seen India' and is ready for anything life may throw at him.

In Skinner's novel Tucker is a feckless but generous Australian, basically uninterested in authority or position, who is happy to throw himself into any adventure and make a joke of it. He specialises in narrow scrapes. In Chapter 7 of *Tucker Sees India*, for example, our hero, who has been in India for only a fortnight, finds himself caught up in the kidnapping for ransom of a young Englishwoman by tribesmen in the Khyber Pass. He disguises himself as a mad mullah and, failing to find himself a 'black tracker'—he claims he would be able to find one in a similar situation in Australia—he travels by camel with a local man, Ali Mohammed, to free the white woman. The events that follow are a comical adventure narrative of stock characters and narrow escapes. As he hurriedly disrobes from his mad mullah outfit after saving the girl who has caused him too much trouble, Tucker remarks that 'if the only way to succeed in such stunts as these is to be the other fellow, we'll get away before the enemy knows I'm me' (Skinner 1937:132). This is of course comical, opportunistic disguise rather than the more subtle merging of personalities in search of deeper understanding that we might find in other kinds of novels or stories. It shows the kind of straightforward narrative adventure tale that DH Lawrence transformed from Skinner's draft in the *The Boy in the Bush*.

The popular British image of an exotic, exciting, extravagant India on which Skinner could draw, albeit with a certain humorous undercutting of British pomposity, is deployed by a number of short-fiction writers in Australian magazines and newspapers of the late 19th and early 20th century. Albert Dorrington's (1871–1953) 'The Mouth of the Moon-God' in *The Australian Town and Country Journal* in 1907 is a good example. Dorrington uses the figure of the legendary American pirate and buccaneer of the Pacific, Captain 'Bully' Hayes, to tell a yarn of an adventure in India after he has landed in Calcutta.

Dorrington's yarn is purportedly told in an opium shop in Port Darwin to a group of 'shellers and bêche-de-mer men'. The story's subject matter and theme hark back to Rider Haggard and forward to *Raiders of the Lost Ark*. 'Bully' Hayes, the storyteller within Dorrington's yarn, is an unreconstructed scoundrel who loots foreign treasure wherever he can find it. The specific adventure he recalls takes place in a Hindu temple in Meeraj, where a guide, Keddah Singh, has taken Hayes and his mate. The guide persuades the men to put aside a sack of their treasure from the floor of the castle where the skeletons of previous looters who died of the plague lie around:

> Some lay in the open courtyard, others sprawled in front of the altars, with silver and gold gee-gaws clutched in their skeleton hands. We could see, too, where the jackals had been and stripped them bare, leaving nothing but the bones and the jewels (Dorrington 1907: 26).

Undeterred, the pirates continue their gothic adventure, but they have not counted on the treachery of their Indian guide. Persuaded by Singh to reach into the jaws of the moon-god to retrieve his tooth, Hayes is trapped when the jaws snap shut on his arm. A bizarre comedy ensues when Hayes's companion, Bill, uses a crowbar to smash the moon-god's face in and free his mate. The fabulous tooth is lost and Jeddah Singh escapes with the loot. No moral is drawn from the tale. Hayes, the loser on this occasion, concludes that much gold and silver remains in Indian temples. The American pirate vows he will return to 'get some more one of these days'. An old dream of imperial India—of a treasure trove to be plundered—is played out for Western readers.

A recurrent feature of exotic India in Australian magazine and newspaper stories in the early 20th century is the life of Majarajahs and their retinues. Australian playwright Louis Esson's (1878–1943) story 'My Friend, the Maharajah' (1910), published in the *Bulletin*, is a witty spoof on excessive wealth and the extravagant styles of living it generates. The chief figure of this story is the sporting Maharajah of Jodhpur, whose tailor has fashioned the Jodhpur riding breeches that became famous around the polo-playing world and beyond. Louis Esson's socialistic views do not lead him to sober criticism of the Maharajah's excesses, however. In present-day terms, his point of view might be described as that of a 'chardonnay socialist'. Indeed, his own Australian-derived love of sport draws him into an affectionately humorous account of quintessential Jodhpur polo among the Maharajah's elite followers and friends:

Was this polo, or was it only a dream? They didn't play that kind of game in Victoria. It was fierce. The Jodhpur team? Well, there was his Highness a reckless rider, famous for his dash, meteoric. There was Fute Singh, as solid as the Rock of Ages. There was Zelim Singh, blue-turbanned, a fierce set look in his eyes, cantering all around the gallant English officers, and giving them naught. And finally there was Dokal Singh, the world's champion.

Who shall describe Dokal? A handsome man, nearly 6 ft. high, 12 1/2 stone, perfect in build, a cavalier in manner, a very Napoleon of polo. As rover he was everywhere, two men trying in vain to stop him. Full back, his defence was as that of Gibraltar. Shooting for goal, he would have bagged all the peanuts in the Eastern markets. His attack was a charge of the heavy brigade, officers, ponies, even his Highness himself, if he were in the road, being bumped, and then scattered like chaff blown before the autumn gale...he was a whole team in himself, a champion, a Caesar. He was the personal factor in history. He moulded events (Esson 1910:40).

The Australian visitor, fêted by the Maharajah, seems to accept and enjoy these sporting excesses—in hunting, horse-races and billiards as well as polo—and the hyperbolic heroes that grow from them. 'The sporting Maharajah takes sport seriously', says an observer, admiringly. His companion agrees: 'The stables—they are the State' (Esson 1910:40).

Esson's visit to India in 1908 also included a string of articles, essays and stories for *The Lone Hand*, an Australian nationalist journal that played up the fear of China and Japan and criticised the morals and manners of the British in India and Australia. This kind of anti-imperialist nationalism, like Esson's rather theoretical socialism, was an avenue to uncertainty and confusion. As David Walker has shown, Esson mocked the 'unedifying mix of racial arrogance, brutality and bureaucracy' in British India and the imperialists' 'tendency to see "sedition" everywhere', and urged Australians to dissociate themselves from the British in India (Walker 1999:35). At the same time, he was drawn to the eccentric individuality of maharajahs and to images of traditional village life in India.

If military life and the high life of British and Indian elites are generally preferred by Australian writers during the Raj to the life of the streets and the ambiguities and troubling doubts about foreign occupation of India, there are, nevertheless, some exceptions. While many writers sketchily refer to beggars or the anonymous life of crowded streets and bazaars, Mary C Elkington's story 'The Soul of the Melon Man', published in *The Lone Hand* in 1908, uses the form of a fable to contemplate foreign ways of thinking and believing and how they may affect giving and receiving. In 'The Soul of the Melon Man," an *ayah* tells her *memsahib* about how, despite being hungry herself, she has given some *pân* to a poor, hungry family. What has helped her to do this, she says, is 'the soul of the water-melon man hovering near'. Then follows a tale about a seller of melons in the bazaar who was once generous but has selfishly and dishonestly grown relatively well-off by cutting thin slices or giving dry, stale pieces of melon to little children and other customers. When a traveller passes, he finds the water-melon man asleep beneath a tree with his soul departed from him in the branches above. The traveller persuades the soul to return to the sleeping body, which, with some grumbling, it does. The traveller then gives the renewed Melon Man two melons to recommence his trade, one to eat himself and one for his soul which, 'if that is starved it is better that a man should cease to be' (Elkington 1908:55). After some temptation, the seller of melons responds to his now indwelling soul and becomes kind and generous again. When the soul grows, he feels it blossoming 'through all his being' (Elkington 1908:55). Thus, the *ayah* tells her *memsahib*, when 'we who pause and put our own needs before the sad lack of others, we hear the rustling wings of the melon seller's soul' (Elkington 1908:55). It is a tale designed to appeal to the better, feminine self of imperious foreigners, which female rather than male writers in English seem more licensed to draw attention to. The contemplation of a single soul in this story transcends the confused messages of the crowded streets of poor people.

By the 1920s, a number of fissures were appearing in the easy confidence expressed by British authorities and their sometimes resistant friends and allies in India, such as the Australians. Mahatma Gandhi had begun his strategy of nonviolent confrontation with India's British rulers in 1920. EM Forster's *A Passage to India*, which showed the near impossibility of an equal friendship even among liberal, educated men of goodwill across the racial divide, was published in 1924. Occasional stories in Australian magazines and newspapers in this decade also showed cracks in the wall.

Such a story is R Francis Strangman's 'Black and White', which appeared in *The Triad* in 1926. The story's title seems to invite the rejoinder, 'There's no such thing [as black and white]'. The first-person narrator is identified early as an Australian who tends to see things in terms of his home country. As he sits on the verandah of his bungalow, where he is lord of all, he surveys the scene at dusk:

Looking before me, I could see the dull-green rolling plain scarred by yellow sheep-tracks; the narrow winding river and the trees, like willows, dotted along its banks; beyond this again the wheatfields, miles in extent, and the little white farm-houses. Away in the distance, dark ranges of hills. What a pity there were no rabbit-proof fences (Strangman 1926:35).

The writer has already shown readers that this Australian newcomer in India is a dreamer who does not see clearly what is before him. He is an unreliable observer. He is sufficiently self-aware, however, to recognise in himself 'the patronising attitude of all newcomers' when he speaks with his servant and bearer Naghu and is mystified when Naghu speaks nervously and passionately about the 'damn Parsees' who are alleged to be taking the best jobs from other Indians. These are deep waters and the Australian is adrift in them. He recognises that in any conversation with an Indian there are 'so many detonators waiting to be touched off' (Strangman 1926:35). He is even more surprised that evening when he learns from his chief that the bearer is using a false name and is suspected of murdering a Parsee a couple of months ago. He must, therefore, be dismissed. But the story has a twist in the tail. The bearer has been using drugs supplied by Europeans—cocaine in this case—and a neat exchange between the newcomer and his chief concludes the story:

'We do cause rather a lot of trouble—by being here, I mean—don't we, sir'?

'Oh yes. That's one reason we've got to stay.'

'Shall I get you a drink, sir?'

'Oh please. Hell of a day this.'

'Yes, sir. Hell of a day.' (Strangman 1926:35)

Such stories hint at an unconscious sphere of colonial relations which Bart Moore-Gilbert has discerned in Homi Bhabha's recognition of 'complicitous kinds of psychic affect circulating between coloniser and colonised' (Moore-Gilbert 1996:5). In the 1920s, even in distant Australia, relations with India can be seen to become more interesting, intriguing, complex and dangerous than the prospect of cheetahs or tigers in the jungle. Yet it must be remembered that Australia was still six colonies of Britain until 1901 and the colonial hangover persisted until at least the mid-20th century.

What must be admitted is that none of the Australian story writers referred to in this essay from the mid-19th century to mid-20th century saw India or Indians with quite the range, depth and perceptive enthusiasm of Alfred Deakin (1856–1919), who was to become Australia's most literate and visionary Prime Minister (and after whom Deakin University at Geelong, near Melbourne, is named). Deakin vigorously promoted a federated Commonwealth of Australia during the 1890s and was a three-time Prime Minister of the fledgling nation in the early 1900s.

At the invitation of the editor of *The Age* newspaper, Deakin visited India for two months in 1890, from which a series of articles and two books, *Irrigated India* (1893) and *Temple and Tomb* (1893) emerged. Deakin's first biographer, Walter Murdoch, remarks that, 'if his stay in India was brief, the preparation for it had been spread over many years of study; he knew the history of the country as few Englishmen knew it' (Murdoch 1923:170). Although he considered British rule a net benefit to Hindus in India ('the net result is a beneficent tyranny'), Deakin remarked that 'Officialdom is nowhere more rampant than in India'. He praised knowledgably the irrigation systems of India and the temples and tombs (Murdoch 1923:172–173). Nor were Deakin's essays restricted to buildings and landscapes. An indication of the broad sweep of humanistic thinking allied with an astute sense of policy development that informs Deakin's *Irrigated India* is shown in the following brief quotation:

> We are near enough to readily visit India and be visited...Its students might come to the universities of our milder climate, instead of facing the winter of Oxford, Paris or Heidelberg. Our thinkers may yet become authorities upon questions which need personal acquaintance with India and its peoples (Murdoch 1923:172–173).

As Australia's first major international statesman, Alfred Deakin needs to be reread and reconsidered. As a man of letters, he reminds us of the traditions, including literature, that provide an avenue of continuing linkage between Australia and the Indian subcontinent as our two-way exchanges increase. He also reminds us that, although stereotyping will continue and is perhaps necessary, imagination and thought together can lead to deeper relationships between countries. The 'family closeness' that novelist Christopher Koch envisaged between the literate peoples of Australia and India needs to be explored further and the links that were being forged back then brought seriously into play once again.

Works cited

Anderson, Ethel 1948, *Indian tales*, Australian Publishing Co., Sydney.

— 1959, *Little Ghosts*, Angus & Robertson, Sydney.

Bennett, Bruce 2003, 'A family closeness? Australia, India, Indonesia', in Bierbaum, Nena et al (eds), *The regenerative spirit* vol 1, Lythrum, Adelaide.

Clark, Greg 1967, *In fear of China*, Lansdowne, Melbourne.

Deakin, Alfred 1893, *Irrigated India*, EA Petherick, Melbourne.

— 1893, *Temple and tomb*, Melville, Mullen & Slade, Melbourne.

Dorrington, Albert 1907, 'The mouth of the moon-god', *Australian Town and Country Journal* 25 December.

Elkington, Mary C 1908, 'The soul of the melon man', *The Lone Hand* 2 November.

Esson, Louis 1910, 'My friend, the Maharajah', *Bulletin* 14 April.

Hingston, James 1879, *The Australian abroad on branches from the main routes around the world*, Sampson Low, Marston, Searle & Rivington, London.

— 1995, 'From *The Australian abroad*', in Gerster, Robin (ed), *Hotel Asia* Penguin, Ringwood, Vic.

Hosking, Rick 2003, 'Realms of possibility in Australia, Britain and India in John Lang's *The Wetherbys*', in Bierbaum, Nena et al (eds), *The regenerative spirit* vol 1, Lythrum, Adelaide.

Koch, CJ 1982, *Across the sea wall*, Angus & Robertson, Sydney. (First published in 1965.)

— 1987, *Crossing the gap: a novelist's essays*, Hogarth Press, London.

Lang, John 1853, *The Wetherbys, father and son; or, sundry chapters of Indian experience*, Chapman & Hall, London.

Lawrence, DH and ML Skinner 1996, *The boy in the bush*, edited by Paul Eggert, Penguin, London. (First published in 1924.)

Lusetich, Robert 2005, 'Unimaginable until now', *The Australian* 1 January.

Moore-Gilbert, Bart (ed) 1996, *Writing India 1757–1990: the literature of British India*, Manchester University Press, Manchester.

Murdoch, Walter 1923, *Alfred Deakin: a sketch*, Constable, London.

Narasimhaiah, CD 1980, 'Introduction', *The Literary Criterion* 15(3/4).

Ramson, WS 1988, *The Australian national dictionary*, Oxford University Press, Melbourne.

Skinner, ML 1937, *Tucker sees India*, Secker & Warburg, London.

— 1992, *The fifth sparrow: an autobiography*, Sydney University Press, Sydney.

'A Strange night-watchman: a story of Northern India' 1889, *Australian Town and Country Journal*, 16 November..

Strangman, R Francis 1926, 'Black and white', *The Triad* 1 June.

Walker, David 1999, *Anxious nation: Australia and the rise of Asia 1850–1939*, University of Queensland Press, St Lucia.

Zach, Wolfgang and Heinz Kosok (eds) 1987, *Literary interrelations: Ireland, England and the world* vol 3, *National images and stereotypes*, Gunter Narr, Tübingen.

Chapter 7

A Traveller's Eye

John Lang's *Wanderings in India*

Rick Hosking

As Victor Crittenden's painstaking research (Crittenden 2005) has established, the Australian-born writer John George Lang published, either in serial or book form, more than 20 novels, several volumes of short stories, four volumes of poetry and at least two plays. Lang also published *Wanderings in India* (1859), sometimes called 'a travel book', and, according to Rolf Boldrewood (Thomas Alexander Browne), one of the best of the lighter descriptions of Indian life ever published. Most of the chapters in *Wanderings in India* first appeared in Lang's English-language newspaper *Mofussilite* in the mid- to late-1840s in India; when they were republished between November 1857 to February 1859 in Charles Dickens' *Household Words*, the travel sketches were offered in eleven parts, with the running title 'Wanderings in India'. In 1857 Lang was living in London and, with the Indian Mutiny very much in the news, Dickens was eager to publish as much background material as he could find about India.[1] While a number of Lang's pieces had appeared in *Household Words* as early as 1853, the majority were published just after the Sepoy Rebellion, allowing readers to set his sketches and stories against the evolving narrative of India's first war of independence.[2] In the complete collection that appeared in the

---

[1] The Indian Mutiny began in Meerut on 10 May 1857 and the rebellion was quashed 13 months later. Dickens wrote 'The Perils of Certain English Prisoners' for the 1857 Christmas issue of *Household Words*, a piece shaped in part by attitudes Dickens revealed in a letter about his desire to 'exterminate the Race [of Indians] from the face of the earth, which disfigured the earth with the late abominable atrocities' (quoted in Moore 2004:194).

[2] Dickens published six of Lang's pieces about India in *Household Words* in 1853, none in 1854, one in 1855, one in 1856, eight in 1857, twelve in 1858, and eight in 1859, including one in the journal's last issue. Dickens also published a number of Lang's Australian pieces.

1859 Routledge edition, Lang used many of his *Household Words* pieces and added two new sketches written specifically for the volume, both of which say something about the Sepoy Rebellion and its aftermath.

At first glance *Wanderings in India* seems best described as travel memoir; its subtitle is 'Sketches of Life in Hindostan'. When Lang began publishing his own sketches in the *Mofussilite* in the mid-1840s, the literary sketch was established as a staple of popular periodical publication. There were a number of influential English-language models available: Washington Irving's *The Sketch Book of Geoffrey Crayon* (1819–1820); Charles Dickens' *Sketches by 'Boz'* (1836–1837); and William Thackeray's *The Paris Sketch-Book* (1840) and *Irish Sketch Book* (1843). All are now considered important in the development of the sketch as a plotless first-person narrative of life and scenes encountered during a writer's travels, often representing a single episode, vignette or scene. Alison Byerly (1999:349) notes that by the 1830s the sketch had emerged as 'a rapidly drawn picture that sacrifices aesthetic finish for a sense of spontaneity'. As one of Lang's narrators says in an aside, '[m]y duty is simply to paint the picture' (Lang 1859:18). With the explosion of newspaper publication all around the world, the sketch rapidly became a staple of popular publishing, although when photography was developed later in the century its word-painting became increasingly redundant.

With the exception of 'Black and Blue', all the pieces in Lang's *Wanderings in India* are first-person narratives. The title—*Wanderings in India*—and the subtitle—'sketches'—encourage a reading of the pieces as memoirs and/or travel pieces. Certainly *Wanderings in India* has been read as such by historians wishing to make use of Lang's reminiscences of people met during his wanderings. Most of the pieces in the collection portray India in the years immediately before the Sepoy Rebellion, so it is not surprising that Lang's work has been read by historians for his views about historical characters such as Nana Sahib and the Rani of Jhansi, both significant players in the rebellion. Surendra Nath Sen's *Eighteen Fifty-Seven* (1957) cites Lang five times, while Pratul Chandra Gupta cites Lang on seven occasions in his *Nana Sahib and the Rising at Cawnpore* (1963).[3] However, while historical personages do appear in *Wanderings in India*, a number of his pieces are not simply 'history' or even memoir; some obviously deploy fictional devices and can be read as short stories, as the naming of their different narrators

---

[3] A number of the pieces subsequently reprinted in *Household Words* and then in *Wanderings in India* were edited for publication after the Mutiny; the post-1857 additions in the main simply note in passing the events of the Mutiny (Lang 1859:102,130,192, 218,229–233,242,244,251).

indicates.[4] 'The Himalaya Club' is the first piece in *Wanderings in India* and in it a Indian landscape is described:

> From the back of the club-house, from your bedroom windows…you have a view of Deyrah Dhoon. It appears about a mile off. It is seven miles distant. The plains that lie outstretched below the Simplon bear, in point of extent and beauty, to the Indian scene, nothing like the proportion which the comparatively pigmy Mont Blanc bears to the Dewalgiri. From an elevation of about seven thousand feet the eye embraces a plain containing millions of acres, intersected by broad streams to the left, and inclosed [sic] by a low belt of hills, called the Pass. The Dhoon, in various parts, is dotted with clumps of jungle, abounding with tigers, pheasants, and every species of game. In the broad tributaries to the Ganges and the Jumna, may be caught (with a fly) the mahseer, the leviathan salmon. Beyond the Pass of which I have spoken you see the Plains of Hindoostan. While you are wrapped in a great coat, and are shivering with the cold, you may *see* the heat, and the steam it occasions. With us on the hills, the thermometer is at forty-five; with those poor fellows over there, it is at ninety-two degrees. We can scarcely keep ourselves warm, for the wind comes from the snowy range; they cannot breathe, except beneath a punkah…We are all idlers at Mussoorie. We are all sick, or supposed to be so; or we have leave on private affairs. Some of us are up here for a month between musters (Lang 1859:2–3).

Mary Louise Pratt (1992:201–202) describes the 'promontory' view represented in the 'monarch-of-all-I-survey' trope which is often found in colonial travel writing, stressing the superiority of the European seer with a perspective that frames the 'relations of contact' (1992:78) and makes 'territorial surveillance' (1992:39) possible. This extract is a classic exemplar of 'promontory' view, often found in writing about India, which, given the willingness of Anglo-Indians to describe themselves as 'heaven-born', is perhaps not all that surprising.[5] The lofty vantage point, while allowing a god-like and essentialising hegemonic perspective, has the consequence that any other human activity below at ground level is simply not registered. What

---

[4] Lang's Australian fiction makes similar use of historical personages; commentators have noted that Lang only thinly disguised some of them (Miller 1940:403).

[5] Prime Minister William Pitt the Elder described Robert Clive as 'a heaven-born general' and the epithet 'heaven-born' was later applied to members of the Indian Civil Service.

is seen is jungle, described as full of game. Even if there are people below, it is only the Europeans who are considered—the *punkah-wallah* on the end of the rope is simply not observed, his presence effaced by what the writer's voice understands as the need for hot Englishmen to be cooled; he leaves no trace on this space that is now the European's through the act of describing. The repeated use of the pronouns 'you' and 'we' suggests a communal or shared vantage point for viewing India; the higher up the European seeing-eye can get, the more all-embracing is the perception, the reality of dominance and appropriation thus made clear. The representation of this landscape as empty, save for hot Europeans and an invisible *punkah-wallah*, reinforces the perception that Lang offers in many places in *Wanderings in India* that India is a terrific place for sporting European gentlemen, without wife or children, who like a drink and a bet, a ramble and outdoor sports.

'The Himalaya Club' may read like a travel sketch, but it is in fact a short story; the narrator is Captain Wall, a member of the Club who has a bedroom there and describes the goings-on in Mussoorie during the 'season'. Captain Wall is a navy man, supposedly on sick leave, who spends his time in what he calls 'utter idleness'—gambling, drinking and visiting various English women who are always writing to their husbands when he calls (Lang 1859:5).[6] Lang deploys a knowing—or perhaps that should be know-all—first-person narrative voice:

> Let us sum up the events of the season. Four young men were victimized—two at cards and two at billiards. Two duels were fought on the day after the ball. In one of these duels an officer fell dead. In another the offending party grievously wounded his antagonist. Four commissions were sacrificed in consequence of these encounters. There were two elopements [which]…led to two actions in H.M. Supreme Court of Calcutta, and seven of us (four in one case and three in the other) had to leave our regiments or appointments and repair to the Supreme Court to give evidence. Some of us had to travel fourteen hundred miles in the month of May, the hottest month in India (Lang 1859:26–27).

Wall's tone is bored, sardonic and cynical and Lang's representation of the British at rest and play in the hill station is hardly flattering; the

---

[6] In passing, while describing the mundane routines of his life at Mussoorie, Captain Wall mentions that he had once been in the navy on a line-of-battle ship called 'House of Correction' which had once visited Sydney. This is one of only a handful of references in *Wanderings in India* to the Lang's country of Lang's birth.

cooly dispassionate tone of Wall's stiff-upper-lip account of the highlights of the season suggests a chaotic, dissipated, amoral and violent colonial world. Given Lang's family break-up, the women who inhabit this world are especially interesting; the confident and assured young grass widows are wives of army officers and other administrative figures. The fact that Wall is required to travel to Calcutta to give evidence suggests, perhaps, a rather closer acquaintance with these dramatic events in the season than he is prepared to recognise openly. His willingness to 'sum up' what had happened through the season reveals his insider knowledge and his confidence in his powers of observation and judgment; he even goes so far as to assert that by the mid-century the moral tone of Anglo-Indian society was improving: 'It is now four years since I heard of a duel in the Upper Provinces—upwards of four years since I heard of a victim to gambling, and nearly three since there was an elopement' (Lang 1859:28).

The second and third pieces in *Wanderings in India* are also short stories— 'The Mahommedan Mother' and 'Black and Blue'. Both represent transracial erotics, with both sympathetic to the predicament of Indian women whose relationships with European men have turned out badly. Representing the difficulties of achieving cross-cultural rapprochement, Lang's works describe racial and sexual differences with a complex sense of moral ambivalence; there is even a little implicit questioning of the assertively masculinist and racist codes that have led to the human tragedies described. Perhaps Lang's own family and marital circumstances made him rather more sympathetic to the predicaments of such relationships than he otherwise might have been. Perhaps it was the case that his second wife, Margaret Wetter, was of mixed race.

'The Mahommedan Mother' is set in Mussoorie and is a powerful and sentimental story. Mr Longford, the first-person narrator, is a former sailor, a Hindi- and Persian-speaking old hand, experienced and knowing in the ways of the world. The story describes an evening during a thunderstorm when he meets Dooneea, a Muslim woman and the daughter of a *moolvee* (law officer) from Agra. She tells him the story of her relationship with an unnamed English magistrate, who is a close friend of Longford, and its destructive and tragic consequences. The magistrate had died of fever, leaving Dooneea with their child—a boy—who had been taken from her by the magistrate's brother when she, in her despair, had taken to opium and *bhung*. Now she waits to see the boy who is attending school, and Longford helps her with an elaborate stratagem to make contact with her son. After Dooneea meets the boy, Longford returns him to his school and tells Dooneea she must not see him again. Dooneea's reaction is to swoon and die, a fortuitous turn of events, in that the long-term consequences of transracial contact are thus neatly avoided.[7] Longford concludes the story with the hard-nosed observation that the son will not only benefit from being raised as an Englishman but will also inherit property to the value of £4,000, and that he 'will, I trust, make good use of his little fortune, when he comes of age' (Lang 1859:58). However, the overall impression of the piece is that Indian women have much more to lose in transracial relationships than their British lovers.

'Black and Blue', the third piece in *Wanderings in India*, describes a relationship between the Honourable Francis Gay (son of Lord Millflower) and Ellen, a young Muslim girl, the daughter of a water carrier. Gay arrives in India in disgrace as a remittance man, a reprobate and a disgrace to his father, but he changes his ways in India. He learns Hindi and Persian, begins to 'live like a native—a Mahommedan', wears the native costume, becomes a vegetarian, abstains from drinking and eventually takes the name Mustapha Khan. He persuades Ellen to convert to Christianity and then marries her. They have a son called Chandee, with 'light blue eyes, exactly like those of his father; but his complexion was quite as black as his mother's'—hence the title of the piece (Lang 1859:66). Francis/Mustapha leaves the military and becomes a trader in jewels, but he is murdered, leaving Ellen and Chandee penniless. Mother and son establish a sweet shop in Delhi and Chandee becomes a 'box-waller', selling odds and ends to the European officers in Delhi, who call him 'Black and Blue'. However, the death of his grandfather and his uncles leaves him with a claim to the titles and estates of Lord Millflower. Chandee accompanies an attorney to London to lay claim to his inheritance and, although the claim is unsuccessful, Chandee never returns to India. Despite the 19th-century obsession with elaborate plots involving inheritance, that Chandee can never claim the title that is rightfully his says a great deal about entrenched racist attitudes in the years before 1857.

The pieces following the first three short stories appeared in *Household Words* under the title 'Wanderings in India'. In the Routledge edition a further title has been added to each of these. 'The Ranee of Jhansi' is the first of the true sketches and was written especially for the 1859 edition. It describes Lang the lawyer's dealings with the Lakhshmibai, the 'best and bravest of the rebels', the woman who would later become (in)famous during the Sepoy Rebellion and would die leading her troops at the Battle of Gwalior in June 1858. Lakhshmibai had approached Lang to act for her against the

---

[7] Lang's novel *Will He Marry Her?* (1858) uses the same plot device to get around the long-term consequences of transracial relationships.

East India Company in an attempt to reverse an order of annexation on Jhansi. Lang describes his trip there in the Ranee's palanquin, which even included a *punkah* and a ready supply of cool water, wine and beer. After stressing the pomp and ceremony of his arrival at the fortress, Lang makes much of an exchange with the Rani's finance minister about removing his shoes when in the Rani's presence; agreement was finally reached that, while Lang would take off his offending footwear, he would still wear his black 'wide-awake' hat.[8] Noting that the piece was especially written just a year or so after her death, Lang describes his amusement at this bargaining; there is a strong sense of his taking a stand, asserting his power over the Rani, demonstrating he can behave as truculently as any of the heaven-born who have treated her and Jhansi with such cavalier disregard. While the piece seems disconcertingly vainglorious after the sympathy for Indian women represented in the first two stories, there are some moments of sympathy and human exchange, for example, when Lang catches a glimpse of the Rani when the purdah curtain is moved:

> I was very curious indeed to get a glimpse of her; and whether it was by accident, or by design on the Ranee's part, I know not, my curiosity was gratified. The curtain was drawn aside by the little boy, and I had a good view of the lady. It was only for a moment, it is true; still I saw her sufficiently to be able to describe her. She was a woman of about the middle size—rather stout, but not too stout. Her face must have been very handsome when she was younger, and even now it had many charms—though, according to my idea of beauty, it was too round. The expression also was very good, and very intelligent. The eyes were particularly fine, and the nose very delicately shaped. She had no ornaments, strange to say, upon her person, except a pair of gold ear-rings. Her dress was a plain white muslin, so fine in texture, and drawn about her in such a way, and so tightly, that the outline of her figure was plainly discernible—and a remarkably fine figure she had. What spoilt her was her voice, which was something between a whine and a croak. When the purdah was drawn aside, she was, or affected to be, very much annoyed; but presently she laughed, and good-humouredly expressed a hope that a sight of her had not lessened my sympathy with her sufferings nor prejudiced her cause.

---

[8] The detail is beguiling. Although 'wide-awake' hats—so called because they had no nap—were certainly worn by Englishmen, they seem to have been particularly associated with the American West and with the colonies. Does the detail suggest the British gentleman, or does it suggest some residue of Lang's 'flash' colonial style?

'On the contrary,' I replied, 'if the Governor-General could only be as fortunate as I have been, and for even so brief a while, I feel quite sure that he would at once give Jhansi back again to be ruled over by its beautiful Queen' (Lang 1859:93–94).

Lang quotes the Ranee: '[m]eera Jhansi nahin dengee' (I will never give up my Jhansi), thus helping to sustain the legend of the Rani and the defiant cry still associated with her. For his services, Lang received an elephant, a camel, an Arab, a pair of greyhounds of great swiftness, a quantity of silks and stuffs (the production of Jhansi) and a pair of Indian shawls.[9]

'Tirhoot, Lucknow, Bhitoor, ETC.' is first of the travel pieces proper in *Wanderings in India*, and in it the beguiling image of Lang the footloose and fancy-free traveller is first encountered. Although Lang says nothing about his personal circumstances after the departure of his wife, after the success of his paper and earning £30,000 from an infamous lawsuit conducted on behalf of Ajoodia Pershâd, he had the economic freedom to wander the *mofussil*—the backblocks of India.[10] While it is more usual to associate the style of the *flâneur* with the stroller in the European cities of the mid 19th-century, there is something of the type in Lang's descriptions of his own wanderings around India. He notes that he:

> was in no way connected with the Government, and was consequently an 'interloper' or 'adventurer'...the terms applied by certain officials to European merchants indigo-planters, shopkeepers, artisans, barristers, attorneys...I had no occupation, was my own master, and had a large tract of country to roam about in. My first step was to acquire a knowledge of Hindoostanee and of Persian (Lang 1859:97).

He claims that on his travels he did not speak English for five months, 'made a point of avoiding my own countrymen, and of associating only with the natives of India', and became a vegetarian (Lang 1859:105). Elsewhere, Lang calls himself a 'wanderer and an interloper', and we discover that he is 32 years old, suggesting he is young and foolhardy (Lang 1859:244,286). Through the accumulation of such detail, Lang adopts the persona of the

---

[9] Lang's legal work for the Rani was described in 'an extraordinarily closely argued and comprehensive memorial', dated Fort William, 8 June 1854 (Lebra-Chapman 1986:36).

[10] Resuming his old career as a lawyer, Lang won a court case for Ajoodia Pershad against the East India Company in 1851, and his fame spread throughout India, bringing considerable wealth and the financial independence to travel (Crittenden 2005:117).

picaresque *flâneur* who consciously goes out of his way to dissociate himself from the 'heaven-born', attempting to engage with the colonised in India, while trying to avoid the most obvious consequences of the coloniser's desire to dominate and rule. Furthermore, in an extraordinary admission, Lang makes it clear that on one occasion he even dressed as a Muslim woman, knowing that women in traditional dress might travel more easily in those parts of India where there was a risk of highway robbery (Lang 1859:120).

In his sketches, Lang uses a strongly individualised narrative voice, allowing the traveller's eye to survey the various and varied human experience revealed through his 'wanderings'. Lang's traveller–narrator typically stands on the edge of the action, watching, listening, recording, and now and again inserting an editorial commentary on what has been witnessed or heard. He is called 'old boy' by the young lieutenant on gold-escort duties near Agra; he is experienced, cynical and laconic, an observer whose conversational prose style encourages readers to accept the validity of the narrative. Some might consider the style presumptuous; Lang had arrived in India in 1842, but within eight years it seems he had had sufficient time to develop the focalising voice of the old hand, the expert commentator on sundry Indian subjects.

The description of Lang's meeting with the Maharajah Peishwa Bahadoor. the notorious Nana Sahib,[11] in Chapter Five of *Wanderings in India* suggests that, although Lang may have liked to think of himself as having 'gone native', he was only prepared, or able, to go so far. Lang describes a meal at some length:

> I had scarcely made myself comfortable, when the khansamah informed me that dinner was on table. This was welcome intelligence, for I had not tasted food since morning, and it was half-past five p.m. I sat down to a table twenty feet long (it had originally been the mess table of a cavalry regiment), which was covered with a damask table-cloth of European manufacture, but instead of a dinner-napkin there was a bedroom towel. The soup—for he had everything ready—was served up in a trifle-dish which had formed part of a dessert service belonging to the 9th Lancers—at all events, the arms of that regiment were upon it; but the

---

[11] Lang calls him Nena Sahib (Lang 1859:116), although he is better known as Nana Sahib. The British have since represented him as one of the leading villains of the Mutiny, much hated by the British for his role, albeit disputed, in the massacres at Kanpur/Cawnpore. Lang describes him as 'not a man of ability, nor a fool. He was selfish; but what native is not? He seemed to be far from a bigot in matters of religion; and…I am quite satisfied that he drank brandy, and that he smoked hemp' (Lang 1859:116–117). Lang concludes *Wanderings in India* with a post-1857 piece called 'Tantia Topee' which offers a further estimation of Nana Sahib (Lang 1859:410–415).

plate into which I ladled it with a broken tea-cup, was of the old willow pattern. The pilao which followed the soup, was served upon a huge plated dish, but the plate from which I ate it, was of the very commonest description. The knife was a bone-handled affair; the spoon and the fork were of silver, and of Calcutta make. The plated side-dishes, containing vegetables, were odd ones; one was round, the other oval. The pudding was brought in upon a soup-plate of blue and gold pattern, and the cheese was placed before me on a glass dish belonging to a dessert service. The cool claret I drank out of a richly cut champagne glass, and the beer out of an American tumbler, of the very worst quality (Lang 1859:107).

Lang may speak Hindi, he may have a decent suntan and may avoid contact with other Europeans, but here he constructs the Indian household as bizarrely different and breaking all the rules of civilised living, offering what we now read as a fascinating and, in Homi Bhabha's terms, hybridised amalgam of India and Europe, that perpetuates rather than challenges stereotypes (Ashcroft et al 2003:118). When Lang notices and records this hybridised space between two cultures, the strength of his own European conviction is enhanced by his self-confident reportage which mocks the confusion of styles. Lang is cocooned as an outsider by the explicit superiority of his 'imperial eye', although he is still able to enjoy his host's hospitality. Lang agrees to be shampooed ('a luxury to which I was always partial'), but here it means massage, four men pressing and cracking away until he slept (Lang 1859:112).

Lang is not always so conventionally and knowingly Eurocentric. Here and there in some of the sketches in *Wanderings in India* he recognises that India is a land saturated with significations *for Indians*, that India is a place of great diversity and richness, that India is a country worth travelling. Lang comes to understand that people might even go about their business in spite of the presence of their colonial masters. Furthermore, he can now and again see Indians as individuals, rather than represent them as a homogenised collective 'them', which was so often the typical colonialist strategy. There are encounters between Europeans and Indians in the collection, even if the people met are usually high-caste Indians and often what might now be called celebrities. These few moments usually coincide with episodes and incidents where Lang participates in the life he seeks to describe, where his presence is partly dramatised, and where he goes a little further than casting himself as a relatively unsentimental observer.

Chapters Six to Eight of *Wanderings in India* are among the most interesting of the pieces, in that they describe life on the road for the nonchalant gentleman-traveller. The narrator meets a motley mob of individuals in his picaresque and picturesque travels along the Grand Trunk Road; he encounters a Treasure Party—a company of 'native infantry' proceeding from Mynpoorie to Agra with £25,000 in the charge of a philosophical Anglo-Indian lieutenant who insists on 'screw[ing] a small chat' out of each of the travellers on the road. The unnamed lieutenant is a whimsical little fellow who wears an odd assortment of British and Indian clothing, travels barefooted, smokes huge cigars, carries a walking stick and seems 'to know everybody in Hindoostan', possibly because he has 60 first cousins in India (Lang 1859:173). Warning Lang about the dangers of drinking tea while travelling, since it spoils the flavour of cheroots, he is blasé about his military status. Along with a Sepoy, a 'powerful Brahmin' named Manu Singh Sipahee, who is ill and thus must share the lieutenant's gig, they converse about various matters concerned with the British in India: how caste affects Indian soldiers' performance of their military duties; the ridiculous nature of many of the General Orders issued from Headquarters; how the marble headstones marking the graves of Englishmen along the Grand Trunk Road are stolen; and so on. As they make their way to Agra—the Taj appears in the distance like a large white cloud—we discover how this magnificent monument was nearly demolished on the orders of the Governor General, Lord William Bentinck.

While these travel sketches are some of the liveliest pieces in *Wanderings in India*, they also offer some manifestly fictional moments. The travellers Lang meets tell him stories; several of his sketches have sentimental or Gothic short stories embedded within them, in the traditional manner used by Geoffrey Chaucer in *The Canterbury Tales* in the late 14th century. In the chapter 'Marching', the 'lighthearted lieutenant' tells Lang a story of a young boy of European appearance who had wandered all over India with an Afghan dried-fruit seller; the lad, who now thinks and speaks as a 'Musselman', is revealed as the son of a sergeant of the Queen's 13th Regiment of Foot and eventually restored to his family when the Afghan trader produces several items of family memorabilia, including a miniature of his mother, a bracelet, a brooch and a pocketbook.

Lang uses often rather ponderous names for his characters, very much in the spirit of the period's fascination with onomastics. In the Agra chapter he makes quite a deal of a colonel he calls Damzè. In a copy of the 1859 edition of *Wanderings in India* in the University of Western Australia Library, someone who must have known who the colonel was has written 'Ramsay' in the margin. Lang obviously had strong memories of Damzè (Ramsay), who cut him dead at a social occasion because he suspected Lang of having written a metrical squib in which he ridiculed the rules of precedence governing Anglo-Indian society. A number of the protagonists in Lang's sketches attract satirical names, which are obvious cultural references intended for his contemporary readers. In the chapter 'Indian Society' there is a complex representation of a 'Bengalee Baboo', a Brahmin of the highest caste whom Lang names Nobinkissen, a particularly pointed conceit; we wonder if it meant then what it means now (Gupta 1959:366–368). He is described as a man who:

> spoke English with marvelous fluency and accuracy, and could read and write the language as well and as elegantly as any educated European. He was…the cleverest Hindoo whom I encountered during my sojourn in the East. His manners were peculiarly courteous and winning, and there was an air of penitence about the man, which, apart from his abilities, induced me to treat him with kindness and consideration (Lang 1859:212).

Nobinkissen, Lang learns, had been a writer for the East India Company and had been jailed for nine years in Alipore near Calcutta for a particularly clever and profitable piece of chicanery. While employed by 'John Company' he had managed to get his British magistrate to sign copies of his judgments that found in favour of both plaintiff and defendant, thus allowing him to sell them to the higher bidder. After nine years in jail, Nobinkissen made his way from Bengal to the Upper Provinces to start afresh. He debates matters of long-term governance in India with Lang and is particularly mocking of missionary attempts to convert Hindus and Muslims to Christianity. Without resorting to the usual denunciations of Bengali conceit and effeminacy found in stereotypes later in the century, Lang rather admiringly notes Nobinkissen's criminal past, his intelligence, his skill with the English language; perhaps Lang had met someone like Nobinkissen when he was in jail, or perhaps Lang responded to Nobinkissen as one 'flash' or clever colonial might to another, although there is little in the text to indicate this (Sinha 1995).

The chapter dealing with Lang's stay in Agra is particularly interesting. He meets Lall Singh, one of the 'Seik' commanders at the Battle of Ferozeshah in 1845, the second battle of the First Anglo–Sikh War. Singh, now a friend of Britain, is in exile in Agra, training as a surgeon. He tells Lang that he had sent some of his Damascus swords to England to be converted into surgical instruments. Lang stays with Lall Singh at Jatnee-Bagh, the 'garden house' owned by Lallah Jooteepersâd [Ajoodia Pershâd], the army contractor for whom Lang acted in a notorious court case in 1851. A curious feature of this scene is that Lang does not admit to being the lawyer—rewarded handsomely—who acted for Ajoodia Pershâd; instead he opines that the case was very controversial and 'the most extraordinary and protracted trial that was ever known in India' (Lang 1859:192). We can explain Lang's omission of mention of his role in the case as uncharacteristic modesty—after all, if the case was so extraordinary, then the readers of the day would remember his involvement, as the number of memoirs that refer to the matter confirm.[12] Lang notes some further post-Mutiny ironies:

> Jooteepersâd cannot have harboured any revenge for the wrongs (involving disgrace and dishonour) which were heaped upon him; for it is he who has fed, for several months, the five thousand Christians during their incarceration in the fortress at Agra; and, amongst the number of civilians there shut up, is the gentleman who conducted the prosecution on the behalf of the Government, and who, in the execution of his duty, strove very hard indeed for a verdict of guilty! Without Jooteepersâd we could not have held Agra! (Lang 1859:192)

Such ironies are the stuff of travel writing, essaying the *zeitgeist*. Lang and his host later stroll in the garden in the evening cool; Lang makes a point of stressing what good company 'the ex-Commander of the Seik Cavalry and the ex-Prime Minister of Lahore' is—a man who bears his altered condition with great dignity and with whom Lang discusses all sorts of topics. A gardener approaches the two men with the news that workmen, digging the foundations in the garden for a vine trellis, have unearthed a *ty-khana* (a vault beneath a dwelling) and Lang learns that in such dark places are perpetrated 'dark deeds'. The following morning Lang returns to the site, the excavations continue, and it is discovered that a young woman had been bricked up in the wall:

> The skin was still upon the bones, which were covered with a costly dress of white muslin, spangled all over with gold; around the neck was a string of pearls; on the wrists and ankles were gold bangles, and on the feet were a pair of slippers, embroidered all over with silver wire or thread; such slippers as only Mahommedan women of rank or wealth can afford to wear. The body resembled a well-preserved mummy. The features were very distinct, and were those of a woman whose age could not at the time

---

[12] On page 192 of the University of Western Australia Library's copy of the 1859 edition of *Wanderings in India* a previous owner has made annotations pointing out that Lang was paid 'a lak of rupees, £10,000' for his services.

have exceeded eighteen or nineteen years. The head was partially covered with the white dress. Long black hair was still clinging to the scalp, and was parted across the forehead and carried behind the ears. It was the most horrible and ghastly figure that I ever beheld (Lang 1859:197–198).

Lall Singh and Lang discuss the significance of the skeletal remains, the Raja suggesting that she might have been the wife of a jealous husband. Digging resumes, and Lang records that *five* more bodies were exhumed, one of a young man bricked up between two young women. Lang notes that as the sun strikes the remains they disappear, one by one, leaving only a heap of bones, hair, skin, jewels and finery. This anecdote is one of the most Gothic of the curiosities Lang collects in his travels. These days we can read the scene as again suggesting the blurring of generic boundaries in mid-century writing. What begins as an evening stroll with a gossiping rajah ends with the high Gothic, the discovery of the entombed woman; travel writing becomes 'sensation' fiction.

While Lang's remarks about Lall Singh and the Ranee of Lahore might suggest an insider's view of India and the 'style...of the gossip-column', Lang's narrator is usually more conscious of his outsider status, which may have had something to do with Lang's own association with outsiders and his colonial origins (Carrington 1955:69). In the Agra chapter he describes himself as both a visitor and a straggler, while in other chapters he seeks out kindred spirits (Lang 1859:201). In the first travel sketch he travels with a French indigo planter, whereas, as we have seen, the only member of John Company with whom he travels for some time is an eccentric lieutenant. He also teams up with 'two interlopers in the East' (Lang 1859:202), the 'German Baron and the French gentleman'. In a later piece called 'The Himalayas' he travels the hill country with them, seeking out the sportin' life. Given their conspicuous consumption during their travels, Lang obviously has the money to enable him to wander the *mofussil* in style, as illustrated by one fascinating incident in this chapter. The adventurers are forced to camp just nine miles from Mussoorie so their servants can return to civilisation to collect several items essential for their comfort: pickles and sauces, a corkscrew, the instrument for opening tins of lobster, oysters and preserved soups—and the Baron's guitar. The trio shoot kakur, bear, pheasant, ghooral, partridge, elk, green pigeon, hill fox, deer and wild dog, and catch fish.

Chapter Eleven of *Wanderings in India* describes a particularly poignant ramble through the Meerut cemetery, as the narrator is given a guided tour by an 'old and very intelligent pensioner...originally a private in a regiment of Light Dragoons' whose only friend is now a cobra capella (Lang 1859:251–252).[13] This chapter is hardly the stuff of gung-ho jingoistic imperial panegyric, but instead offers a wistful and, once again, rather Gothic insight into one aspect of imperialism's human toll, the casualties of empire, including the children of the *sahib*s and *memsahib*s buried in the children's corner of the cemetery. Lang is mindful of those who had died and been buried in such cemeteries and makes a parenthetical remark:

> (Whilst I write, it has just occurred to me that this old soldier [his guide] and his family perished in the massacre at Meerut on the 10th of May. He was in some way related to, or connected by marriage with, Mrs. Courtenay, the keeper of the hotel, who, with her nieces, was so barbarously murdered on the disastrous occasion) (Lang 1859:261–262).

Such moments of reflection show where Lang's sympathies ultimately reside, the aside undoubtedly written especially for publication in *Household Words* and intended for British readers still appalled by the events of 1857–1859. As Lang himself admits, the convention was well established by the 1850s that travel writing by foreigners about India should be critical. While it is clear that *Wanderings in India* does not stray too far from mainstream views of the British rule in mid-century India, there are still a number of scenes dealing with the foibles and follies of that administration, and Lang joined the debates about imperial practice by critiquing the petty, bureaucratic behaviour of many of the employers of 'John Company', especially their snobbery and narrow-minded social divisions. Several sketches represent such moments. In one mentioned above, Lang notes how close the Taj Mahal came to being demolished on the whim of a Governor-General; in another he mocks the social divisions between the 'red' (the military) and the 'black' (the civilians) in Agra.

Lang also has a great deal to say about the common soldier, both British and Indian, in pre-1857 India and writes of improving their lot, especially about the need for better housing for the married enlisted men and their families with air-conditioning provided by *punkah-wallah*s. Lang also comments on those who have become instant experts on India. In the chapter 'Returning', Lang stays with a friend at Bijnore—a district magistrate and old India hand. A travelling member of parliament, Lord Jamleigh—a 'Lord Sahib', as he is announced—arrives, intent on acquiring a bird's-eye view of India. Lang

---

[13] Ruskin Bond included this as the second chapter of *The Penguin Book of Indian Ghost Stories* (1993:4–44).

describes the MP as a man who knew all about India long before he touched the soil, for he had read a good deal in blue books and newspapers.

John Lang's *Wanderings in India* is a remarkable book. Although today's readers come to it as a travel book—the first by an Australian about India, it demonstrates how generic distinctions between memoir, fiction and travel writing had not fully emerged in the 1850s when it first appeared. His sketches test the boundaries between essay, travel writing, short story, memoir and travelogue in ways that may now seem very modern. Indeed, some of the characteristics of his writings anticipate the achievements of Rudyard Kipling's short stories four decades later. We still read Kipling and celebrate his achievements, whereas Lang has been largely forgotten.

Works cited

Ashcroft, Bill, Gareth Griffiths and Helen Tiffin 2003, *Post-colonial studies: the key concepts*, Routledge, London.

Bond, Ruskin (ed) 1993, *The Penguin book of Indian ghost stories*, Penguin, New Delhi.

Byerly, Alison 1999, 'Effortless art: the sketch in nineteenth-century painting and literature', *Criticism* 41.

Carrington, CE 1955, *Rudyard Kipling: his life and work*, Penguin, Harmondsworth.

Crittenden, Victor 2005, *John Lang: Australia's larrikin writer: barrister, novelist, journalist and gentleman*, Mulini Press, Canberra.

Gupta, Anil Chandra Das (ed) 1959, *The days of John Company: selections from* Calcutta Gazette, West Bengal Government Press, Calcutta.

Gupta, Pratul Chandra 1963, *Nana Sahib and the rising at Cawnpore*, Clarendon Press, Oxford.

Lang, John 1858, *Will he marry her? a novel*, Routledge, London.

— 1859, *Wanderings in India and other sketches of life in Hindostan*, Routledge, Warne and Routledge, London.

Lebra-Chapman, Joyce 1986, *The Rani of Jhansi: a study in female heroism in India*, University of Hawaii Press, Honolulu.

Miller, E Morris 1940, *Australian literature from its beginnings to 1935* Part One, Sydney University Press, Sydney.

Moore, Grace 2004, *Dickens and Empire: discourses of class, race and colonialism in the novels of Charles Dickens*, Ashcroft, Aldershot, Hants.Pratt, Mary Louise 1992, *Imperial eyes: travel writing and transculturation*, Routledge, London.

Sen, Surendra Nath 1957, *Eighteen fifty-seven*, Ministry of Information and Broadcasting, Delhi.

Sinha, Mrinalini, 1995, *Colonial masculinity: the 'manly Englishman' and the 'effeminate Bengali' in the late nineteenth century*, Manchester University Press, Manchester.

Chapter 8

Up the Hooghly with James Hingston

David Walker and Roderic Campbell

James Hingston (1830–1902) was born in London and arrived in Victoria in 1852, where he practised as a notary public, an agent authorised to draw up legal documents (Walker 2005:179–180). He built up considerable personal wealth from investing wisely in commercial opportunities following the goldrush era in Melbourne. Hingston never married and lived for over 30 years in his bedroom at the George Hotel, St Kilda, amid large piles of books and papers and a growing reputation for eccentricity. An indefatigable reader, he knew Shakespeare's plays almost by heart and was considered one of Melbourne's great raconteurs. He died at Exmouth, in England, in 1902.

Hingston's first travel writing was published in the late 1860s, but his overseas travel began in the late 1870s when he took an extended world tour through India, the Middle East, Japan, China, Cochin-China, Malacca, Singapore and Java. He travelled by himself, sometimes meeting other travellers along the way, and took particular pride in journeying without benefit of guidebooks, feeling that 'it is a great advantage to the traveller to have read none of them' (Hingston 1885:iv). He declined to clutter his mind with the opinions of others and claimed to have recorded what he saw and what he heard while actually in the locations themselves and when his impressions were still fresh. He contributed articles to the Melbourne *Argus*, compiling a chapter at each destination. From the kindly welcome their regular appearance received, he was prompted to collect his separate pieces into a book, which was first published in two volumes in London, one in 1879 and the second in 1880. Hingston felt that the one-volume popular edition, *The Australian Abroad on Branches from the Main Routes Round the World*, published in Melbourne in 1885, better met 'the spirit of the times and the needs of the reading public' (Hingston 1885:iv). Although his contributions to the Melbourne press continued into the 1890s, he did not publish any more books.

Hingston tells us in the Preface of *The Australian Abroad* that he had no intention of creating a guidebook, although he did think his book might be 'a companionable one' for those taking the sea routes in or out of Australia. Its structure would be well suited 'to travellers on long or short journeys, and to desultory readers', since each chapter was wholly discrete and the book could therefore be picked up and put down at will. His narrative of travel was continuous and had no plot or storyline, which he hinted was ideally suited to the rhythm of travel. 'At sea or on land, on board ship, on the rail, by the bedside of the invalid, or for the travelling bag of the tourist, the book is one equally adapted for beguilement of otherwise unoccupied hours' (Hingston 1885:iv-v).

His objection to guidebooks is not made clear, but it may have had something to do with his projection of himself as a practical sort of fellow who liked to make up his own mind about things. This does not stop him collecting in his notebook, as he moves from place to place, a great deal of apparently factual information of varying reliability—historical detail and statistical information, particularly—much of which he appears to have obtained from his guides and some of which he recites in his account. If he did not read guidebooks he probably would not have noticed the regular warning that appeared in contemporary Baedeker guidebooks to be wary of local guides and the quality of their information, which was why the Baedeker guides went out of their way to provide comprehensive details as correctives for the educated traveller (Baedeker 1898:xxxv). But, as Hingston said of Shah Jehan's claim to have created paradise on earth at Delhi, you have to take someone's word, and it seemed that the word of the local inhabitants, of hotel-keepers, and especially of the guides he hired was good enough for Hingston.

Hingston's tone is largely conversational, reminiscent of the Victorian clubman, settled in the corner with a good drink and a fund of well-worked stories. In keeping with his ideas about the rhythm of the book, each chapter is one of these stories and, perhaps surprisingly for this kind of book, the writing exhibits considerable skill and literary sophistication. It is measured, even if liberally laced with literary allusions or analogies drawn from his experience, and well organised in the marshalling of its elements. His style appears as the measure of the man himself—bluff, idiosyncratic and reflective, with the good storyteller's sense of timing.

Arrival

Hingston's first sight of India is from a steamer anchored off Madras, when he gazes across the turbulent breakers dashing on the shore half a mile away and spots the dark shapes of the famous surfboats hurrying out to meet them (Hingston 1885:256). He's not impressed. He can see the low-lying city of Madras and finds it somewhat unprepossessing. It lacks any harbour or breakwater, and their only means of getting ashore is to risk life and limb boarding the surfboats heading out to pick them up. It's an inauspicious start.

By the time he reaches Delhi, a median point in his trip through India, he has come to regard his journey as taking an upward trajectory as he moved from Madras to Calcutta, and thence up country through the fertile Ganges plain to Benares, Lucknow and Delhi; these places are all, as he puts it (falling unusually into the third person), 'on the ascending scale in the traveller's estimation, and for that reason he is glad that his curiosity has led him onwards' (Hingston 1885:286). And back at Madras, when he finally gets ashore it is largely through his curiosity that he manages to surmount his lack of enthusiasm for the place.

His curiosity is aroused by the sight of some jugglers performing on a hotel verandah. Their repertory involved swallowing pebbles and swords, breathing fire, and a variety of substitution tricks, all quite mystifying. For Westerners travelling in India witnessing a performance of jugglers and magicians was one of the standard sights, and a conventional Western view of their trickery was that it was the devil's work, a trope Hingston rejects yet continues to play with whenever he encounters similar activities. Here, he observes that, with 'their black colour and unprepossessing features', one might 'believe that their clever doings were really *diablerie* in all senses of the word', but Hingston clearly respects their undoubted skills, asserting that 'these men were the best of their kind that I ever saw' (Hingston 1885:257). When, later on in Calcutta, he has the opportunity to attend some Western entertainment, he prefers instead 'a Hindoo entertainment' on the street. Again, extraordinarily proficient sleight of hand and swallowing tricks leave him pondering material and spiritual questions. Previously, he says, 'I had but a half belief in miracles, but I retired that night convinced that there was more in heaven and earth to understand than he thinks for who sits in the seat of the scorner' (Hingston 1885:268).

Hingston does not care to be one of the scorners; rather, he travels as one who prefers to reflect upon and draw what understanding he can from what he sees about him. At times it even resembles a self-education project as he

Figure 1: The Traveller and Guide in Delhi Palace

Hingston's view of India was mediated as much by his literary reading as by the words of his guides, whom he sought out on the spot, convinced of their superiority over published guidebooks. This illustration from *The Australian Abroad* depicts the studious traveller inside a Delhi palace being instructed by his guide in the mysteries of India's past, which Hingston saw as 'the transformation scene of an extravaganza'.

Source: Hingston's The Australian Abroad on Branches from the Main Routes Round the World, William Inglis and Co., Melbourne, 1885, p 286.)

probes and questions, ponders and draws his conclusions. He suggests at one point that travel is the key to broadening one's understanding of human nature (Hingston 1885:297). 'Never believe what you see' is one maxim he takes from watching these performances; 'In one way or another we are all throughout life the fools of our senses, to which we so pin our poor faith' (Hingston 1885:257–258). Beyond that, though, his open, inquiring mind searches for what this can tell him about the country he finds himself in. All this conjuring 'may be called the poetry of illusion, and…makes "the thing that is not seen as though it were"', but at the same time he recognises its specifically Indian character and long history:

> Such art is a specialty of Hindoostan. Practised for ages, and handed down from father to son, it has reached that fine finish that takes from it all semblance of art. In that way, the world has not its equal to show (Hingston 1885:269).

Similar thoughts occur to him when, spotting an abandoned Juggernaut car in Madras, he contemplates the awful nature of its purpose, now thankfully prohibited by the English. What 'a fine curio' it would make now, he thinks, its strange appearance creating 'a good show in some distant land' (Hingston 1885:256–257). This also is a tension he constantly explores—the nature of the British rule and its transformative or reductive effect on the ancient, vibrant, sensuous, but also pitiless culture now controlled through subjugation to imperial rule. Looking at the Juggernaut's wheels, he cannot help thinking of how many people had been crushed by them. Nevertheless, he can appreciate the complexity of issues involved in such prohibitions and their unexpected consequences, such as the lot of the poor widow after the banning of *suttee*. A widow has nowhere to go; she can neither remarry nor return to her own family, so for most women there is 'no refuge whatever but to become the slave of her mother-in-law!…thenceforth for the rest of her life the most miserable of all womankind' (Hingston 1885:278). The Juggernaut is for Hingston the first in a long series of ambivalent reminders of India's past.

The history of Madras has significance for the British visitor as it was the first place the British settled and built their first fort, Fort St George; it became the first of the Indian presidencies and was also where the English and French fought their first battle (Hingston 1885:258–259). Even though, as he says, for all these reasons Madras is properly the first city that one should visit in India, 'the mere visitor will not wish to make a long stay' here, and he is glad enough to leave, despite having to encounter again the indignities and dangers of the surfboats to rejoin his steamer. If he ever revisits Madras, he concludes, it will be on urgent business only and from the landward side (Hingston 1885:259).

Up the Hooghly River

From Madras, Hingston's steamer heads up the coast to enter the complex delta system of the Ganges on its western branch, taking on a Hooghly pilot who attracts Hingston's attention as one of a special breed unrivalled in the world, and slowly winds its way along the Hooghly River towards Calcutta. The boat by now is fairly empty, since, as Hingston explains, this means of arriving at Calcutta has largely been superseded by the new cross-country railway which has reduced the travel time by several days from Bombay, where ships now prefer to land mail and passengers. The creation of the railway network has not just made travel easier; it also has economic consequences for major centres, changing the commercial balance of the old India. It has made Bombay's fortune and significantly diminished Calcutta's trade, although some smaller boats that do not need pilots to negotiate treacherous sandbars continue to trade along the river, including two vessels he sees bound for China loaded with a cargo of opium. Later, as he travels across the plains to Benares and Lucknow, he'll see the vast poppy fields, but his first sight of 'this disgraceful traffic' is here (Hingston 1885:262). This leads him to contemplate the complex relationship Britain has with its subject peoples in India—something he continues to dwell on.

In Hingston's view, the opium trade is odious and as morally reprehensible as the slave trade: 'It is about equally profitable, and equally disgraceful and demoralizing', and should be suppressed too; nor should the opium be forced on the Chinese 'at the point of British bayonets'. Yet, he suggests, the very benefits brought to India by her new rulers, the British, are largely subsidised by the profits from opium, 'for years the best paying of Indian exports' (Hingston 1885:262–263). It is as if the nub of the complex, ambiguous, imperial relationship is encapsulated in the opium trade. Here Hingston argues that it is to Britain's credit that she does not enrich herself with the profits of either the opium trade or any other Indian produce: 'Every penny that is raised from India is spent upon the government and improvement of that country', he says (Hingston 1885:263). India's vast revenues 'are, within a few pounds, expended there in promoting protection, civilization, and the progress and bettering of its people', which he contrasts with the lack of protection Indians had previously enjoyed, being 'robbed by their rulers, and sacrificed to please their whims' (Hingston 1885:263).

On the other hand, Hingston has no illusions about the importance of India for Britain's standing in the world. It's a morally fraught conundrum reasoned away by claiming that if Britain is beneficent to its subject peoples then it is worthy of the prestige derived from holding such a great dominion, which is, in fact, 'the brightest jewel in the British crown'. Some people, he says, have diamonds to sell and profit from, but Britain holds tightly onto its jewel 'very much for the reason that all folks keep jewels—to show the world that they can afford to do so' (Hingston 1885:263). There is no mistaking, he adds, 'that the possession of this vast India alone places Britain in her foremost position among the powers of Europe. To lose it would be to sink to a second-rate place in the world's regard' (Hingston 1885:263). There is a conflicted kind of pride here for Hingston, giving way to his imperial sympathies, conflated with the pride Britain has in showing off its jewel to the world. And as his journey continues through the dominion, he is constantly amazed by the disjuncture between this vast empire, the Raj, that is 'as large as all Europe…and has more square miles of land than I know how to write without help; that has two hundred and fifty millions of souls' and of which 'the little island of Britain with its small thirty-eight millions is really the owner' (Hingston 1885:265). How would it be possible for so small a country to keep such a large, disparate territory in check if its rule were not benevolent? Such is the nature of the thoughts he retires with on his first night in Calcutta, as sleep overtakes him:

> I dream of the empire into which I have thus wandered…Is it anything but a dream—all that relates to such romance of a land that has had every great nation of the past at some time for its owner…? None of those great nations of the past have held greater power in it than little England, and none have held it longer. It is something wonderful to obtain of such a land even the bald and barren idea that writing can only convey. To *see* it is to satisfy one that there is an object in life (Hingston 1885:265).

It is perhaps no surprise, then, that with such thoughts circulating in his mind, he feels the need for the refreshing cynical asperity of the colonial viewpoint as a corrective and enjoys the moment at the Calcutta Customs House when an Australian, incensed by high-handed treatment from customs officials, 'taunts the officials of this great India as being only the servants of "a Crown Colony" and having no discretionary powers or liberty to exercise them in favour of a free and independent colonist like himself' (Hingston 1885:263–264). He does not say who this was, but, for all that he is English-born and an apparent closet imperialist, we should not forget that Hingston is also, as the title of his book firmly asserts, an 'Australian Abroad'.

Britain may have firm charge of its great, seething empire but the old India has a habit of irrupting in ways that form part of its fascination as signs of the mysterious East, as well as in other less reassuring ways. In Calcutta his guide shows him the site of the infamous Black Hole, now occupied by the post office building. It may now be subsumed beneath or behind the quasi-European facades of Dalhousie Square and out of sight, but it is a sign that the Mutiny[1] continues to lurk beneath the consciousness of the ruling power as still having the potential for appalling instability. On arrival there, Hingston remarks that an early recollection of Calcutta has to do with the story of the Black Hole, from which most people have 'an unpleasant impression of the place', and it is scarcely surprising that it should be in his mind since the events of the Mutiny occurred barely 20 years before his arrival in the country. They were events that shocked European self-confidence deeply and changed the way India was administered, as he recorded when he saw on their approach to Calcutta the prison-palace of the last king of Oude spread out along the Hooghly riverbank (Hingston 1885:262). It was, he said, the avaricious deposing of this king by the Honourable East India Company that was one of the main triggers for the Mutiny, and that, in turn, led to the deposing of the Company itself and the imposition of direct British rule and the creation of the Empress. For Hingston the sight of this palace was too redolent of what he calls 'the saddest pages in Indian history' and he thought it was 'bad taste to place this prison palace where it is. Such unpleasant features of the country should be set further back' (Hingston 1885:262). Out of sight is out of mind, perhaps. However, adopting his own symbolism, the imprisoned king 'caged a magnificently large and very restless Bengal tiger' on his water frontage in full view of all who passed by—a gesture whose meaning would be plain to all (Hingston 1885:262).

Throughout his journey Hingston encounters further traces of the Mutiny—marks on a city gate where Europeans were massacred, ruined and abandoned palaces, memorials for the dead—or else indications of its lingering effect. He is curious, for instance, about the grandiose railway stations he encounters all over the country, even at small towns, until he realises that they've been constructed as fortresses in case of future unrest, and that the rail network, too, is more than just an improvement in travel delivered for the country by benevolent rulers. 'With the network of railways

---

[1] It is usual nowadays to avoid the term 'Mutiny' for the overall Indian revolt in 1857–1858; in this chapter the term that Hingston used is adopted here for the revolt, as well as for placenames that have since changed.

throughout Hindoostan a series of forts have been thus built that may one day be needed' (Hingston 1885:293). His arrival at Cawnpore is a moment when memory of the Mutiny and lurking fear of another similar episode will become crystallised in one place and one time.

For now at least, in Calcutta he feels no sense of apprehension about 'the natives'. In fact, as he walks around he finds the disparity in population numbers between them and the Europeans almost reassuring, since 'it says something for good government, that one hundred and fifty thousand should dwell so peaceably, as a governing people, among two hundred and forty millions' (Hingston 1885:267). As a people, Indians 'are of temperate habits', he decides, with little inclination to change their situation: 'The way of life of the majority, wretched as it may seem, no doubt best suits them' (Hingston 1885:267). He has already formed a mental idea of Indians as pliant and supple like a willow branch, bending to the prevailing wind and letting change—and a succession of rulers—simply blow over them. 'They have ever bent where they should rebel. To that which ill-uses them they kneel. Their destroyer they worship. Of their trinity, the favourite god is the destroying Shiva' (Hingston 1885:260).

It is another of Hingston's themes that the East is unchanging and, regardless of what goes along on the surface of events, beneath it things continue much as they were. This was an orientalist view that chimed with his image of the romance of India of old, as 'the proper home of all that is imaginative, fantastic, sensuous, and extravagant' (Hingston 1885:291). While Delhi probably became for him the highest expression of this sentiment, wherever he went in India he found this element of the unchanging nature of the East to pervade.

Benares, the 'Holy City'

Travel from Calcutta onwards is now by train and with the change in mode of transportation the journey itself begins to take on a different hue. It is as if Madras and Calcutta have been like a foretaste of the real thing and Benares, supposedly 'of the most ancient of all habitations of men in this world' (Hingston 1885:272), is where the real journey begins—into the past and into the spiritual world of India.

In Calcutta Hingston had briefly noticed the places of worship of the three main faiths, commenting that only at the Muslim one was he forbidden entry. His observation then of the Hindu temples was that they reminded him more of small museums, being 'so full of carvings and curiosities' (Hingston 1885:270). In Benares, however, he's confronted by the full panoply of Hinduism at work—the multifarious shrines and temples and myriads of people crowding around him 'working out their salvation in the waters and in the temples; the priests ever at their elbows—and pockets' (Hingston 1885:274). His views seem to have undergone some subtle transformation as he realises that what he saw in Calcutta as just so many curios were much more than this. He mentions 'Professor Max Müller's lectures on the origin of religion' (Hingston 1885:272), which may have guided this change.[2] For he has now come to understand their individualities and what they represent as well as something of their origins, which he gives some account of, despite still finding the multiplicity of divine forms 'bewildering' (Hingston 1885:272–273). Here, he says,

> is to be seen all the idolatry and grovelling to graven images of which we read such denunciation in the Scriptures, and are so apt to think as a thing of a bygone period; and not, as it is, the form of religious worship followed by over one hundred millions of the inhabitants of Hindoostan (Hingston 1885:273).

After he had viewed the cave temples in southern India and had the Hindu pantheon explained to him more fully, he came to a deeper understanding of what he first saw at Benares (Hingston 1885:319).

It is this realisation that something so apparently ancient continues as a living religious force in the lives of so many which is at the heart of his understanding of India generally, not just its religious culture. Benares is the past as well as the present: 'Its antiquity…is the chief ingredient in that sanctity to which its crowds of temples only help'. He claimed that Benares, as one of the oldest cities in the world, rivals even Damascus and that Hinduism is one of the most ancient of religions, which 'has been described as the natural religion of humanity, and as the outcome of our ordinary devotional instincts, unguided by any revelation' (Hingston 1885:272). In Benares Hingston has been drawn in by this all-encompassing religious atmosphere to discover something he had probably not previously suspected. Of course, he's by no means the only 'European', or even Australian, to fall

---

[2] Max Müller (1823–1900), a German-born Sanskrit scholar and Professor of Comparative Philology at Oxford, was then well-known for his work on philology and comparative religion, as a translator of Hindu classical literature, and for this popular series of lectures first given in 1878.

under the sway of this ancient wisdom, at a time when widespread interest in Indian religion was developing, largely because of Müller's scholarly work and translation of texts. I have written elsewhere of other Australians who were attracted by India in this way, including Alfred Deakin, who pursued his own pilgrimage there slightly later (Walker 1999:20–25).[3]

Nor was Hingston's approach uncritical. Some aspects of Hinduism still trouble him, especially 'its fakirs—a class of fanatical beggars peculiarly holy and filthy' (Hingston 1885:273). Hingston cannot shake from his mind the connection between cleanliness and godliness, which colours his perceptions of *fakir*s, when he observes them in Benares and again in Lucknow, where he attempts to 'interview' one, as he puts it. This *fakir* had been living up a tree, where he desired to become imprisoned in a cage of growing branches, but British soldiers pulled him down and he remained in a deserted palace gardens, a 'most gruesome, grimy creature'. Hingston is appalled by the disfigurement and strange practices adopted by *fakir*s he met along his way and is not backward in expressing his 'disgust' (Hingston 1885:282). Despite these cavils, Hingston decides that in Benares 'the phenomena of faith can be well studied here—in this its head-quarters' (Hingston 1885:274). In a characteristic pose he determines, once again, not to be a 'scoffer' and throws himself into a maelstrom of investigation, bathing in the Ganges and drinking from the Well of Knowledge, while at the same time attempting to preserve a dignified impartiality.

His attempts to complete his pilgrimage, performing the same devotions that any Hindu would, are baulked by the intransigent guardians of the Well of Purification, who refuse his attempts to partake of its waters because he is not a Hindu; once again he discovers that, unlike what Europeans generally believe in Asia, some things are not to be bought (Hingston 1885:275). His cynical disposition has not been set aside, however, as we discover when he contemplates the kind of knowledge that might well afflict him after drinking 'that nasty mixture', the stinking waters from the Well of Knowledge. Equally, his bathe in Ganges made him feel 'all the better for it' but not, he suspects, for the same reason as those around him; in his case, it was because he now felt 'as one always does after a bath in this climate'

---

[3] There is never any suggestion that Hingston's interest is anything other than curiosity; he shows no signs whatsoever of interest in Theosophical views; for instance, Hingston refers to 'some spiritualistic imposters from America' at one of the theatres in Calcutta when he was there, and, intriguingly, Mme Blavatsky was in 1879–1880, conducting her own tour of India and giving various spiritualist performances, in which she visited many of the places Hingston visited, including Calcutta (Blavatsky 1892).

(Hingston 1885:274). He speculates that climate may have something to do with this worship, as he contemplates all those around him who 'believe in this sanctifying power of the Ganges with a strength of faith that we, born of a cold northern hemisphere, scarcely comprehend' (Hingston 1885:273). It is as if, here, Hingston is exploring the limits of his own tolerance.

He appears to be no longer in holiday-maker mode but to have taken on the role of an explorer or adventurer, as he surmises when pondering his motives for wanting to involve himself so directly at personal risk.

> Why we do such things these can well answer who risk their lives in climbing to dangerous peaks which have proved already fatal to many adventurers. No knowledge is to be gained by doing such risky climbing, but here the case was different; and I followed only the example of thousands whom I have no right to say were less wise than myself (Hingston 1885:275).

There is a suggestion, perhaps, that he has personally determined to test the Müllerian hypothesis on the plurality of religions and to leave himself open to the possibility that his own religion is not the sole valid profession of faith. This is the virtue of travelling, as he has already found; it teaches us about other possibilities—'If we learn in travelling what fools there are in this world, we also learn how we have been equally befooled at home in other ways' (Hingston 1885:275).

Benares has affected him in many ways: it has stimulated his curiosity and his bent for seeking knowledge and understanding; it has aroused his distaste and natural scepticism, but at the same time he has been deeply touched by it. He develops an admiration for Indian culture that informs what he sees in the rest of his journey, from the palaces and magnificent buildings of Lucknow and Delhi to the ancient remnants of old destroyed cities there and at Allahaba, and the temple-caves carved from the rock. Most of all, perhaps, Benares moved him in a way that must have taken him by surprise when he witnessed a cremation on the waterfront.

In Calcutta he had stumbled across a cremation, drawn, he said, by the smell of roast pork. It is perfunctorily described as something discovered by a sightseer, who then moves on (Hingston 1885:270). At Benares, however, his mind is undoubtedly transformed by all that he has seen; the cremation he sees is 'the most impressive sight, next to a hanging, that I ever saw'. He witnesses the complete ceremony as the pyre is built and the young widow takes the torch, walks round the pyre before setting it alight and then retires to watch her husband consumed in the flames. For Hingston, there is a poignancy in this scene as well, perhaps, as something symbolic of what he has learned here in Benares about the antiquity, continuity and vitality of Indian cultural life. It is something that will be, he says, 'a lifelong recollection—one of the most enduring that all India leaves with me' (Hingston 1885:277–278).

Lucknow and Delhi

The journey to Lucknow passes slowly through the same kind of landscape as before, but differs in other respects. This section of the railroad is the Oude and Rohilcund line and 'about the worst to be found in India', with dirty, old and uncomfortable carriages in which sleep is all but impossible. Yet, it turns out to be a more sociable leg of the journey when he encounters 'an old Australian acquaintance' who is a stationmaster at one of the stations on the line, and three Americans on the train 'who are travelling with no better reason for doing so than I have' (Hingston 1885:279).

Picking up on a long-running theme, the Australian bemoans the climate, saying he now understands why extreme heat was designated the chief post-mortem torment, and he misses Australia. The Americans are 'good company', Hingston finds, which makes up for the discomforts of this journey, as well as for the difficulties he had had in holding a conversation on the previous leg to Benares, when he 'had but Hindoos for company, and conversation therefore rather flagged' (Hingston 1885:279). Lest we do not grasp the point, Hingston adds 'which is but a mild way of saying that I could not understand a word that I heard said by those around me' (Hingston 1885:279). Hingston's difficulty in understanding Indians speaking English is one of his constant gripes, almost from the moment he first lands when he engaged a guide at Madras 'who, lyingly, said that he knew English' (Hingston 1885:256). However, the sense of companionship with the Americans, one of whom is a lady, is obviously mutual, as they keep company beyond Lucknow to Delhi and Agra, even adopting little subterfuges on the way to Delhi to keep Indians from entering their compartment (Hingston 1885:284).

They reach Lucknow early in the morning and, after tea and toast at 5 am in his hotel, Hingston sets out to wander around the town. He calls it the 'City of Palaces'; it is the 'City Beautiful', located in 'the very garden of Hindoostan', but he's really talking about a city 'that was so grand-looking but awhile ago' (Hingston 1885:280)—in other words, before the Mutiny.

This is the perpetually looming presence that marks the moment when the extraordinarily delicate and refined beauty of a dream city crashed in ruins. For Hingston's experience of Lucknow is in reality an experience of what once was rather than what is now, and he exerts his imagination, fuelled by his repository of literary knowledge, in an attempt to recreate the former glory of Lucknow that resides inside his head. Similarly in Delhi, where he celebrates the extraordinary richness and vitality of Moghul culture by reference to a long poem written by the Irish poet Thomas Moore, Hingston seeks out a world that has, to all intents and purposes, passed him by. In a telling observation there he laments that 'the traveller through India thus finds here that he is a day after the fair, and must see Delhi in all its glory in the mind's eye only' (Hingston 1885:287).

In contrast to the way in which he presented Benares, Hingston's experience of Lucknow, Delhi, and Agra is treated primarily as an architectural excursion; it is principally the buildings and town planning that attract him and form the substance of his commentary. He is captivated by the palaces, towers, mosques and gardens that constitute what remains of 'that once magnificent city' of Lucknow (Hingston 1885:281) and the 'wonder of a city' that is Delhi (Hingston 1885:285). In so doing, he has reverted to a familiar kind of tourism—the concentration on past glories now suggested only by the grandeur of their ruins. It is the kind of tourism that took travellers to the ruins at Athens and Rome to contemplate the achievements of the classical world or to Egypt to marvel at the legacy of the Pharaohs. It was also the kind of tourism that by this late stage of the 19th century was influenced by Ruskin. The tone of Hingston's treatment of the former architectural splendours of Lucknow and Delhi recalls some of Ruskin's writing on the decayed greatness of Venice.

The recital of the names of these places, such as the Chutter Munzil and the Kaiser Bagh gardens in Lucknow, the Shalimar gardens and the Red Fort in Delhi, evokes for him, and for the educated British reader, a certain exoticism. Hingston's account of what he sees in them is replete with the tropes of orientalism and of decayed civilisations—of decline and fall. In Lucknow and Delhi he imagines languid courts and reclining *houris*—all the sensuousness that practical Englishmen, perhaps wistfully, associate with the soft, sinuous East. In Delhi particularly, his mind's eye is full of the images supplied by his reading of Thomas Moore's *Lalla Rookh* (1817), which was in part, he points out, set there. Indeed, he suggests that the reason he was so keen to see Delhi was that he owes his earliest knowledge of it to this poem: 'Moore's pleasant imagery and word-painting take hold of the reader, and remain in the memory—thus giving to Delhi a poetical, equally with an historical, interest' (Hingston 1885:285).

However, in viewing India through this particular lens, Hingston is following an already well-established tradition for the British traveller. It has been suggested that the poem's continued popularity long after its first publication in 1817 influenced the kind of exotic imagery used by British visitors to India for most of the 19th century (Archer & Lightbown 1982:104–106). As early as 1838 one traveller in Kashmir, GT Vigne, remarked, 'At one glance we have before us the whole of the localities described in *Lalla Rookh*. I use the word described, for there is great justice in the ideas of scenery to be collected from the poem' (Archer and Lightbown 1982:109).

In fact, Delhi was one for Hingston of the highlights—if not *the* highlight—of his tour of India. It was a place he had yearned to see— 'Youthful impressions being of the strongest, Delhi so draws me to it, irresistibly' (Hingston 1885:285)—and he is not disappointed by all it offers. It is at one of the old sites of Delhi that he sees the Kootub Minar, a 250-foot high minaret, 'simply the largest shaft, the grandest pillar, the tallest and most costly column, that the world can show!'; seeing this 'alone is worth the journey to Hindoostan' (Hingston 1885:290–291). His enthusiasm for such a large object of this shape might cause some to snigger, when it is presented so baldly, but what Hingston is suggesting here is that the structure suggests a kind of sublimity evoked by a combination of its antiquity (it was constructed in 1190), its architectural detailing and carving (the Koran is beautifully carved around the column as it ascends), and, most of all, the views of it and from it and what they suggest. This again is a familiar trope of tourism, but one more commonly associated with natural views of mountain peaks and high thundering waterfalls. The tower impresses Hingston 'as a grand combination of architectural ideas, in all of which elegance is allied with great strength' (Hingston 1885:291), but, as usual in these discussions, he clarifies his aesthetic appreciation by describing the affective impression it makes upon the viewer and what it engenders in the spectator who adopts it as a viewing point.

> The effect on the visitor is according to temperament; the excitable are full of loud admiration; but others seem dazed and subdued to quietude by a majesty that approaches the sublime, so far as stonework can represent it. Hours are spent in wandering around and sitting about at different points of view to gaze at what so fascinates one. The ascent is, from the large size of the pillar, made with the greatest ease—the four

hundred steps leading one around to the summit with scarcely a feeling of fatigue. The view from that position is over a scene of desolation and ruined greatness that is quite deplorable (Hingston 1885:291).

Once again, we are brought back to the feelings of decay and loss and former grandeur which Hingston presents as the prevailing message of the stones of Lucknow and Delhi.

'The rest', he says, 'can be filled in by the imagination of those who look now upon that which is left' (Hingston 1885:287), which is what he invites us to do. Literature can certainly help in this process and Hingston's recourse to Byron and Moore, and even to *The Thousand and One Nights*, in this context is instructive; it is no surprise that the complete title of Moore's poem is *Lalla Rookh: An Oriental Romance*. Of Delhi, he comments 'Literature has helped to its great fame' (Hingston 1885:285). It is not too much to say, however, that Hingston is seduced by the buildings and that his reading has assisted in this process. He describes Lucknow's Chutter Munzil as 'a building that, in a sort, invites the visitor and woos him to visit it' (Hingston 1885:281). He has a similar reaction when he first sees the Taj Mahal by daylight in the distance: 'Now that one so sees it, there is no help but to go, as all further resistance to its fascination is ineffectual. It is as if Venus, fresh risen from the sea, had beckoned one to come' (Hingston 1885:302). When close to it, his reaction is similar to the impression created by the Kootub Minar. He sits gazing upon the Taj Mahal in companionable silence with his three American friends, 'but we are each as if we were alone'.

> So seated, every sense within one seems to run all to eyesight…hearing is gone…The enchanter architect who inspired this pile has waved his wand, and spell-bound one. He was a true Prospero, and one gazes as if one would never cease gazing at this 'dainty Ariel' of a palace, which he has here called into existence (Hingston 1885:302).

The eye may have taken over momentarily, confounded by the sublime prospect unlike any other sight in the world (Hingston 1885:304), but literature is deeply implicated in his response and has not been forgotten:

> If you ever thought that the 'Arabian Nights' was all nonsense and romance, and 'Lalla Rookh' all imagination and fancy, what think you now?—now that you have looked around upon the scene that has filled the last four hours as if but a few minutes. You have looked

upon Lucknow and its palaces—you have seen what Delhi and its surroundings have had to show—and have now come to this wonder of all wonders. Are your thoughts what they were; or what say you? You are silent, and silence is the all-sufficient answer (Hingston 1885:304).

Yet, while Hingston—and, indeed, any 'European' or, more specifically, British visitor—may stand in front of these buildings mysteriously drawn to them, with their heads full of romantic imagery of the East, there is no question that a denizen of Lucknow or Delhi or Agra, standing by his side, would have his head filled with a different kind of imagery. This is more especially so of Lucknow and Delhi, where the recital of the names of palaces and forts and mosques Hingston endows with romance are precisely the same names and places that only a short while before carried terrible associations of massacres, appalling privation, war and heroic battles, and carnage. Hingston does mention the Mutiny—he could hardly avoid doing so—but only in passing and only from a British perspective; he does not allow recent history to draw him in with the same attention to detail that he applies, say, to the workings of Shah Jehan's court. He talks of the British losses but does not ponder the Indian ones. This is a significant omission, since the relief of Lucknow by the Highlanders supposedly marching in to the sound of the bagpipes was one of the almost archetypical moments in the Mutiny—a moment fixed in the popular Victorian imagination and recreated endlessly in drawing-room prints. What did not impinge on the Victorian imagination in the same way was what occurred in the moments after the relief. These events were recorded in old photographs, such as Felice Beato's 1858 photograph of the courtyard of the siege-battered Sikanderbagh building strewn with the remains of about 2000 'rebels' slaughtered by the British forces after they regained control (reproduced in Chaudhary 2005:63) and in another contemporary image showing the British military looting the Kaiser Bagh (Russell 1860:I, facing 333)—a place, according to Hingston, of 'bewildering prettinesses', which was built just seven years before its destruction at huge cost by the same ruler of Oude imprisoned on the prison-palace on the banks of the Hooghly (Hingston 1885:280). These images, which suggest there is an alternative story to be told, might accord better with local memories of these events and be closer to the associations these placenames prompted in the minds of the local inhabitants.

The fact that Beato's 1858 photograph is constructed does not detract from the force of its imagery. Without going into his reasons for doing so, one can surmise that Beato reconstructed a scene that he felt had some kind of veracity.[4] Beato's reconstructed scene represents a narrative, just as Hingston does with his construction of the meaning of the buildings he sees. Each is an act of imagination related to architecture. In Hingston's case, however, the touristic concentration on the architecture allows him to elide the uncomfortable recent past, whereas Beato's representation highlights it.

Hingston has postponed his reckoning with the Mutiny until he comes to Cawnpore, as he acknowledges upon arriving at Delhi, saying that in his haste to get there 'I overrun another city by the way, to which I must return, as it has a name in the story lately made more prominent even than this great Delhi, though from other and sadder causes' (Hingston 1885:285). He clearly does not want the Mutiny to get in the way of *Lalla Rookh*. Just as Beato's photograph is a set piece, Hingston has reserved a special chapter for his own set piece on the Mutiny.

In the meantime, he tours Lucknow, Delhi and Agra, determined to take in their historic buildings and the remoter history they suggest, as well as taking what opportunities he can to remind us of the benevolence and achievements of British rule. For all his admiration of their beauty and refinement, Hingston remains mistrustful of the motivations behind their construction and the way they were built, arguing that 'slave labour is the secret of the wonders of architectural India' (Hingston 1885:288). These differ from the motivations of the British, of course, whose construction of such things as bridges and railways is more practical and democratic, being aimed at providing benefit for the Indians without exploiting them. His readership is, after all, among the 'British' (in the wider sense of that term). He is also, in the end, more comfortable with the 'British'; he has slipped back here into being once more the colonial gentleman on tour—and hard work it is, too, all this sightseeing (Hingston 1885:283). If only he could 'have been here in the last century—about 1738—to have seen Delhi in all its glory, ere the Persians then despoiled it' (Hingston 1885:285) (or even in about 1855, before the modern-day equivalent of the Persians despoiled it?). Fortunately there is still *Lalla Rookh* to paint the scene for us. Hingston may well have possessed one of the many illustrated editions of this book. Richard Westall was the first artist to provide illustrations for *Lalla Rookh*, for an edition published in 1829, but the best-known portrayal of Moore's vision was in Sir John Tenniel's illustrations for the 1861 edition (Nolan

---

[4] About 4–5 months after the event, Beato had the bodies disinterred from their shallow graves in the vicinity, where they were only partially buried, and arranged them across the courtyard for his photograph (Chaudhary 2005:68–70).

2008: 80,84).[5] This was the India[6] Hingston had specifically sought out and was why Delhi represented for him in so many ways the pinnacle of his journey.

> India is the land of the wonderful, and the proper home of all that is imaginative, fantastic, sensuous, and extravagant. Its past has been as the transformation scene of an extravaganza. It is something, I think as I leave Delhi, to have, in so seeing it, realised 'Lalla Rookh' (Hingston 1885:291).

Departure

India has challenged Hingston and charmed him. To paraphrase the words of Whitman, it is large and contains multitudes, and Hingston has done his best to take them in, travelling around filling his notebooks and consulting his sources, including the ones he only lets slip, perhaps by accident, some of which have been discussed here and some speculated upon. For it is clear that he has, after all, done much reading and, as he sits on the Bombay wharf waiting for his steamer to leave, he drops another name, that of Colonel Cory, which tells us he was thinking imperially about India at this juncture—about the 'Great Game' and the threat from expansionist Russia in the north.[7] He quotes Cory's assessment of what a catastrophe for British wealth and might the loss of India would be. Cory quotes Peter the Great's description of India as 'the storehouse of the world' and Hingston wonders

---

[5] An important part of Moore's project was to use the orientalist setting to cloak his critique of British imperialist policy and of the Protestant Ascendancy in Ireland—'Moore created an Orient in *Lalla Rookh* which was integral to an anti-imperialist stance' (Majeed 1992:120). It seems unlikely that Hingston would have been aware of this aspect of *Lalla Rookh* or favourably disposed to it.

[6] Work by the scholars Javed Majeed and Mohammed Sarafuddin has reappraised Moore's orientalism more favourably, placing more focus on the ambiguity of *Lalla Rookh* as a political allegory and discovering in it a more sympathetic understanding and even a more accurate representation of Islamic or Moghul life than some previous Western commentators have given it credit for; so perhaps in this respect at least Hingston may not have been totally wide of the mark (Majeed 1992:97,104; Sharafuddin 1996:138,141–142,213).

[7] Colonel Arthur Cory, a former officer in the Bengal Army, was the first co-editor and managing proprietor of the Lahore edition of the *Civil and Military Gazette* (from 1877) and later edited the *Sind Gazette* in Karachi. He was the author of *The Eastern Menace, or, Shadows of Coming Events* (1881) and was regarded as an expert on the politico-military strategic issues affecting northern India (Carter 2000:12; Marvin 1882:45,336–337).

aloud 'whether Russia's gradual advance to the gates of Afghanistan' is a continuation of Tsar Peter's policy (Hingston 1885:330).

All Hingston's observations have now come together in this imperial viewpoint. His tour has taught him that the British presence on the subcontinent is tenuous:

> The feeling of the traveller throughout India is, that he is in a foreign land…and liable at any time to be kicked out of it…If England cannot, for climatic reasons, colonize India, what chance has she of permanently holding it? (Hingston 1885:331).

None of a succession of previous rulers, he reminds us, not even the colonising Mongols could hold onto it in the past.

> What Colonel Cory tells us is well-known to the nations of the world, and such a many-times transferred country as India is will be certainly looked upon as fair prey for any Power at variance at any time with England (Hingston 1885:331).

But, for various reasons he concludes that 'British power has nothing to fear from those that are now in India' (Hingston 1885:331) and has great faith in its civilising mission, which, by providing education and elevating the living standard, personal security and civil status of the ordinary Indian, will continue to prevail, he argues, so long as Indians recognise the benefits conferred upon them (Hingston 1885:334). The process of 'adopting the Hindu into the British family' (Hingston 1885:334) will pay off in the end and, ultimately, will even bring about the passing of what Hingston regards as one of India's greatest evils and impediments to progress—caste, which he describes as 'a tree of great toughness, ancient growth, and wide-spreading roots and branches. Yet it is marked for falling at some distant date' (Hingston 1885:332).

For the rest, after spending barely any time there at all compared to what is needed to do it justice, his visit to India has been like a dream—so much so he can scarcely recall all he's seen:

> An Arabian Night's sort of dream will India be to prince or peasant who may run through it all…bent only on seeing everything with the eye of the curious. The recollections of it will jumble in the confused manner of dreams (Hingston 1885:333).

Already it is time to leave and, as the deck-gun lets off its farewell, one-gun salute, Hingston gazes back from the stern of the mailboat. His last view of India, like his first, is from the sea.

Works cited

Archer, Mildred and Ronald Lightbown 1982, *India observed: India as viewed by British artists, 1760–1860*, Victoria and Albert Museum and Trefoil Books, London.

Baedeker, Karl (ed) 1898, *Egypt: handbook for travellers* 4th remodelled ed, Karl Baedeker, Leipsic.

Blavatsky, Helena Petrovna 1892, *From the caves and jungles of Hindostan*, Theosophical Publishing Society, London.

Carter, Jennifer MT 2000, 'A tale of two poets', *Kipling Journal* 294.

Chaudhary, Zahid 2005, 'Phantasmagoric aesthetics: colonial violence and the management of perception', *Cultural Critique* 59 (Winter).

Cory, Arthur 1881, *The Eastern menace, or, shadows of coming events*, Kegan, Paul, Trench & Co., London.

Hingston, JH 1885, *The Australian abroad on branches from the main routes round the world*, William Inglis and Co., Melbourne.

Majeed, Javed 1992, *Ungoverned imaginings: James Mill's* The history of British India and orientalism, Clarendon Press, Oxford.

Marvin, Charles 1882, *The Russian advance towards India*, Sampson Low, Marston, Searle and Rivington, London.

Moore, Thomas 1817, *Lalla Rookh: an oriental romance*, Longman, Hurst, Rees, Orme, and Brown, London.

Nolan, JCM 2008, 'In search of an Ireland in the Orient: Tom Moore's *Lalla Rookh*', *New Hibernia Review* 12(3).

Russell, William Howard 1860, *My diary in India, in the year 1858-9*, Routledge, Warne & Routledge, London.

Sharafuddin, Mohammed 1996, *Islam and romantic orientalism: literary encounters with the Orient*, IB Tauris & Co., London.

Walker, David 1999, *Anxious nation*, University of Queensland Press, St Lucia.

— 2005, 'Hingston, J. H. (1830–1902)', in *Australian dictionary of biography*, Supplementary Vol, Melbourne University Press, Melbourne.

Chapter 9

Critics, Crucibles, and a Literary Career

Inez Baranay and Her Indian Novel, *Neem Dreams*[1]

Alison Bartlett

When Inez Baranay's seventh book, *Neem Dreams*, was released in September 2003, it met with wide critical acclaim in India, yet was barely noticed in Australia. Baranay had been publishing in Australia for almost 20 years, but this novel was published in India, indicating a shift in her publishing career. While *Neem Dreams* continues Baranay's interest in issues of Third-World development and with Western tourism, travel and trade, I propose in this chapter that it also engages with Australian literary criticism, especially in postcolonial debates. *Neem Dreams* was released almost a decade after Baranay's nonfiction text, *Rascal Rain* (1994), which met with fierce criticism. That decade was one in which Baranay addressed that criticism, contemporary theory and the academy. I argue, therefore, that *Neem Dreams* signals Baranay's uneasy relationship with Australian writing, publishing and identity, as well as her changed attitude to the academy and contemporary theory. While the back cover blurb of *Neem Dreams* alerts us to the neem tree 'acting as a kind of crucible for India', I want to argue that, in many ways, postcolonial theory is the crucible for this book. In this chapter then, I offer a reading of Baranay's literary career from 1994 to 2004 through its encounters with the academy, with *Rascal Rain* and *Neem Dreams* operating as bookends. Her substantial and productive career means that shifts in institutional and political discourses become evident in tracing the ways in which Baranay's

---

[1] This chapter is a revised version of Chapter 1 of *Australian Made: A Multicultural Reader*, edited by Sonia Mycak and Amit Sarwal (Sydney University Press, Sydney, 2010), which was first published in *Antipodes* December 2007.

texts and career are read (and written). I am interested in the kinds of questions a career such as hers raises about the imbrication of theory and fiction and the circulation of authority among writers, critics and the academy.

Neem Dreams

Inez Baranay's seventh book, *Neem Dreams*, was published in India by Rupa & Co. In many ways it is fitting that it was published in India, as the novel revolves around the lives of mainly four characters in India. Pandora is an Australian whose PhD was on women and development in the Third World. She is an ecofeminist and wants to write about a local women's project that involves the collection of neem seeds. The project has been organised by Maneeksha, an Indian woman who was educated in the United States and returned to India to be married to Prashant. Prashant and his cousin run the local neem factory, producing skincare products which Jade, another Australian, wants to buy in bulk. She works for an upmarket store in SoHo named Orientalisme, which offers urban New Yorkers the commodities of the East. Jade is particularly attracted to the marketability of the raw brown paper wrapping of the neem soap. Andy is a gay English lawyer in India to cast his lover's ashes into the Ganges and to find out more about neem as a potential answer to AIDS. The collision of these lives with the politics of globalisation, rural aid, trade agreements, corporate greed, packaging, traditional knowledge and ownership, and postcolonialism all spiral around the neem tree, 'a kind of crucible', as the back cover calls it, and a symbol of India. The narrative structure is sophisticated, repeating the same few days from different narrative points of view and covering continents as personal histories are filled in. Interspersed are seven chapters on the myths, remedies, folklore, business, politics and potential patents of the neem tree.

Following the book's release, reviews from India were glowing. Almost all of them admire Baranay's skill as a foreigner in capturing an authentic India. Eugenie Pinto's review in *Crossings* claims that 'Inez Baranay's perception of India is truly amazing. She has put her finger on the pulse of the country—nothing has escaped her keen observation' (Pinto 2003). Meenakshi Kumar in the *Hindustan Times* was slightly more hesitant at giving out accolades to a foreigner writing about India:

> Like most foreigners who are bitten by the India bug, Australian writer Inez Baranay too, is in love with the country. But unlike most

foreigners, it's not the unwashed sadhus, bedecked elephants or snake charmers who fascinate her or form a part of her writing. Her latest book, *Neem Dreams*, steers clear of dishing out an exotic India (Kumar 2003).

Swati Pal, in another Indian newspaper, *The Sunday Pioneer* was similarly happy that the writer does not use India as an exotic backdrop' (Pal 2003), while Padmini Devarajan, in *The Hindu*, raised the possibility that gender is another potential hurdle that Baranay overcomes: 'Baranay has risen above her feminine voice and foreigner perspective to strike a neutral unbiased language as far as basic values and issues are concerned' (Devarajan 2003). Pal made the claim that Baranay 'uncannily conjures splashes of Indian reactions, attitudes or relationships with as much authenticity as she does the American, Australian and British ethos' (Pal 2003). Publishing this novel initially in India was important to the reviewers, perhaps as evidence of Baranay's commitment to the Indian literary establishment, authenticating her involvement in Indian cultural life, which the reviews applaud as getting it right. But it is also an aspect of representation that Baranay argues is rooted in shared class and cultural values. Outlining her immersion in Indian novels, newspapers, magazines, music, conversations, as well as her travels in India while preparing the manuscript, Baranay suggests that 'the middle classes have a culture that overlaps several other categories of cultural identity such as nationality and ethnicity' (Baranay 2004a). On this basis, she suggests that the educated middle-class Indian characters she writes are probably closer to her own cultural identity and sense of self than an Australian woman of a class and life experience different to her own. While this argument is crucial to Baranay's critical position in representing India, it does not explain why this novel was barely noticed in Australia. Only one online review appeared on an Australian site (*API Review of Books*), written by an Indian reviewer two years after the novel's publication (Prasad 2005). While *Neem Dreams* continued Baranay's enduring interest in travel, tourism, and development, in other more complex ways it marked her active engagement with academic criticism and postcolonial theory.

Critics

Neem Dreams came almost a decade after the publication of *Rascal Rain*, Baranay's first nonfiction book, which narrates her experience as an

Australian Volunteer Abroad with a women's development project in Papua New Guinea. In contrast to the strong reception given to her earlier fiction, *Rascal Rain* was not well received by reviewers, who focused on its cultural politics as if it were 'a defence of imperialist projects and attitudes' (Baranay 2003b:224). One critical article, in the North Queensland journal *LiNQ*, explored the shortcomings of the book in detail (Ash 1997:44–54). Interested in the discourses that operate to construct the tourist, the traveller and the aid worker, Susan Ash notes that Baranay 'conspicuously demonstrates political and personal awareness. For example, she recognises the travel industry's slogan "Papua New Guinea is for travellers not tourists", as nothing but a "wise-ass distinction"' (Ash 1997:47). Ash then asks, 'can [Baranay] avoid colonizing, exoticizing operations in language? The answer is emphatically no, but what does surprise is the degree and intensity to which she employs "staggeringly"…offensive images of local people' (Ash 1997:47) and lists examples, including one description of a young boy as a 'beautiful…fine-boned black-skinned just-out-of-childhood beauty' (Baranay 1994:1). Ash critiques this by writing,

> She calls him a 'young god.' (1) In other words, here we have the stock aestheticised, eroticised and sexualised body of the native. In fact, [Baranay] subjects everybody she meets to this penetrating inspection by the Western eye, selecting and filtering the visible for signs which, when translated into narrative, will enter a web of signification already familiar to the Western reader (Ash 1997:48).

In short, Ash concludes that 'the resulting narrative invokes base, derogatory stereotypes' (Ash 1997:49).

In the next issue of the journal *LiNQ*, Baranay wrote a reply to Susan Ash titled, 'Theory Couldn't Help Me', rebutting many of the points Ash made and repositioning herself as a creative writer who does 'know' theory but does not find it helpful in her writing. In telling the story of her year in New Guinea, Baranay argues that *Rascal Rain* was,

> a strenuous attempt to make sense of the experience, while looking at ideas of what is a story, woman, race, culture, postcolonialism, development/aid and so on, and whether so-called women's development in third world countries—these terms I use in implicit multiple inverted commas—obligatory po-mo irony— is feminism or not or should it be or must it not be (Baranay 1998b:54)

In protesting her position as knowing subject rather than naïve writer, Baranay mobilises satire and allusion in her angry defence: 'to scold about… the "Western eye" is ludicrous. What are writers supposed to do, put out our eyes? To not ever write anything about non-Western people?' (Baranay 1998b:54–55).

Around this time I had more than a passing interest in Baranay, so I feel obliged to introduce myself as a character in this story of critics, crucibles and literary careers. This part of the story begins in 1992 when, as a beginning graduate student, I wrote to Baranay asking for an interview as part of my doctoral work which sought to position the writer as knowing subject, as theorist of her own work. Baranay was still living in New Guinea. We corresponded briefly. She was moving to Cairns in North Queensland where I had lived and asked advice on where to live. A couple of years later, we ended up living around the corner from each other as I finished writing my PhD and as *Rascal Rain* was published. The interview took place in March 1993, when Baranay was 'trying to make sense of the chaotic experience of the year before' (Baranay 2003b:226).

'Send me some theory' she asks, on women's development, on postcolonialism, on the latest feminism. 'I don't have any truck with universities', she tells me, nor did she have any contact with 'us' academics. She met some academics in Goroka, she tells me, but they were nice people. She isn't joking. 'I went to university [in the 60s] when the English school was extremely conservative. I was much more interested in the sex, drugs and rock'n'roll of that era. But I didn't see that reflected anywhere in the way the classes were conducted or in what we were reading [or] how it was talked about' (Bartlett 1998:220).

When I ask if she had come across any of the French feminists I was using, she says they were 'just names to me, and they've been on my Must Read This One Day list, but haven't fallen into my lap…I mean, where do you? You have to go to university don't you, to come across that sort of thing?' (Bartlett 1998:216). So I sent her some theory. I sent some Irigaray and some Cixous and a commentary by Elizabeth Grosz. I sent some Spivak and Chandra Mohanty's 'Under Western Eyes' (1984), which seems to have become an enduring trope in Baranay's institutional reception. This was the theory that 'couldn't help', and maybe it indicates some of the limits of theory for articulating politics that have been lived rather than imagined. Baranay presents a compelling quandary for writers who are informed of theoretical debates of cultural representation. Writing in retrospect in 2003, Baranay suggested that the book's reception was partially over-determined by the pressing social concerns of the time. It appeared, she reminds us, after the 1988

Australian Bicentenary, which officially celebrated 200 years of colonisation in Australia and provoked increased political and social movements to recognise the traumatic Indigenous history this involved. Ash's critical article coincided with the publication of the Stolen Generations report *Bringing Them Home* (1997), which documented the systematic removal of Indigenous children from their parents in order to dilute Indigenous culture. *Rascal Rain* appeared, therefore, 'in a period of increasing anxiety over Australia's ongoing shame-making history, and many took pains to demonstrate their difference and distance from the increasingly evident racism inherent in the nation's structures' (Baranay 2003b:227). Baranay rues the fact that 'the book's serious treatment' of women, race, culture, postcolonialism, development or aid and feminism was 'generally neglected' in its reception (Baranay 2003b:227).

I feel deeply implicated in the matrix of relations being played out here, which I now seek to construct as a narrative of a literary career reshaped by changing cultural formations. It is not coincidental that Susan Ash's article was published in *LiNQ* when one of my doctoral supervisors was editor and that Baranay was given the opportunity to respond to Ash's criticism. In the special issue of *Meanjin* on Papua New Guinea, in which Baranay's 'Fraught Territory' (Baranay 2003b) was published, editor Drusilla Modjeska attributes Baranay's dilemmas to the genre of memoir. But the cultural politics of representation are also infused in her latest fiction. If the neem tree is 'a crucible for India' (Baranay 2003a), then postcolonial criticism and Australian literary politics also function as crucibles for *Neem Dreams*.

Crucibles

Neem Dreams is conscious of its engagement with the fraught politics of postcolonial theory. In one scene, the materialistic Jade wants to talk clothes with Pandora, the highly ethical women's development worker:

> 'I secured a special little selection of *salwaar kameez*, these embroidered ones', [she says] patting her own ample dimensions, 'perfect for a New York summer'.
>
> Pandora didn't say anything. She had emphatically not 'gone Indian' in her own dress, in fact she never wore a dress…There was an appropriation issue she avoided by dressing as someone who is fine with the way she usually is (Baranay 2003a:186)

The novel touches on *suttee*, the practice of widow-burning, by having Pandora think 'that it is too easy to condemn the practices of other cultures by imposing the standards of our own practices of honour' (Baranay 2003a:205). Local politics and religious loyalties are conveyed as complex mechanisms, as representations of national identities that are understood to be multifaceted. As Meenaksha tells us, 'She says there is not a single India and I say there is not a single West' (Baranay 2003a:223).

The novel, therefore, is acutely aware of the cultural politics of representation. At one particular scene this becomes quite pointed as Pandora—the ethical one—polices herself. Pandora thinks of an Indian boy named Jolly as 'sweet':

> Uh-oh, hang on a minute, she checks herself, am I allowed to think of Jolly as *sweet*? Sweet, that word meaning a gentle, attractive demeanour, you can't call just anyone sweet, sinister meanings are attributed to adjectives applied to identifiable Others. Let's decide, she decides again, that there are sweet people in all the locations of the world and that I mean the same thing by it wherever I am, though that's not the end of it according to the professional perversities of certain pundits, critics keen to crow over forbidden perceptions, and whatever you might say about Others is forbidden. Never mind.
>
> 'The tea's really good' she said (Baranay 2003a:56).

This does not need a 'Dear Susan' for the traces of literary criticism to be readable. In fact Baranay spells it out in the authoritative space of *Meanjin*, saying that 'Writing this book was, in effect, an answer to, or defiance of, the objections made to my *Rascal Rain* and the foreseeable objections to the very project of writing a novel set in India with Indian characters' (Baranay 2003b:225). *Neem Dreams* seems to offer a responsive example of a text affected by institutionally regulated reading formations, which David Carter (1997:x) argues can 'govern how texts get to be written and get to be read'.

Literary careers

It is easy to read the decade of Baranay's career from 1994 to 2004 as being driven by the need to defend her writing. But I do not want this to turn into a story of the lone writer accosted by academic critics and then spending years in her turret, or travelling the world, writing back to the academy. Instead, my interest is in the shifting cultural formations at work in shaping her writing, reputation and reception. David Carter elegantly articulates the ways in which literary institutions—of writing, of theory, of criticism and publication and reviewing—can 'be discovered as textual or narrative effects which in turn will depend for their significance on the institutions governing what counts as literariness, as authorship, as appropriate reading, as a "serious" career in a specific literary system' (Carter 1997:xi). Such cultural formations cannot be figured, Carter argues, in dichotomous terms like inside/outside, creative/critical, because they generate affects on each other—they form relationships.

Baranay's construction as a writer in the public domain exemplifies this. In the late 1980s and early 1990s, Baranay's reputation could easily have been read, as I read it in my doctoral work, as pivoting on her position as a multicultural and a woman writer at a time when multiculturalism was still a federal directive and feminism a powerful social movement. Small presses actively published writers like Baranay. Even though Baranay has been dubious of being labelled in these ways, she benefited from their cultural currency, contributing to Sneja Gunew and Jan Mahyuddin's *Beyond the Echo: Multicultural Women's Writing* (1987) and to Sneja Gunew and Anna Couani's *Telling Ways: Australian Women's Experimental Fiction* (1988). Her biography on the Austlit Gateway emphasises her multicultural dimension, saying that she writes in English and that she has worked for the federal Department of Immigration, among other things.

Now, however, when positions like 'multicultural' or 'woman' writer are barely noticed in federal policy or publishing priorities, Baranay's biography demands to be read quite differently. Her biographical details as she presents them on her website begin by positioning Baranay as only provisionally Australian:

> I was born in Naples, Italy of Hungarian parents who emigrated to Australia when I was a baby. I was educated in the western suburbs of Sydney then moved to the inner city. I lived in Malaya with my parents as a teenager for two years, and began my adult travels with a trip to Bali in the late 1970s (Baranay 2012).

Note how her parents emigrated rather than immigrated, locating the subject elsewhere in relation to Australia. This gesture is repeated through listing other international locations for growing up and a continuing adult life of travel that 'began' in Bali. Her writing history is also decidedly charted through her travels, through her connections with and movement between other places:

> *The Edge of Bali* (1992) marked the end of 40 years based in Sydney (including travels in South-East Asia, Europe, Morocco and India)…I went to Papua New Guinea with Australian Volunteers Abroad in 1992 (the subject of *Rascal Rain: a year in Papua New Guinea* (1994))…I lived in Far North Queensland for the next few years, in Cairns and then Torres Strait Islands. In 1997 *Sheila Power* was published. During this time I also spent time in the USA, mostly New York City, with a stay in 1995 at Yaddo, the artists' colony in Saratoga Springs, and I India, where I have been several times to study yoga. Other trips to India have included a period as writer-in-residence at the University of Madras (2001) and a Literature Residency granted by Asialink (2002). India is the setting for my novel, *Neem Dreams* (2003) and was first published there (Baranay 2012).

I read this biography as a claim to be much more than an Australian writer. There seems to be a distancing of the writerly self from Australian literature, and more of a positioning as global citizen. Indeed, in an interview for *The Hindu* in 2003, Baranay maintains that 'nativity doesn't define us…After World War II, [my parents] happened to land up in Australia with a random throw of the dice. Italy is now just a name to me and being an Australian is only a twist of fate…I became an Australian only by leaving the country' (Baranay 2003c). If 'multicultural' and 'woman' writer are labels that are relics of the 1980s publishing and literary worlds, then Baranay seems to have adopted the markers of a newly cosmopolitan globalised economy to position her work and her career.

In this discourse, Baranay's identity and career have been resignified in order to do the work of authorising, as Carter suggests happens continually in the drive to authorise authorship:

> To write involves situating the text in a particular career trajectory the possibilities of which will be determined by the other texts and careers circulating in the relevant literary system…The writer's own prior texts and careers will be part of what is at stake, part of the structuring context, in any new act of writing; and any new writing which is granted status within the career will work to re-order, to re-write, this prior history (Carter 1997:xii).

This sort of reworking of prior history is evident in granting status to *Neem Dreams*, for while multiculturalism and woman writer are displaced for a more cosmopolitan cultural currency, Baranay mobilises that history in new ways to shore up her engagement with the literary politics of postcolonialism. She argues in a 2004 critical article that while she is so obviously a 'foreigner' in India, it is not a new experience for her: 'I grew up in an Australia where reffos like my family were foreigners, so a sense of foreignness, of parts of myself as essentially Other, had become part of my sense of myself' (Baranay 2004a). Even as she writes this, however, there is still a willingness for shift-shaping again, as she claims 'the writer goes on being shaped and changed by new texts and new characters, both other to and inextricable from, her sense of self' (Baranay 2004a; also 2004b).

Such a rewriting, or rereading, of Baranay's career, also tacitly suggests a displacement from Australian literary establishments. Indeed, this is evident in her relations with Australian publishers, who told Baranay that there was 'no market' for *Neem Dreams* (Baranay 2003b:228) and that the India and its characters in the book 'were not recognisable to them' (Baranay 2004a). She cannot persuade publishers to reprint her previous works, most of which are out of print (Baranay 2004d). In order to sustain the circulation of her writing, she has consciously taken control of her publishing and distribution. In 2004 she released *Three Sydney Novels*, which packages her previous books, *Pagan* (1990), *Between Careers* (1989) and *Sheila Power* (1997) in one cover and she has distributed *Neem Dreams* outside of India herself. This perhaps indicates much about the market-driven publishing industry, but also suggests a shift in the business of being a writer and an Australian writer in particular. Writers have for some time been obliged to market themselves as commodities—for writers' festivals and for creative writing courses—and Baranay suggests that self-publication and self-marketing is the next step. But this step also suggests a more conscious control of a career, of rewriting prior texts and future career trajectories. This need not be judged in a cynical or a celebratory way, but seems an extension of narratives of globalised corporations and trade agreements, individual packaging and ownership issues—the very themes of *Neem Dreams*.

In addition, Baranay's association with universities has been irrevocably changed since 1994. Not only has she been writer-in-residence and taught creative writing at universities, but she has also completed a PhD. Her second book of nonfiction, *Sun Square Moon: Writings on Yoga and Writing* (2005), includes material that began as part of her PhD. Baranay reviews, gives conference papers, and publishes monographs and academic papers, but still consciously positions herself as a creative writer for whom university is one of the fields in which she operates. But if Baranay's literary career has been reshaped through her textual interactions with academia, is the opposite also evident? Does the interaction between creative writing and academic writing as it merges in the form of doctoral graduates disrupt the sedimented divisions between writers and theorists? If Baranay now has academic credentials, does it change how we read her work? Will she receive the serious treatment she imagined for *Rascal Rain*? Can a writer like Baranay be regarded as doing postcolonial work in the form of fiction? Can a writer's ethics and aesthetics be considered as seriously as a critic's? Somehow, I am not so optimistic about these possibilities, although I should be. These questions prod and stretch the institutional formations through which we read and write careers, including our own.

Works cited

Ash, Susan 1997, 'Aid work, travel and representation: Inez Baranay's *Rascal rain* and Alice Walker's *Warrior marks*', *LiNQ* 24(2).

Baranay, Inez 1989, *Between careers*, Collins Australia, Sydney.

— 1990, *Pagan*, Angus & Robertson, North Ryde, NSW.

— 1992, *The edge of Bali*, Angus & Robertson, Pymble, NSW.

— 1994, *Rascal rain: a year in Papua New Guinea*, Angus & Robertson, Pymble, NSW.

— 1997, *Sheila power: an entertainment*, Allen & Unwin, St Leonards, NSW.

— 1998a, 'Creativity: review', *TEXT* 2(2), www.textjournal.com.au/oct98/baranay.htm, viewed 12.3.2012.

— 1998b, 'Theory couldn't help me', *LiNQ* 25(1).

— 2003a, *Neem dreams*, Rupa & Co., Delhi.

— 2003b, 'Fraught territory', *Meanjin* 62.

— 2003c, 'Speaking through her work', [interview with] TA Hafeez, *The Hindu: Literary Review*, 2 November, www.hindu.com/thehindu/lr/2003/11/02/stories/2003110200110400.htm, viewed 12.3.2012.— 2004a, 'It's the other who makes my portrait: writing self, character and the other', *TEXT* 8(2).

— 2004b, 'Multiculturalism, globalisation and worldliness: origin and destination of the text', *JASAL* 3.

— 2004c, *Three Sydney novels*, The Three Sydney Novels Project, Sydney.

— 2004d, Personal communication, 2 February.

— 2005, *Sun square moon: writings on yoga and writing*, Sun Square Moon, Sydney.

— 2012, 'Inez Baranay', www.inezbaranay.com, viewed 12.3.2012.Bartlett, Alison 1998, *Jamming the machinery: contemporary Australian women's writing*, Association for the

Study of Australian Literature, Toowoomba.

Carter, David 1997, *A career in writing: Judah Waten and the cultural politics of a literary career*, Association for the Study of Australian Literature, Toowoomba.

Devarajan, Padmini 2003, 'Unbiased perspective', *The Hindu: Literary Review*, 2 November, www.hindu.com/lr/2003/11/02/stories/2003110200100400.htm, viewed 12.3.2012.

Gunew, Sneja and Jan Mahyuddin 1987, *Beyond the echo: multicultural women's writing*, University of Queensland Press, St Lucia.

Gunew, Sneja and Anna Couani 1988, *Telling ways: Australian women's experimental fiction*, Australian Feminist Studies, Adelaide.

Human Rights and Equal Opportunity Commission 1997, *Bringing them home: report of the National Inquiry into the Separation of Aboriginal and Torres Strait Islander Children from Their Families*, Sydney.

Kumar, Meenakshi 2003, 'Writer from down under sells' *Hindustan Times* 4 September.

Mohanty, Chandra Talpade, 1984, 'Under Western eyes: feminist scholarship and colonial discourses', *Boundary 2* 12(3)/13(1).

Pal, Swati 2003, [Review of *Neem dreams* by Inez Baranay], *The Sunday Pioneer* 14 September.

Pinto, Eugenie 2003, 'Indian dreams', *Crossings* 8.3, http://pandora.nla.gov.au/pan/13231/20040203-0000/asc.uq.edu.au/crossings/8_3/indexa7f8.html?apply=dream, viewed 12.3.2012.

Prasad, Ch A Rajendra 2005, '*Neem dreams* by Inez Baranay', *API Review of Books* June, www.api-network.com/main/index.php?apply=reviews&webpage=api_reviews&flexedit=&flex_password=&menu_label=&menuID=homely&menubox=&Review=5429, viewed 12.3.2012.

Chapter 10

Connecting with India

Australian Journeys[1]

Susan Cowan

Geographical isolation and innate curiosity have long motivated Australians to leave their shores and travel far and wide to broaden their horizons and experience cultural and social differences with countries established long before explorers began to map Australia. As well as responding to the touristic impulse, there is also the patriotic one of planting Australia's name abroad, particularly in times of war. This essay looks at the writings of some of the travellers who converged on India, long before the hippy trail of the 1970s, through a historical lens, and compares these writings with a sample of those written later in the 20th century and the shifts in their perceptions and social and cultural awareness which evolved in modern times. India, which had long been purely a brief stopover on the P&O route for Australians, became a desirable place in its own right in the late 20th century, a mysterious subcontinent that signified high adventure and the exoticism of the other.

Colonial India: Lang, Skinner and Anderson

The earliest of these Australian writers, John Lang, was born in 1816 and has the distinction of being not only the first Australian-born novelist, with his

---

[1] Part of this revised paper appears with the title 'Glimpses of India: A Military Dekko', in Sarangi, Jaydeep and Binod Mishra (eds), *Explorations in Australian Literature* (Sarup & Sons, New Delhi, 2006).

authorship of *Legends of Australia* (Earnshaw 1974:58–59), but, according to CD Narasimhaiah (1980:xxi), the first Australian-born novelist to set foot on Indian soil. Lang's career and writings on India are explored elsewhere in this volume.

Born 60 years later than Lang, Mollie Skinner, a qualified nurse and midwife, went to India in 1913 at the age of 37. Four years later she joined the Australian Imperial Force, remaining at the base hospital at Jardee (Wilde, Hooton & Andrews 1994:699). The roguish hero of her 1937 novel *Tucker Sees India*, Richard Smith (Tucker), sees India from a variety of angles within and outwith the military from which he has absconded. A reluctant enlistee into the Australian Light Horse, Tucker, en route to the Great War, misses the boat after a hefty drinking session and remains in Bombay. Sent on his way by his cousin Reggie who happens to be serving there, he takes off on a series of adventures around India in many different guises.

Any preconceived ideas of the stereotypical Australian encountering India for the first time are swept away as the unusual hero Tucker adlibs outrageously and becomes variously a food tester, a nurse—a midwife even—while supposedly serving in the Indian army. Unlike some of his compatriots, Tucker moves among the throngs and feels uplifted by the 'stream of dark life' (Skinner 1937:22). Like John Lang's Wetherby, and indeed like Skinner herself, he quickly masters some Urdu and Hindi and travels all over India, connecting at times with military personnel whom he treats with a marked lack of deference, and with the locals whom he sees as equals, carrying out assigned military tasks and, chameleon-like, rearranging his persona to suit the occasion. He is fascinated by the military presence in India:

> Military police and doctors, so many little white threads holding back the huge dark mass of Indian humanity—how do they do it? Because of the divisions below, Hindu against Mussulman, caste against caste. Or because of the fear inspired by the great white powers over the seas. Was it out of fear they bowed down to the officials in their uniforms, representatives of the British Empire and the princes? Or from indifference? A great mystery it was (Skinner 1937:181).

For one who is so ready to learn about local customs, language and history, imperialism is an imponderable for Tucker. Distinguished towards the end of the novel as a 'gallant hero' for his conduct during a train raid, Tucker is modest, refusing to accept a bravery award from the very imperialists that he questions.

The larrikin Tucker faints at the sight of blood which gives rise to the suggestion that Skinner may also have wished to 'minimize, even eradicate the ubiquitous notion that all Anzacs were bloodthirsty sharp-shooters or vicious sabre-wielding killers' (Coates 1999:119). In *Tucker Sees India*, Skinner speaks with authority of her wide experiences in India and depicts Tucker, with the quintessential characteristics of the laid-back Australian, a rascal, filled with curiosity, challenging authority. He exploits his position by turning his so-called tour of duty into a touristic journey, evading the military, seeking cultural opportunities and trying to fathom the mystery of India and its people. Skinner softens the image of the bronze Anzac and questions the motives of the military presence and its effect on the local people.

Another Australian writer, a contemporary of the artists Thea Proctor and Grace Cossington-Smith and a fifth-generation Australian, Ethel Anderson lived for ten years (1904–1914) with her British military husband in several parts of India. Anderson sought to escape the boredom and loneliness of being a military wife by honing her accomplishments in writing, painting and music and became a lively chronicler of events in India, writing for the Indian *Pioneer* (as did Kipling in 1887 as a 16-year-old). Unfortunately few of these writings are extant, but those that have survived are well informed, colourful and sprinkled with Hindustani words (Foott 1992:74), giving a further edge of credibility to her work. HM Green (1961:1170) has described Anderson's work as 'in some respects near being a masterpiece'.

While Anderson's husband Austin, a British gunner, served with his battery in Campbellpore, Dinapore, Lucknow and finally at Nainital, Anderson put her mind to learning about India and its history (Foott 1992:65). She successfully draws on her observations of military life as a basis for her stories. She learned to ride side-saddle (Foott 1992:65) and caused quite a stir by winning the army sports day event with the four-in-hand, having been coached by Bombardier Gwyllam of whom she wrote a spirited autobiographical short story 'Bombardier Gwyllam's Night Out' (Anderson 1948).

Her best-known story, 'Mrs James Greene' from her *Little Ghosts* collection (Anderson 1959), arose out of a request by Lord Kitchener to Austin Anderson to look into the rumour that an Englishwoman had survived the Indian Mutiny in 1857 and had been taken into protection by Mirza Khan, an Indian *sowar* or cavalryman in James Greene's regiment (Anderson 1959:77). In Lucknow there is a memorial to the many who died at that time and Mrs James Greene's name quite erroneously appears on it.

The romantic side of this story would seem to have appealed to Anderson as the theme of mixed liaisons fascinated her. It is this aspect around which she bases this richly textured novella.

Mrs James Greene's husband is killed in the Mutiny and she escapes with her baby daughter and ends up in Mirza Khan's household, ostensibly until it was safe for her to rejoin her own people. Anderson romanticises the actions of her heroine who earns the respect and love of the *sowar*'s womenfolk for sharing her knowledge of 'the simple arts she had learnt in her English country home: tatting, knitting, the making of peculiarly good cheeses, and of various preserves, comfits, jams, pickles and sauces...which they sold with profit in the bazaar in Sitapur' (Anderson 1959:77). These 'simple arts' would have been exceedingly unusual talents for a 16-year-old Englishwoman of her class.

Observed admiring Mirza Khan as he bathes in the courtyard, Mrs James Greene tries to make plans to return to her friends in Lucknow. Not in a hurry to despatch his houseguest, however, Mirza Khan deems it unsafe for her to do so. She is saved again and is dressed in Indian clothing, when one of the mutineers visits the household and catches sight of her blue eyes shining out of her dyed brown face. Mirza Khan has no option but to kill the marauder and it is at this moment, dressed as she is in his wife's clothing from her wedding-night, that romance sparks and the dynamics of the household change. In the Spring Mrs Greene follows tradition, lays out her love mat—a quilt of neem flowers and jasmines—and waits for Mirza Khan to visit her (Anderson 1959:86).

The story jumps some 40 years when Mrs James Greene, having chosen to relinquish her British origins and remain with her lover, is observed by 'a famous traveller' dressed in the tattered rags of extreme poverty, with her Indian protector. Her loyalty to the now blind Mirza Khan is evident in her tender solicitude towards him and she ensures that he at least is wearing 'garments of a much better quality, clean and neatly darned' (Anderson 1959:86).

This female conventionality redeems her, and allows her, as Paul Sharrad (2004:101) observes, 'to appear as the titular heroine of a tale whose historical context might otherwise erase her, safely leaving her marked only by an official monument as a racially/culturally pure and dead victim of perfidious native violence'. The young widow, who appears to have grieved only briefly for her slaughtered husband, is highly regarded in the household of Mirza Khan, and as the mutual respect and admiration eventually turns into love, Mrs James Greene is prepared to sever connections with her own people to live like a pauper with her Indian lover. Like John Lang, writing nearly 100 years earlier, Ethel Anderson clearly recognises the fascination with and exoticism of the 'other', and she explores the possibilities that arise from the story of the legendary Mrs James Greene and makes the case for her to see it through to its logical conclusion.

Ethel Anderson's interest in mixed liaisons prompted her to write 'The Eurasian' (Anderson 1959), in which she gently mocks Eurasians by overdoing the *chee-chee* dialogue of her characters and giving them outlandish names with a Spanish/Portuguese flavour. Don Manoel Jeronimo Henriques William de Azevdeo, who is the head of the household, had been a lieutenant in the Goanese army. One of his daughters, Khujasta, is saved from drowning on the night of the Festival of the Lamps by the typically dashing hero, Major Hew Adam, who is later accused by the jealous colonel of trying to defraud her. Both men are subsequently killed on a night march. A colleague of Adam's, Major Wylde, investigates the story and finds the true culprit. Yet again, the ending redeems Anderson, as she marries off the sole remaining daughter to Major Wylde who adores her, not just because she has inherited a plantation and great wealth. In contrast to Mrs James Greene who accepts the poverty that goes with her love for Mirza Khan, this story gives the impecunious English officer his heart's desire and the wealth that goes with it. For the romantic Anderson, both women get their men.

Described as a 'unique figure in Australian letters' (Thompson 1958:177–178), Anderson explored and profited from her experiences with the people whom she had grown to love in India. The long periods of enforced loneliness as a military grass widow do little to dampen her high spirits, but fuel her curiosity particularly about women and their relationships. Although she enjoyed interacting socially with upper-class Indian women, she did not concern herself with the lot of the oppressed and underprivileged. In no way did she seek to be a radical reformer or challenge the conventions of the status of women. Anderson died in 1958, a formidable and feisty 75-year-old who sported a silver ear trumpet. Her lively voice, which is little heard today, nevertheless makes a rich and important contribution to literary studies.

Post-colonial India: Clark, Koch, Stivens

In his review essay 'Last Mango in Pondicherry', Sunil Badami takes up the cudgels against books not only by Western writers affected by their visits to India, but 'in more recent "postcolonial" times, by native-born writers who have left India and write about it in English far from home' (Badami 2004:200). Badami includes Rushdie, Seth and Mistry on his hit list and views their work as 'mango novels'—'exotic-looking fruits of the imagination that conjure up colourful mirages of magical-realist wonders (or thrilling terrors) in faraway places' (Badami 2004:200). Badami grew up in Australia, speaks no Indian languages and questions the authority of anyone to speak on India at all. He asserts that on a visit to India the 'greatest peril of travelling in India is not catching Delhi belly, but…it's constantly being told by other travellers *what India is*'. Badami delights in bringing these pseudo-experts back to earth by reminding them of the caste system, dowry deaths and communal rioting (Badami 2004:201). Perhaps it is easier for expatriate Indians to view their homeland through a rosy prism, where Western writers expect to feel confronted and uncomfortable by their first impressions of life on the subcontinent.

Three contemporary writers whose perceptions and cultural consciousness have been partially formed in postcolonial India include the well-known Australian historian, Manning Clark, who wrote a collection of short stories that included a satirical piece 'A Democrat on the Ganges' (Clark 1969). The story describes the changing perspective of a rather clueless couple, Jack and Val Howell on their first trip to India. Clark clearly enjoyed writing this short story, drawing on observations made on his short time in India and dwelling on the concerns of the less worldly as they undertake an experience of a lifetime.

Nominated by the University Labor Club to travel to India on a goodwill mission, the Howells are bewildered from the moment they set foot on the subcontinent. They attempt to be open-minded, 'democratic', and struggle to be egalitarian. For a social scientist, Jack is peculiarly unskilled in social and cultural contexts: 'Why not…see the sights on Mother Ganges—see the burning-ghats before decent education and decent conditions give these people an adult attitude to death?' (Clark 1969:85). He is likewise puzzled that his students in Delhi would find his pamphlet 'The Role of Social Sciences in Underdeveloped Areas' offensive. On the one hand, Jack acknowledges the poverty that he sees, yet to save money he attempts to show 'these Indians the meaning of democracy. I'll carry the bags up to the room', thus confusing 'democracy' with choice and overlooking the needs of the hotel staff (Clark 1969:88). Clark's tongue-in-cheek portrayal of the besieged pair doesn't let up as they stagger from crisis to crisis, forking out rupees at every turn, while differentiating themselves from Americans and the English, thus making it possible 'to be matey, and friendly and nice to Indians' (Clark 1969:88).

The perennial problem of gratuities, which infuriates Jack Howell as Val tries to rein in what she considers to be his excessive tipping, causes him to hire a boat on the Ganges which he attempts to row himself. Obviously not as fit as he was in his university rowing days, Jack collapses in the bottom of the boat to the sound of the guide telling him unhelpfully, his lips practically touching Jack's ear, that 'All Hindus believe if they die on Ganga their souls go "straight to paradise"' (Clark 1969:92). Dwelling on his dislike of the physical intimacy of the Indian men he has observed, he feels he has 'got mixed up with a pack of queens' (Clark 1969:92). The story ends with the hapless Howells surrendering their rupees in begrudged acquiescence to pay to be rowed back to shore. It seems that Clark himself had a few difficulties in his interactions in India and is thus able to satirise so successfully the plight of the Howells in 'A Democrat on the Ganges'. Clark clearly took pleasure in sending up a social scientist and his long-suffering wife, who, for their part, desperately and unsuccessfully attempted to show that they were culturally aware and socially conscious on their first trip to India.

Alur Janaki Ram (1980:24) has noted that

> Insularity and isolationism have been the conspicuous features of Australian writing for many years. It is only in recent years, starting with the mid-sixties that Australian writers…have increasingly made use of Asian settings, mainly the South-east Asian and Indian settings, as a source of symbols for defining the inner psychological concerns of their characters.

One such example is Dal Stivens' 1979 short story 'The Strange Business at Bombay and Madras'. As well as being a cricket story, a sport that has historically provided a forum for great competitive ferocity between the two countries, it also has symbolic and psychological elements at its heart. The Madras cricket match begins and the pragmatic Australians' game rapidly begins to fall apart as the Indian bowler appears to bowl snakes, grenades, spiders and scorpions at the batsmen. Initially the Australians put it down to hallucinating in the heat, but the images continue and, although shaken and upset, they try to rationalise the phenomenon as hypnotism or autosuggestion. The protagonist of the story seeks advice from one of Madras's leading psychiatrists, Dr Bhaya, who rules out hallucinations and hypnotism and, while he doesn't accept auto-suggestion as an explanation, he doesn't rule it out: 'This is an odd exotic land, hag-ridden with myth and legend and strange transcendental things the rational mind can't explain away' (Stivens 1979:36). He suggests that somehow their phobias have taken a physical form and been planted in their minds, and advises that the team should start afresh in Bombay. The turning point comes when a blue-eyed baby's head appears to the batsman in place of the ball. Shortly after this phenomenon Dr Bhaya reports to the Australians that the Indians, too, have started to see the things that they fear springing at them in place of the ball: 'Rabid dogs are greatly feared here. Also bats. A couple of players saw bats. One even saw a tiger!' (Stivens 1979:44). The story ends with the ball no longer metamorphosing into phobic horrors, but does not offer a satisfactory explanation for the phenomena.

Stivens has drawn on images of Indian rope tricks, superstition and shimmering mirages to give this cricket story bizarre and humorous twists. Both teams apparently try to infiltrate their opponents' minds to dwell on morbid fears that exist subconsciously to put each other off their game. Stivens' introduction of the Indian psychiatrist as an objective confidant of both teams prevents the story from developing into farce while retaining its comedic nature.

The interests of another contemporary writer, Tasmanian Christopher Koch, lie in spirituality and cultural identity. He recalls his backpacking journey through India in 1955, seven years after Independence, in his 1987 essay 'Asia and the Australian Imagination'. In those days it was quite an unusual event for Europeans to be travelling thus and he notes that they were left in no doubt that the Raj was a 'two-way affair of love and hate' (Koch 1987:6). He and his travelling companion were assigned the role of 'surrogate sahibs' (Koch 1987:6) and it is only with distance from that time that Koch has ruminated on Australia's place in the new Asia-Pacific scene. His affinity with India and Indians is expressed in the similarities he finds between Australians and Indians: 'Indians can scarcely doubt the essentially European spirit that is within them' (Koch 1987:14) and they are linked by way of both being ex-colonies of Britain. Koch suggests that Australians tend to think of '"turning to Asia"—as though it were a new adaptation' (Koch 1987:16). But it has always been there for those prepared to explore it.

Koch's experiences in his months travelling in India in 1955 led, ten years later, to his edgy novel, *Across the Sea Wall*, in which he explores the attitudes of some Australians to a recently independent India. The innocent Robert O'Brien sets off on a trip to Europe and, like Mollie Skinner's Tucker, gets no further than India. In O'Brien's case he is inveigled into exploring India with two women and an outspoken westernised Indian, Sunder Singh, with whom he is only casually acquainted. He is smitten with Ilsa, the coarse Latvian immigrant to Australia, but it soon becomes clear that she is more foreign to him than the locals he encounters. There are few tourists in the early decades after independence and they attract much attention from beggars and businessmen alike. As Bruce Bennett (2009) has noted, the novel is unusual 'in presenting a strong Indian voice that challenges Australian opinions and outlooks'. When Koch's O'Brien and Sunder Singh are in Madras and O'Brien is airing his mistrust of India, they come across the statue of Queen Victoria on Marine Drive, and Singh accuses him of being 'as bad as the rest…Scratch you people hard enough and the pukka sahib comes out, doesn't it?' (Koch 1965:94). O'Brien tries to laugh it off but Singh retorts 'You see, O'Brien…you bloody Australians don't know what you are. You don't think much of colonialism, but then suddenly you're waving the Union Jack. It's disheartening' (Koch 1965:95). O'Brien looks at the statue of Queen Victoria and is surprised to feel 'a certain wistfulness. Relic of the Raj, bereft in independent India' (Koch 1965:95). This interchange reveals a nostalgia for the different routes that India and Australia have undertaken, with India gaining independence in 1947 and Australia still retaining the monarchy 60 years later.

O'Brien is impressed with the courtesy and dignity with which he and Ilsa are received by Singh's father, yet he is not prepared to investigate the dress rules before entering a Delhi nightclub and looks shabby and dishevelled compared with the immaculately groomed Indians. Mrs Singh is less than tactful when Ilsa appears draped in a sari and surprisingly tells her in English 'Western women cannot wear saris' (Koch 1965:16), despite the fact that she claims to speak only Urdu.

Koch's interest in the Hindu gods can be seen in his comparisons of the cruel and destructive dancer Kali with Ilsa the dancer, displaced person and deceiver of men who tramples on O'Brien's passion for her. Through the eyes of Koch's character Sunder Singh one gains a perspective on Indian attitudes to the visiting Australians. While it seems that the book represents a sense of missed opportunities for O'Brien, he succeeds in having his 'European experience' through his doomed relationship with Ilsa. As Helen Tiffin (1982:329) suggests, by aborting his proposed journey to Europe in Asia, 'on the allegoric level…in becoming Ilsa's lover, he has already come in contact with ancestral Europe, making the continuation of the journey unnecessary. A wiser and more culturally aware O'Brien returns home with more of a sense of self and promising himself that 'he would go abroad again: and this time, he would reach Europe' (Koch 1965:134).

Conclusion

The three Australian writers who travelled to colonial India all took up military themes but their experiences differed greatly. They all had a deep love of India gained during the years spent there. While Lang was unhappy with the ruling military class in *The Wetherbys*, this attitude softened in his short story 'The Mohammedan Mother' to depict the more inclusive attitude of the narrator. Skinner was before her time in portraying the egalitarian nature of the larrikin Tucker; and Ethel Anderson steeped herself in the history of the country and was interested in cross-cultural relationships. All three, however, demonstrate a stronger social and cultural awareness of their Western characters; with the exception of Lang in 'The Mohammedan Mother', they keep the natives, the others, mainly as silent actors off centrestage. The three contemporary Australian writers mentioned here portray India and Indians as more challenging, and chart their characters' adaptation and shift from naivety to acceptance and understanding. Clark's 'A Democrat on the Ganges' takes the Howells through fear and distrust to a resigned acceptance of the way things work in India. The subconscious fears of the cricketers of both sides in Dal Stivens' short story are presented in dramatic, psychological and physical forms which they confront and eventually overcome with professional assistance. Koch's O'Brien receives some unwelcome home truths from a fierce and challenging friend, Sunder Singh. These stories all portray credible journeys and build on the perspectives put forward in the earlier writings. Only Dal Stivens' story could be said to be an ironic form of 'mango' of mirages and magic-realism, or it could just be a case of fronting up to your fears.

The influence of India in Australia has existed since the early days of British settlement, through trading and shipping connections that were established to supply the new colony. From those early links, Australian writers, starting with John Lang, have taken up the challenge of discovering India; Lang was the forerunner in an impressive stream of writers to experience the paradoxes of India. In doing so, they have often discovered more about themselves and deepened their cultural and social understanding. In colonial times, these writers tended to assign the Indians in their stories to a subservient position—darkly mysterious and in the background. The postcolonial writers have brought their Indian characters into the foreground to challenge and shape their attitudes.

Works cited

Anderson, Ethel 1948, *Indian tales*, Australasian Publishing Co., Sydney.

— 1959, *Little ghosts*, Angus & Robertson, Sydney.

Badami, Sunil 2004, 'Last mango in Pondicherry', *Meanjin* 63(2).

Bennett, Bruce (ed) 2009, *Of sadhus and spinners: Australian encounters with India*, HarperCollins India, New Delhi

Clark, Manning 1969, *Disquiet and other stories*, Angus & Robertson, Sydney.

Coates, Donna 1999, 'Guns 'n' roses: Mollie Skinner's intrepid great war fictions', *Southerly* 59(1).

Earnshaw, John 1974, 'Lang, John (1816–1864)', in *Australian dictionary of biography* vol 5, Melbourne University Press, Carlton.

Foott, Bethia 1992, *Ethel and the Governor's General*, Rainforest, Paddington, NSW.

Green, HM 1961, *A history of Australian literature* vol II, 1923–1950, Angus & Robertson, Sydney.

Koch, Christopher 1965, *Across the sea wall*, Angus & Robertson, Sydney.

—1987, *Crossing the gap: a novelist's essays*, Chatto & Windus, London.

Narasimhaiah, CD 1980, 'Introduction', *The Literary Criterion* 15(3–4).

Ram, Alur Janaki 1980, 'Chris Koch, India and *Across the sea wall*: some observations', *Literary Criterion* XXIII(3).

Sharrad, Paul 2004, 'Trading yarns: India, Australia and Ethel Anderson', *New Literatures Review* 41.

Skinner, Mollie 1937, *Tucker sees India*, Secker & Warburg, London.

Stivens, Dal 1979, 'The strange business at Bombay and Madras', *The demon bowler and other cricket stories*, Outback Press, Collingwood, Vic.

Thompson, John 1958, Obituary, *Southerly* 3.

Tiffin, Helen 1982, 'Asia, Europe and Australian identity: the novels of Christopher Koch', *Australian Literary Studies* 10(3).

Wilde, William H, Joy Hooton and Barry Andrews 1994, *The Oxford companion to Australian literature* 2nd ed, Oxford University Press, Melbourne.

Chapter 11

Through an Australian Lens

Explorations of India in Jane Campion's *Holy Smoke!*

Lisa French

Introduction

In the half-light, a black man's hand strokes Ruth's neck. She flicks him away like an insect, oblivious to the sensual energy she radiates. This is how filmmaker Jane Campion introduces Ruth (Kate Winslet), the central character of her 1999 film, *Holy Smoke!* This opening scene, of Ruth on a bus amidst the colour and vigour of a busy Indian city can be read not only as representing an experience common to Western women abroad in Southeast Asia,[1] but also as emphasising that Ruth is a luminous and irresistible beauty. This chapter begins by outlining the role India plays in *Holy Smoke!* (the film and the novel), then gives an overview of what makes this an Australian film (despite being made with international stars and money), followed by a discussion of how Campion uses the luminousness of her film's central character to explore Western female experience,[2] and

---

[1] Web sites for women travelling in India (for example, Journeywoman: The Premier Travel Resource for Women 1997–2011) warn that Indian women do not ordinarily travel alone and that this can make Western women a curiosity. Touching members of the opposite sex is also a taboo.

[2] Female experience is taken to mean an ongoing process by which female subjectivity is constructed semiotically and historically—a definition taken from Teresa de Lauretis (1984). De Lauretis (1984:182) offered experience as meaning effects 'resulting from the semiotic interaction of "outer world" and "inner world", the continuous engagement of self or subject in social reality'. Note that the concept of 'female experience' here is

finally, examines how the film explores ideas of how men and women might exist together in the world—or, what it is to be human.

Jane Campion was apparently inspired to make a film in India following a trip there (Polan 2001:142), and the film and the novel of *Holy Smoke!* Were both released in 1999. Campion wrote the novel with her sister, Anna Campion; the film is directed by Jane, but written by both of them. Although structured differently, the film and the book have the same story. An Australian woman, Ruth, backpacks through India with her friend Prue. In New Delhi, she finds herself drawn to an ashram and decides not to return to Australia because she has found truth and the meaning of life. Prue returns home to tell Ruth's parents that a guru has indoctrinated her. The family flies into a panic[3] and lures Ruth back to Australia to a waiting cult-exiter, the American PJ (Harvey Keitel), and most of the film and the book, centre on this process.

Exploring India

While the film begins in India, the novel begins with the cult-exiting and Ruth explains early in the book what had occurred, using the past tense

> We'd travelled to India...we didn't really know why we were going, we could have gone to many places. Anywhere that wasn't known. Our knowledge was zero—pathetic as you'd expect. Taj Mahal, saris, elephants...no one persecuting you. Indians don't get on your case, they don't judge you, they judge themselves, self-deprecating (Campion & Campion 1999:13).

Although Ruth is critical of her initial contact, which brings forth the notion of Western travellers seeking the exotic or salvation, stereotypes of

---

complex and contested and understood not as homogenous, but rather as to be viewed as multitudes of perspectives that might be considered.

[3] Campion constructs the Barrons' panic about Ruth's subscription to a cult as unwarranted. In the film's *mise-en-scène* she makes it clear that Ruth has not been indoctrinated when she stages her in front of her bedroom mirror back at home in Australia. Ruth places her hands together in religious prayer, but this is a moment of narcissism; what Ruth is most interested in here is in observing her own image as she does this. Moments later she has moved on and she lights a cigarette, or perhaps a joint. Ruth's own remarks to PJ reflect that it is not a religious experience what she seeks; what she seeks is in relation to her selfhood and she admits that she had hoped Baba would help her grow.

places in the East, Campion's film does not explore India. The film presents India as an imagined place, a hippy utopia of the 1970s and, despite an opening scene that evocatively captures the look and feel of the place, it does not present India in a serious way that attempts to offer insight or understanding of the complex country that it is. It is a tourist's eye that sees India in *Holy Smoke!* and, thus, the song of love, belief and miracles that features in the opening of the film, Neil Diamond's *Holly Holy* (1969), perfectly captures the stereotype, the 1970s ambiance and the themes of the film. The 'smoke' of title of the film and the book evokes not just India's temperature, but Ruth's luminousness—her heat; she is hot. To be hot comes from the idea of being on heat and denotes that she gives off, or is charged with, sexual heat. Colloquially, 'to be hot' refers to arousing the interest of others in the hot person, who is sexually excited and has strong sexual desire. But the 'smoke' of the title also evokes a spiritual search for the fire of the soul, and is perhaps also about relationships—as Kathleen Murphy (2000:30) suggests, 'falling in love (with a guru, God, or guy) might have somewhat to do with smoke getting in your eyes', echoing Louis Armstrong's song *Smoke Gets in Your Eyes*, in which love is blind 'when your heart's on fire'.

Although India itself does not receive any serious treatment, there is, however, a respect for the values or ideals that India represents to the West. What the film and book do is use India as a metaphor for different ways of thinking, particularly about spirituality. Campion has said, 'I'm hoping that…the film will open up a line of inquiry about ways of Western thinking' (quoted in Murphy 2000:30) and that she is 'not really fascinated by cults, but…interested in the question of how you have a spiritual life in the 90s and in the connections of spirituality, eroticism, and love' (quoted in Taubin 1999:138). Critic Kate Pullinger (1999:10) has described *Holy Smoke!* as centring on 'the contradictions and complications of spirituality, a timely commentary on the West's continual misappropriation of eastern mysticism'. While it could be argued that Campion misappropriates Eastern mysticism, it is true, however, that spirituality has been a recurring theme in Campion's work from the beginning of her career as a feature filmmaker.[4]

---

[4] Her films are scattered with symbols of faith and superstition, from reading tea leaves in her first film *Sweetie* (1989) to the buddha that sits outside Pauline's door in *In the Cut* (2003). Ruth's family, the Barrons, are represented as spiritually barren. That the name Ruth is from an Old Testament story of family emphasises the theological themes of redemption and kindness. (In the film Ruth refers to the Dalai Lama's message of the importance of kindness.) Australian cinema throughout the 1970s and 1980s depicted

An image that connects with India and with spirituality comes towards the end of the film where PJ, prostrate in the desert, hallucinates and has a vision of Ruth as a six-armed goddess. The Hindu iconography signifies India, as does the abrupt change in aesthetic, which is reminiscent of the spectacular qualities of Bollywood, particularly the saturated colour. This image is more than his view of her and more than any decorative reference to the many six-armed goddesses in the Hindu religion; it is a signifier of how luminous and magnificent Ruth is, which becomes evident if one considers what the goddesses themselves signify. While there is no research that indicates whether Campion was referencing any particular deity, the goddess that comes to mind is Rati, the Hindu/Balinese 'goddess of desire' (Davies and Dowson 2003:146), also known as Mayavati or Reva. Rati not only rules sexual desire, lust, love and sexual passions, but also regeneration, revenge, fear and dark magic, and she is a protector of women. The myth tells that, after a battle, 'the gods, led by Kama-deva's wife, Rati implored Tripura-Sundari to restore the god of love, whom Siva had destroyed. She does so, and desire is restored to the world' (Kinsley 1997:116–117). Rati cried

> What have you done?'…Without desire, the bull will forsake the cow, the horse the mare and the bees the flowers. There will be no homes, no families, for men and women will not love each other. Society will collapse and life will be devoid of its very essence. Desire may be the cause of suffering; but it is also the reason behind joy. What is life without it? (Storl 2004:86).

Coupled with the idea of Ruth's luminousness, which I discuss and describe below as 'girlshine', the vision of Ruth as a goddess links two ideas—that desire and sexual passion are necessary for the natural order of things and, more particularly, that the goddess is about the idea of painful humiliation leading to joy and enlightenment, which is an important theme of the film and book discussed later in this chapter. Gods and goddesses have shadow aspects, in the Jungian sense; like archetypes, they have multiple shades, some positive and some negative. The reference underlines the complexity, or duality of identity, and the epic journey of coming to know one's self and others—another central investigation of *Holy Smoke!*

Australian suburbia as what Simpson (1999:24) has described as a spiritual and cultural desert, a depiction that Campion continues ten years later in *Holy Smoke!*.

An Australian lens

Jane Campion's filmmaking career has for some years been international in its reputation and scope. Born in New Zealand, Campion trained as a filmmaker at the Australian Film and Television School (AFTS) in Sydney. She now lives and works from an Australian base and has 'called herself an "Aussie directress"' (Rueschmann 2005:9). While some of her films are more directly linked to New Zealand (*An Angel at My Table* (1990) and *The Piano* (1993)), others engage in a dialogue with Australia (*Sweetie* (1989) and *Holy Smoke!* (1999)). She is, however, a transnational filmmaker because she can work across a range of industrial contexts, and attract international money and talent. She is one of a handful of women who have been able to work continuously in features in Australia and other countries, including in Hollywood. It is important for Australian filmmakers to be transnational, not just because the local market is so small, but because cinema is a global industry—national cinema is also international. Nevertheless, although it is transnational, *Holy Smoke!* is also strongly inflected with a sense of Australia as a place and draws on Australian cinema as a referent.

The link to Australian cinema is no more evident than in the characters of the family at the centre of *Holy Smoke!*. They are a significant reason for the film's description as having been compiled from offcuts from Stephan Elliott's *The Adventures of Priscilla, Queen of the Desert* (1994) and Rob Sitch's *The Castle* (1997) (Hall 1999:12). This is partly because of characterisation,[5] and partly because some of its actors appeared in other films of the 1990s; for instance, Daniel Wyllie, who plays Ruth's brother Robbie, is a family member in Paul J Hogan's *Muriel's Wedding* (1994). His presence works intertextually to signify some themes of *Muriel's Wedding* and *Holy Smoke!*, such as dysfunctional families and the search for identity, particularly the idea of being yourself, which was a prevalent theme in Australian cinema from the 1980s. This is particularly true of the successful glitter-cycle films that preceded Baz Luhrmann's *Strictly Ballroom* (1992), *Muriel's Wedding* and *The Adventures of Priscilla, Queen of the Desert*. *Holy Smoke!* also shares

---

[5] The Barron family as characters also work to construct an ironic voice in the film—a postmodern feature—and Campion has described them as a 'Greek chorus' (Hessey 2000a:8). In *Holy Smoke!*, the choral interludes are the briefing of the family: her capture at Emu Farm, watching the cult film at the farm, Day three at the pub, and the rescue. The classical Greek chorus gathered to comment on what was going on in the play. Thus Campion's use of this description could indicate that she has used them as a way of structuring the story. Through images linked to Australian cinema, the family help to point to the incongruous state of things—that things are never what they seem and can suddenly shift ground.

a sense of the bizarre that many of the glitter-cycle films champion. For example, when the Barron family gathers in the lounge room, a sheep casually wanders around with snack food placed on its back. The characters in *Holy Smoke!* intertextually reference characters from other Australian films. They reference them as pastiche—for example, the bizarre visual spectacle of a car with reindeer antlers speeding across the red landscape (shades of the silver figure on top of a bus in *The Adventures of Priscilla, Queen of the Desert*)—and also enter a postmodern dialogue with these figures of Australian cinema (for example, the character type, Yvonne, played by Sophie Lee).

The casting of Sophie Lee in *Holy Smoke!* is important because it creates an intertextual link and dialogue with the typecast roles Lee has played in several very successful Australian films. Lee plays character type in *Holy Smoke!* that is the same as the types she plays in other films released at the time that *Holy Smoke!* was in development and pre-production: *Muriel's Wedding*, *The Castle* and Robert Luketic's short film *Titsiana Booberini* (1997). Lee's character Tracey in *The Castle* is an affectionate portrayal, but in *Muriel's Wedding* and *Titsiana Booberini*, Lee plays characters that are foils, particular comic types set up for ridicule—the self-obsessed, vain and highly sexual young woman. The character of Tania Degano in *Muriel's Wedding* exemplifies this comic type. When she does not get her way, Tania says in disbelief, 'but I'm beautiful!'. This is in marked contrast to Campion's representation of Lee's character in *Holy Smoke!*, which is filled with empathy for Yvonne's plight as a housewife and mother trapped in very ordinary domesticity. Although she is still a young woman, she is starting to realise that her dreams of what her life could be are not going to be fulfilled. Campion recognises how Yvonne's hopes for life have left her disappointed and makes her function in the film to offer the specifically female subjectivity of a woman whose luminous first flush of youthful beauty has passed who is wondering what happened to all her hopes and dreams of romance and intimacy. She is presented as someone cognisant of the passing of her youth, but who has not yet come to terms with it. She is sad, fearful and emotionally needy, and Campion offers a particularly empathetic female view of her character type and another way of understanding her.

An example of how sad, fearful and needy Yvonne is can be seen in the scene in which she comes to the halfway hut to bring clothes for Ruth. She meets PJ at the gate and tells a story of how Robbie thinks she is having an affair because he has found love letters addressed to her. Yvonne confesses that she wrote them herself and that she finds them romantic and beautiful. In this poignant moment Campion exposes Yvonne's pain, disappointment and need. PJ laughs, however, and then so does Yvonne, thus illustrating that PJ is unable and uninterested in Yvonne's call for help, which she makes more than once in the film and which is never answered. Yvonne has oral sex with PJ, and later, in an echo of this scene, Ruth accuses PJ of being interested in a particular kind of Barbie Doll woman and of hating women. He says that he doesn't hate 'ladies', causing Ruth to scoff at his use of 'ladies' (indicating gender) instead of women (indicating sex). This scene reveals his construction of gender and how it filters how he is able to understand and interact with women. Following this exchange, PJ accuses Ruth of extracting the ultimate revenge against men by taking her beauty off to the ashram, as if her beauty rightfully belongs to men.

Another notable way in which *Holy Smoke!* is particularly Australian is in its representation of the landscape. The film sets the landscape up as a backdrop without mythologising it as many Australian films have.[6] The outback in *Holy Smoke!* appears as a representation rather than a realistic vision. Ruth drives through it, but it appears very much as a backdrop, as in other films such as *The Adventures of Priscilla, Queen of the Desert*, Tracey Moffatt's short film *Night Cries, A Rural Tragedy* (1990) and Alex Proyas' *Spirits of the Air, Gremlins of the Clouds* (1989). Thus both the city and the outback are presented as artificial and an urban/rural juxtaposition that differs from that in early Australian film and in films of the revival is taken up, because the outback, while beautiful, is not a character and does not have mythic dimensions in *Holy Smoke!*. This use of landscape as backdrop locates *Holy Smoke!* in Australian cinema of the 1990s.

'Girlshine' and female experience

Jane Campion has described her central character Ruth as being full of

> a fascist and fundamental energy. It's elemental, beautiful, transforming, and it's only available for a short period of time. It's a kind of girlshine; as she learns more about life it will be shadowed. That is the nature of

---

[6] In early Australian cinema the landscape was represented as eternal, monumental and mythic in films such as Charles Chauvel's *Jedda* (1955) and Harry Watt's *The Overlanders* (1946). Many films of the revival, including Nicolas Roeg's *Walkabout* (1971) or Peter Weir's *Picnic at Hanging Rock* (1975), perpetuated this representation. There is some evidence that there is a return to the early interest in the landscape in recent cinema. For example, Baz Luhrmann has said that the landscape was used to amplify the emotion and drama of the story in his film *Australia* (2008) and refers to *Jedda* and *The Overlanders* as influences (George 2006).

growing up. *Holy Smoke!* begins in joyous mystery before the shadowing (quoted in Murphy 2000:32).

I have taken the term 'girlshine' from Campion's description of Ruth and adapted it as a concept (French 2007). It refers to women aged 16–21 or thereabouts, and denotes a time when young women experience a particular physical flowering and have a sense of power without the caution that age and experience impose. It is a brief, transient and liminal phase. Although women vary in their physical attributes, it is the proposition here that all women of Campion's particular Western, socioeconomic and historical grouping go through this period/experience, whether they are cognisant of it or not, and, as such, it is a commonality of female experience.[7] As I have argued at some length elsewhere (French 2007), 'girlshine' is a central exploration in *Holy Smoke!*, which offers a unique examination of in regard to female experience.

All the elements of the film's production work to underline that Ruth embodies pure sensual energy, from the hand that touches her on the bus to her arrival at Emu Farm, where she blissfully sings and dances to Alanis Morissette's 'You Oughta Know' from *Jagged Little Pill* (1995). The song 'celebrates a young woman's life force, her soul. It's a mantra. One can be on an amazing journey, while others are oblivious even to the possibility' (Campion quoted in Murphy 2000:32).[8] Anthropologist Piya Chatterjee has observed that it is no accident that Campion mines a tradition, which Chatterjee describes as Indian, 'that from the beginning has seen spirituality and sexuality as completely entwined and has revered and, more significantly, feared the power of the female principle and female sexuality' (quoted in McHugh 2001). The idea of entwined sexuality, in which a woman's art, body and sexuality are described as entangled is arguably not only linked to India but also to Campion's other films, such as in the character of Janet Frame, the writer in *An Angel at my Table*, and the singing Sweetie in *Sweetie*.[9]

---

[7] Although all young women experience the flowering of youth, the experience may differ in non-Western cultures because of their different material conditions.

[8] Campion was noting that the song was proposed by Kate Winslet. The song has been described as a 'pop anthem to feminine rage and power' (Bush 1999:249). Although it connects with feminine power, the idea of rage doesn't appear to have the sense in which in is used here. The chorus, "Cause the love that you gave that we made wasn't able / to make it enough for you to be open wide' strongly connects to the idea of human connection, such as that between Ruth and PJ in *Holy Smoke!*. However, it could be read as signalling the rage that is to come.

[9] The idea of creativity as central to the evolution of the self is a prevalent theme in Australian cinema from the 1990s, including in glitter-cycle films such as *Strictly Ballroom*, *Muriel's Wedding* and *The Adventures of Priscilla, Queen of the Desert*.

Female *jouissance*

Ruth encounters the guru in *Holy Smoke!* in a scene where his touch leaves her with a third eye and light streaming from her forehead. Hilary Neroni (2004) describes this as a moment of female eroticism and the spectacle of Baba's touch as female *jouissance*[10]—a concept linked to sexual, spiritual, physical or conceptual joy or ecstasy. *Holy Smoke!* thus places female experience of corporeality and enjoyment in the foreground. It is not Ruth's emotional trajectory, however, but the reaction of the other characters, especially as Neroni (2004:219) has observed, to Ruth's moments of *jouissance*, that is significant in the film. The film explores how Ruth affects those around her and in doing so provides an example of how Campion's films are structurally different to conventional Hollywood movies. Instead of working towards her character's desire throughout the whole film, Campion stages Ruth's desire and her *jouissance* for the audience up front. Campion is 'less concerned with following the path of desire than with dwelling in a particular experience and the web of relationships that are connected to that experience...[and] how it disrupts and reconfigures the surrounding social reality' (Neroni 2004:217).[11]

In conventional storytelling, the 'happily ever after' of the fairytale is never interrogated, so the ultimate satisfaction of the conclusion or the underlying ideology it masks is left unquestioned. At the end of Campion's films we are left with many questions about the future of the central protagonists, and a certain 'happily ever after' is never confirmed, although the characters hold out the promise of their own resourcefulness as a possibility for optimism.

Human communication: men and women in the world

In a perplexing scene in *Holy Smoke!* Ruth stands naked in front of PJ and urinates. Just as gods and goddesses have a shadow aspect, or a duality, 'girlshine' also has an inverse, an abject side, which is signified in Ruth's urinating. While this representation might appear to be at odds with the concept of 'girlshine', it is essentially a reminder that iconic beauty is only surface, and that we are all human.

---

[10] The term *jouissance* is used by French feminist theorists, such as Luce Irigaray (1991), who stress its multiple, ambiguous and fluid nature. For further discussion, see Grosz (1989:115–116).

[11] Neroni (2004) notes that Campion has at times described her films as presenting an experience rather than a story.

There are several possible ways of reading this scene. The most evident for those who know Campion's films, is that women urinating outside is a resonant theme from her early short films and features, including her most lauded film, *The Piano* (1993).[12] In her short film *Peel: An Exercise in Discipline* (1982), the sister/aunt character (played by Katie Pye) squats in the grass and urinates by the roadside, and in her first feature, *Sweetie*, Sweetie (played by Genevieve Lemon) urinates next to her father's car. These scenes are linked to the urination scene in *Holy Smoke!*. In urinating on herself, Ruth is doing something ostensibly animalistic, although animals avoid doing this by cocking their legs or squatting; animals do, however, seek dominance and mark their territory through urinating or spraying. When female characters urinate in Campion's films, they are generally involved in power struggles with men. In *Holy Smoke!* the urination occurs when Ruth accuses PJ of wanting young women because he wants to show others what a 'beautiful post [he] got to piss on'.

One way of reading the urination motif is through the lens of Campion's own comments, which strongly brings to mind that human bodies are abject and that to be human is to leak and seep; as Julia Kristeva (1982) has written, the 'abject confronts us...with the fragile states where man wanders in the territories of the *animal*' (quoted. in Bloom 1999:93). The motif can also be read as an exploration of the concept of the abject across Campion's films. Kristeva has written that 'abjection is above all ambiguity...abjection acknowledges it [the subject] to be in perpetual danger...[it is that which] does not respect borders, positions, rules, that which "disturbs identity, system, order"' (quoted in Creed 1993:8). Through the character of Ruth, the act of urinating signifies Campion's resistance to social and cultural conformity or homogeneity. Thus Campion breaks the taboo in our culture towards representing such fluids—confronting the horror of fluids[13]—and reminds us that the idea of a sealed and 'proper' body is impossible. PJ tries to cleanse Ruth's mind with the implication that her body will fall into line,

---

[12] Kaja Silverman (1988:218) has noted that there are 'nodal points' in any director's work—'the sound, image, scene, place, or action to which...[the author's work] repeatedly returns'. This idea can be directly applied to *Holy Smoke!* in relation to female *jouissance* and the repeated motif of urination. Silverman has claimed that a 'nodal point' is often a sound, image or a scene that is 'marked by some kind of formal "excess", indicating a psychic condition such as rapture...fixation...[or] intoxication'. Campion's film can be understood as part of what Silverman has described as a libidinal economy—a 'fantasmatic' cinema of desire.

[13] Using the arguments of Irigaray, Grosz (1994:195) locates the horror of the fluids as being because they are culturally unrepresentable within prevailing philosophical ontological models. Because of the implicit association of fluids with femininity, maternity and corporeality, all of which have been subordinated to the masculine, Campion can be understood as inserting the feminine here through her use of fluids.

but his failure to do so challenges the concept of the supremacy of the mind over the body.[14] This spectacle of female will is something that Campion's central protagonists all share,[15] and provides particular identification for female audiences.

It is interesting to note that the abject is also linked to the 'gothic'—a form Campion has had an interest in, particularly in romantic gothic melodrama.[16] According to Gerry Turcotte (1993:132), the gothic often deals with scatological or 'the abject' and is 'a mode that explores borderland positions, which engages with the grotesque, which allows sexes to blur to the point of transformation, and which speaks the supposedly unspeakable remarkably well'. The gothic is something that has been regularly present in Australian film from the 1970s and also has a strong place in New Zealand culture.[17]

Another way of reading the urination scene is in relation to how it has been critically received. Some critics have seen *Holy Smoke!* as man-hating. One of these, Phillip Adams (2000:32) wrote that he could not think of the 'versa' of misogyny (which would be misandry) but, if there were such a word, it would be called for in regard to Campion's 'apparent detestation of blokes'. Adams reads the scene of Ruth urinating while standing like a man as providing 'powerful symbolism of Campion's hostility to the penis-wielding gender'. Critic Stanley Kauffmann (2000:26) also implied this in writing of PJ that, when he wears 'the lipstick and red dress that she has put on him—in ridicule of his sexuality', he does so because he has accepted that 'he is her slave'; 'After several more twists, she pities the reduced and now-impotent man' and PJ falls for her. According to Stuart Klawans (2000:35), he falls 'abjectly for a woman who was supposed to have been his conquest'.

---

[14] Throughout history there has been a historic dualism—a mind/body split—in which women have been associated with nature and men with culture. Campion's film effectively works against such distinctions between the sexes.

[15] Many writers have observed this; Klinger (2006), for example, has referred to extreme versions of 'female will' and the confrontation between the 'obstreperous female and her dominators' in *The Piano*, which is emphasised by a line of dialogue; Stewart tells Baines that he has heard Ada in his head, and points between his eyes and says she is afraid of her will because it is 'so strange and strong' and that she wants him to let her go.

[16] For example, much of the writing about *The Piano* has considered the influence of the gothic and her film *In the Cut* was screened at the Australian Centre for the Moving Image in 2005 as part of a focus on the female gothic. Numerous articles deal with the gothic in Campion's films, including pieces by Michael Davis (2002), Cyndy Hendershot (1998) and Moana Thompson (1999).

[17] New Zealand film has been described as gothic by Philippa Mein Smith (2005:241).

These accounts reflect the fury and disgust[18] of some critics, and most likely some viewers, but they do not take into account the bond that develops between Ruth and PJ, which is evidenced, for example, when Ruth sits in the back of the ute cradling PJ towards the end of the film. In the final scene they write to each other about their connection and the profound effect they have had on each other.

Campion has been quoted as saying that she feels for men who desire women but for whom this desire is not reciprocated. She says that men 'feel completely disempowered in relationship to [their desire]' (quoted in Barber 1999:6). While Campion's characterisation highlights PJ as self-deluded, chauvinist and sexually vain, she is not trying to demean men. Others have also noted this point. Dana Polan (2001:41) has observed that Campion's most recent films involve 'an effort to redeem men or at least to find mitigating circumstances for their inadequacies'. What Campion is much more interested in is exploring how men and women interact in the world and how one's gender influences those interactions. For example, Campion has said that the film demonstrates Ruth's awareness of how she is seen and objectified—her 'girlshine':

> Ruth has a kind of battle cry...She acts toward PJ out of the full force of knowing what it is to be sexually objectified: to only be seen in terms of one's beauty—which is not to be seen at all. This is why she dresses him up in the red dress, so that when he looks at himself he is seeing a woman of his own age, someone sexually undesirable. She wants to appal [sic] him with his own double standards (quoted in *Holy Smoke!* Press kit 1999).

While he is a man in drag, rather than a woman, his remark that he 'was young once and handsome too' and that she would have been 'impressed' indicates that he is making the connection Campion describes. She forces him to face the fact that his own beauty has passed; perhaps that the testosterone-driven days of his own boyshine are long gone. He admits, 'I'm a dirty old man'.

---

[18] This scene is singled out because of disgust, a reflection of the cultural horror of the materiality of the female body. Kristeva offers that the cost of the clean and proper body emerging is what she terms abjection—'the affect or feeling of anxiety, loathing and disgust that the subject has in encountering certain matter, images and fantasies—the horrible—to which it can respond only with aversion, nausea and distraction' (Longhurst 2001:28).

The defence of PJ has been seen by critics, such as Kate Pullinger, as a mediation or attack on the ludicrous Hollywood convention of pairing old men with young women. Pullinger (1999:10) writes that 'Ruth doesn't go for PJ because he is powerful and authoritative and fatherly; she goes for him because she has spotted his Achilles heel—he is unable to control his libido. The moment Ruth sees this, he is lost'. While this describes what occurs, it fails to notice that he enlightens her in regard to her own state, which she comes to see and understand through her interaction with him.

David Stratton (1999:14) wrote that once PJ has sex with Ruth, 'this proves to be his undoing...[she] demolishes the vanity of her tormentor and, in the process, negates his power'. This negation of power may be a crucial objection to the film for those wanting the myth of the male seducer to be maintained. PJ loses his symbolic identity, the power of that identity is dissipated and the social order threatened; he loses power both as a man (in the sense he has understood his masculinity until this point) and as an exit therapist (the surrogate god/guru). This demonstrates a way in which Campion's cinema deconstructs dominant paradigms. Conventional cinema represents women as 'a mystery for him [the man] to master and decipher within safe or unthreatening borders' (Grosz 1994:191), but Campion's films do not represent or allow the mystery to be mastered or deciferes, because Campion creates a threatening representation. Her film is without masculinist privilege in the sense that it does not favour the male symbolic and devalue the female symbolic, as feminist writers such as Kristeva have argued that society and culture have traditionally done. It is possibly this that unsettles, threatens or enrages some critics, especially male critics.[19]

Other critics, mostly female, have an alternative view to Adams, Klawans and Kauffmann. Ruth Hessey (2000a:8) has observed that Campion's investigation offers the position that 'humiliation, though painful, can lead to enlightenment'; for example, the wearing of a dress signifies humiliation, in the light of PJ dismissal of Baba (the guru) early in the film because he wears a dress, and, therefore, a link between Baba and PJ is signified when PJ wears a dress. Hessey (2000a:8) also writes, 'Ruth subjects PJ to a humiliation so total it represents what every man probably fears when he lets

---

[19] This chapter is not arguing that *all* male critics react negatively to Campion's work, David Stratton clearly warms to her films, but many of the most indignant reviews are by male critics and I raise this here to offer some discussion of the meaning these men are taking, or not taking, from the films. It is possible that these threatening representations would equally enrage female critics with a patriarchal worldview. However, my research has not found evidence that female critics have responded in this way.

a woman get on top'. However, Campion says '[h]umiliation is an important part of the process…[h]umiliation of the ego can be a very positive thing' (quoted in Hessey 2000b:34).

Holy Smoke! is focused on, and offers a profound insight into, the foibles and failings of humans and what they might become through their interactions with and experience of each other. In her review of *Holy Smoke!*, Stella Bruzzi (2000:48) observed that 'it is essentially a film about the tenuousness of most people's sense of self—our decentredness, our malleability, our vulnerability in the face of our own desires and the manipulative skills of others'. Campion explores the development of a sense of self and the unequal power in human relationships, and is quoted as saying that what she was interested in developing and what interests her is that Ruth and PJ

> fundamentally alter each other…even married couples, might never have such an intimate or naked experience as these two share. I admire them for the courage to stay in dialogue with each other however confronting and raw and even cruel it got. In this way, PJ shows his love. It is also why she cannot forget him. He is the first man to really love her, to risk his life for her. In fact to frighten her with her own erotic power (quoted in *Holy Smoke!* Press kit 1999).

Ruth is altered in that she becomes more compassionate, comes to understand her power and makes contact with her own core values, such as the importance of kindness. The interesting thing about this is that she is not offering relations between the sexes as a binary of powerful/powerless. While Ruth finds this experience frightening, Campion is not portraying this trauma as a negative, but rather as part of the process of understanding. PJ emerges from the experience able to see himself with greater clarity, as Ruth does, and Campion seems to imply that they are now both better able to negotiate the future.

Works cited

Adams, Phillip 2000, 'Holey smoking reputation', *Weekend Australian Review*, 5 February.
Barber, Lynden 1999, 'Holy spirits', *Financial Review* 24 December.
Bloom, Lisa (ed) 1999, *With other eyes: looking at race and gender in visual culture*, University of Minnesota Press, Minneapolis.
Bruzzi, Stella 2000, '*Holy Smoke!*', *Sight & Sound* 10(4).
Bush, Christopher E 2000, 'Smoke and fire', *Christian Century* 1 March.

Campion, Anna and Jane Campion 1999, *Holy Smoke!*, Bloomsbury, London.
Creed, Barbara 1993, *The monstrous feminine: film, feminism, psychoanalysis*, Routledge, London.
Davies, John and John Dowson 2003, *Classical dictionary of hindu mythology and religion, geography, history and literature*, Kessinger, Whitefish MT.
Davis, Michael 2002, 'Tied to that maternal "thing": death and desire in Jane Campion's *The Piano*', *Gothic Studies* 4.
De Lauretis, Teresa 1984, *Alice doesn't: feminism, semiotics, cinema*, Indiana University Press, Bloomington.
Diamond, Neil 1969, *Holly holy*, Prophet Music, New York.
French, Lisa 2007, 'Centring the female: the articulation of female experience in the films of Jane Campion' PhD thesis, RMIT.
George, Sandy 2006, 'Baz sees the big picture in Australian landscape', *The Australian* 23 November, www.theaustralian.com.au/news/arts/baz-sees-the-big-picture-in-australian-landscape/story-e6frg8n6-1111112569954, viewed 12.3.2012.
Grosz, Elizabeth 1989, *Sexual subversions: three French feminists*, Allen & Unwin, Crows Nest, NSW.
— 1994, *Volatile bodies: towards a corporeal feminism*, Allen & Unwin, St Leonards.Hall, Sandra 1999, 'There's smoke but little fire', *Sydney Morning Herald* 23 December.
Hendershot, Cyndy 1998, '(Re)visioning the gothic: Jane Campion's *The Piano*', *Literature Film Quarterly* 26(2).
Hessey, Ruth 2000a, 'Lord, it's hard to be humbled', *Sunday Age* 9 January.
— 2000b, 'Where there's smoke…', *Independent Filmmakers (IF)* December 1999 / January 2000.
Holy Smoke! press kit 1999, Miramax Films and Jan Chapman Productions.
Irigaray, Luce 1991, *The Irigaray reader*, edited by Margaret Whitford, Blackwell, Cambridge, Mass.
Journeywoman: the premier travel resource for women. 1997–2011. www.journeywoman.com/traveltales/her_periodical1.html, viewed 12.3.2012.
Kauffmann, Stanley 2000, 'A passion in the desert', *The New Republic* 7 February.
Kinsley, David R 1997, *Tantric visions of the divine feminine: ten Mahavidyas*, University of California Press, Berkeley.
Klawans, Stuart 2000, 'Rescuer down under', *The Nation* 31 January.
Klinger, Barbara 2006, 'The art film, affect and the female Viewer: *The Piano* revisited', *Screen* 47(1).
Kristeva, Julia 1982, *Powers of horror: an essay on abjection*, translated by Leon S Roudiez, Columbia University Press, New York.
Longhurst, Robyn 2001, *Bodies: exploring fluid boundaries*, Routledge, London.
McHugh, Kathleen, 2001, 'Sounds that creep inside you: female narration and the

voiceover in the films of Jane Campion', *Style* 35(2), www.highbeam.com/doc/1G1-97074180.html, viewed 12.3.2012.

Mein Smith, Philippa 2005, *A concise history of New Zealand*, Cambridge University Press, New York.

Murphy, Kathleen, 2000, 'Jane Campion's passage to india', *Film Comment* 36(1).

Neroni, Hilary 2004, 'Jane Campion's *jouissance*: *Holy Smoke!* and feminist film theory', in McGowan, Todd and Sheila Kunkle (eds), *Lacan and contemporary film*, Other Press, New York.

Polan, Dana 2001, *Jane Campion*, British Film Institute, London.

Pullinger, Kate 1999, 'Women directors: soul survivor', *Sight & Sound* 9(10).

Rueschmann, Eva 2005, '"Out of Place": reading (post)colonial landscapes as gothic space in Jane Campion's films', *PostScript*, 24(2/3).

Silverman, Kaja 1988, *The acoustic mirror: the female voice in psychoanalysis and cinema*, Indiana University Press, Bloomington.

Simpson, Catherine 1999, 'Suburban subversions: women's negotiation of suburban space in Australian cinema', *Metro: Film, Television, Radio & Multimedia Journal* 118.

Storl, Wolf-Dieter 2004, *Shiva, the wild god of power and ecstasy*, Inner Traditions, Rochester VT.

Stratton, David 1999, 'No place like Om', *Financial Review* 24 December.

Taubin, Amy 1999, 'Fear and desires: Jane and Anna Campion make a religious-cult classic', *Village Voice* 30 November.

Thompson, Kirsten Moana 1999, 'The sickness unto death: dislocated gothic in a minor key', in Coombs, Felicity and Suzanne Gemmell (eds), *Piano lessons: approaches to The Piano*, John Libbey, Sydney.

Turcotte, Gerry 1993, 'Footnotes to an Australian gothic script', *Antipodes* 7(2).

Section II

Personal Journeys

Chapter 12

Mad in India[1]

Sophie Cunningham

I slept all afternoon & when I woke I thought it was morning, I didn't know where I was. I had no name for India (Ginsberg 1970).

On 5 and 6 January 2004, I was at the Sydney Cricket Ground to watch Steve Waugh's last test match. It was against India. Many Indians I heard interviewed, especially those who had had contact with Waugh through his work with lepers in Kolkata, had reached a sporting compromise; they wanted Waugh to get a century but India to win the test. I am Australian but India is a country I have visited several times, want to visit again, read and write about. I wondered whom, when it came down to it, I would barrack for.

India disorientates. Like Ginsberg, you find you sleep in the heat of the afternoon, you wake up confused. You try to rest at night but are woken by barking dogs, wedding dancing, loud radios and beating drums. You might find yourself in an airless room. Or you might find yourself in one that is over-air-conditioned for the tourist. You might take some local drugs and have things go wrong, or, as in the case of a friend of mine, drink a Bloody Mary in which the barman has reversed the ratio of tomato juice to Tabasco and spend the night throwing up. In the chaos India causes you don't just forget India's name, you forget your own. Or in remembering it feel no connection to it. My name is Sophie but in India I tell people my name is Sophia because that name seems to register more easily. It is something to do with the broadness of my Australian accent. Your name and the life that goes with it cease to make sense.

---

[1] First published in 2004 in *AustralAsian*, special issue of *Meanjin* 63(2) and available also on the author's website (www.sophiecunningham.com/travel/india/mad_in_india/).

When I first went to India I barely slept for three months. When I returned to Australia I was ill. I could not drink alcohol (a tragedy when doing your first round of 21sts), my heart raced, and I swung from sleeping not at all to sleeping for hours and days at a time. As it turned out, this state of body and mind wasn't just culture shock, it was an antimalarial drug called Lariam. Nowadays it is acknowledged that the drug can trigger depression and psychosis, but when I took it in 1984 no-one mentioned a thing.

In 1999, Roche USA advised against prescribing Lariam for patients with 'active depression or with a history of psychosis or convulsions'. The drug's labels and literature were reworded even more strongly in 2002 to say the following:

> Mefloquine [Lariam] may cause psychiatric symptoms in a number of patients, ranging from anxiety, paranoia, and depression to hallucinations and psychotic behavior...adverse reactions...[include] severe neuropsychiatric disorders (tremor, ataxia, mood changes, panic attacks) [and] rare cases of suicide (though no relationship to drug administration has been confirmed) (Roche Pharmaceuticals 2002).

I have read articles that claim there is evidence to suggest that the killings by soldiers at Fort Bragg in North Carolina in the summer of 2002 may have been related to the use of this drug.

I didn't kill anyone back in 1984; I just lost it with rickshaw drivers. One day I stood in a street in Delhi fighting with an autorickshaw wallah who would not put on his meter. I grabbed the pole the meter was perched on and used it as a kind of lever to rock the whole vehicle, violently, from side to side. 'What is this?' I screamed. 'A fucking Christmas tree?' When I recovered from my rage I looked around to see a dozen men pointing at me and laughing. I was yet another ridiculous Westerner.

Thousands, if not millions of travellers have been given the drug, and India is, in many ways, the land where dodgy products are dumped. That's not history; it still happens. On my last trip to India I met a man called Jhunmun whose first daughter had died when she was only a week old after being fed a milk formula made up with local water. It's the water that kills of course, not the powder, but the products are sold without regard for the fact that people's access to clean water is limited.

So, it seems fair to say that in India 20 years ago I was MAD IN INDIA. Fair to ask then, why I love it so much and why it is that I go back.

As a small child I would spend all my pocket money (all of $2 or so) at a shop called Cargo Hold. It smelt of incense and there were lots of pretty floaty fabrics and objects, such as frog wastepaper baskets, made of cane. They always had a small label: 'Made in India'. MADE IN INDIA. I would repeat the phrase over and over to myself. I would look at photos of the places where these things were made. India. Once the labels said Hong Kong, and then Korea, I lost interest.

As I got older, India became eroticised for me. I fell in love with a high-school teacher who went there each year and came back wearing Indian shirts and earrings and silks. He was a hippy. I started to dress in clothes that were MADE IN INDIA (actually, I still do). He would talk of his trips and what he had seen. He would show me maps.

But you notice? A lot of talk about clothes and fabrics and things. The relationship of a consumer to a favoured shopping centre. Capitalism at work. So is that it? I like India because there is some really beautiful stuff there and I want to buy it? Because India is cheap?

People attach themselves to other cultures and countries. They become obsessed with Italy or Bali, Peru or Egypt. Barry Miles, in *The Beat Hotel*, discusses the Beat Poets' (and, by extension, many others') fascination with Paris: 'As non-French speakers, they had no involvement with French culture and the issues of the day, nor were they restricted by rules with which the French lived, simply because they were ignorant of them' (Miles 2000:19). So perhaps one of the reasons I, and many others, love India is that it is not where we come from. In this analysis, one is falling in love with an 'absence' of culture, an absence created by one's own ignorance. The place becomes an exotic slide show that serves to make the stories we tell about our travels more colourful.

I use to know all about Lacanian theories of the Other and I wrote my thesis on the subject before that first trip to India in 1987. But that kind of theory doesn't explain why people pick a particular country. Why did Helen Darville (1995) choose the Ukraine and Jewish people on whom to dump her damaged psyche as Helen Demidenko? Is it because, like her, the Ukraine is a country with boundary problems? A country attempting to create a coherent history out of many separate cultures that do, nonetheless, have some shared history? I have asked myself this many times since the indignity of being the only publisher at Allen & Unwin available on the night of the Miles Franklin award to take her for a drink. She tried to make me dance with her, and circled around me dramatically, arms in the air, peasant blouse and all. She is an extreme case, but she is not the first, nor the last, to take up the causes of a nation she has no business with (something akin to cultural harassment, in which you make unwanted advances to a country that clearly wants nothing to do with you).

Australia has often been a dumping ground for New Age trips. A few years ago there was an American bestseller called *Mutant Message Down Under* (Morgan 1991). It was an account of the spiritual odyssey of an American woman in Australia. I quote:

> An American woman is summoned by a remote tribe of nomadic Aboriginals, who call themselves the 'Real People', to accompany them on a four-month long walkabout through the Outback. While traveling barefoot with them through 1,400 miles of rugged desert terrain, she learns a new way of life, including their methods of healing, based on the wisdom of their 50,000-year-old culture. Ultimately, she experiences a dramatic personal transformation.
>
> Mutant Message Down Under recounts a unique, timely, and powerful life-enhancing message for all humankind: It is not too late to save our world from destruction if we realize that all living things—be they plants, animals, or human beings—are part of the same universal oneness. If we heed the message, our lives, like the lives of the Real People, can be filled with this great sense of purpose (HarperCollins 1991).

One of the particularly dicey things about this book is that when it first came out it was unclear to the reader whether it was nonfiction or fiction. *Mutant Message Down Under* claimed for itself some kind of essential connection with indigenous Australia that bestowed a deeper understanding of the environment. No doubt many non-native writers on India, or indeed on any country that is not their own, could be accused of this—of drawing on some kind of figment of authentic culture to give their work spice.

So, to write about India or not to write? My ambivalence about this subject has led me to represent the heroine of my novel *Geography* (2004) as a woman who is also ambivalent about such matters. She is travelling in India, but is uncertain of her status as a tourist. She is cynical about the search for 'authentic' experience, which means she moves through the country without trying to get close to it. This, she comes to realise, is as awkward as trying to get too close. Since I wrote *Geography* I have become braver. Perhaps because I have now read so many books about India and been there so many times I think I can find a way to say something that is true, even if only in a modest way, even if only in a way that makes sense of Westerners' experience of that country. A large part of my next novel is set in India and Nepal, though I am still searching for some sense of internal authority that will enable me to write these scenes with confidence.

Another *mea culpa*. Reading about, writing about, trying to understand India allows me not to read about, write about or understand Australia. I find our country's appalling human rights records distressing but I find myself lapsing into a kind of pessimistic passivity whenever I think about it. Easier, perhaps, to worry about poverty overseas than down the road. India is, in that sense, an easy way out.

None of this explains why my particular obsession is India (it just explains why I feel awkward about it). Here is one thing I expected of India on my first trip there. I went because it was a spiritual place. I wanted to be a spiritual person. On that in many ways ill-fated trip, I wandered from amazing place to amazing place in the hope of becoming, you know, spiritual. Like spirit was just one of the many bugs you could pick up there. I really believed that if I had a destiny with a particular religion I would bump into it, our eyes would meet across a crowded room and I would become—ta da—Hindu or a Muslim or a Buddhist. At that age I am not sure I even knew the real difference between those religions. They're all Eastern, right?

Perhaps I am being harsh on myself. It is true that I felt a real connection with the Buddhist temples I visited (which were, on that trip, mainly in Nepal (Buddha's birthplace)). Something did shift in me at that time and drove me to try to figure out what I actually meant by spirituality and what Buddhism, in particular, was. After first visiting Kathmandu's Monkey temple and the stupa at Bodanath I had vivid dreams, which affected decisions I made for many years to come.

Buddhism complicates my relationship with India, as that religion was displaced from India around the seventh century. Most of the temples I visit in India are Hindu, not Buddhist, and the larger Buddhist communities are a result of the influx of Tibetan refugees since 1959. This means many of the places I visit in India are refugee communities such as Dharamsala in the far north, where there is, predictably, tension between the local Indians and the more recent arrivals.

'Who do you like best, the Indians or Tibetans?' one person I met in Dharamsala asked me, as if that place was some kind of ethnic zoo. It was a common question. Dharamsala and the current struggle to save Tibet, culturally and politically, from China's heavy hand led to another argument about authenticity. Who is more Tibetan now, those who left Tibet and live in India, or those who stayed and suffer China? Where, as Patrick French asks in *Tibet, Tibet*, does one find the mind's Tibet?

Each year India is swamped by millions of pilgrims from Southeast Asia, Japan and Korea as well as Tibetan refugees and Western Buddhists. They come because it is on the great plains of India that Buddha once used to walk and teach. Many of them descend on the place where he was enlightened, Bodhgaya, and the temple first built by an Indian emperor around 250 BC to commemorate that event. Some claim the bo tree there is the very one that Buddha sat under on the night of the full moon, but that seems unlikely. What is likely is that it is a sapling taken from a sapling of the original tree. There is no doubt that for Buddhists this is a special place.

There is a hitch, though. This temple is in Bihar state, one of the poorest, most corrupt states in India. As William Dalrymple puts it in *The Age of Kali*, 'Two thousand years ago, it was under a bo tree near the Bihari capital of Patna that the Buddha had received his enlightenment; that, however, was probably the last bit of good news to come out of the state' (Dalrymple 1998:3). People do not drive there at night for fear of being held up by armed robbers. I met several people (Westerners and Indians) who had had guns held to their heads. Murder and poverty are an intrinsic part of life there.

When I was there the Bodhi temple was fighting for World Heritage status, but that goal would only be achievable if the beggars and the villagers who sell you flowers and postcards on the way in could be induced to move away from the area round the temple. A World Heritage site, it seems, cannot be a place of commerce. This was going to be tricky, because what else was in this Buddhist business for the locals other than the chance to make some money? Many of the villagers are Hindus. Over the centuries they have used bricks and stones from the temple to build their homes. For them Buddha only has meaning as one of ten avatars (emanations) of Visnu. That is, he is one of many gods, while those who come to worship him are just more of many tourists.

India is chaotic. India is aesthetic. India is cheap. India has good food. India is confusing. India wears its history for all to see like so many colourful, dusty and sometimes shiny bangles. The bangles are a case in point. They are made in beautiful colours, glass flecked with gold. You can buy them by the yard and line your limbs with them. Child labourers make these bangles. A friend of mine who lives in India, who is helping to build a nunnery in Himachal Pradesh, no longer buys them for this reason and suggests I don't either. There is another thing. Once you put on these bangles you cannot break them off. That is what the Indian woman at an Indian takeaway food store in Richmond told me. So, even though my arm sweated under them, even though they jangled and woke me as I turned at night, I never removed them. After a year or so, an Australian friend who'd had it with listening to me complain about the constant jingling, grabbed me by the wrist and cut the bracelets off with tin snips. 'It's enough', he said. 'with the superstition.'

In India you have to give up control. In India you have to learn patience. In India the spirit, like sport, matters; it is nothing to be embarrassed about. One reason India can be so invigorating is that it does not separate the spiritual from the secular. This is also, of course why horrors, most notably Partition, and the emergence of extreme-right Hindu groups like the Bhartiya Janta Party (BJP), Vishwa Hindu Parishad (VHP), Bajrang Dal and Shiv Sena have occurred.

There is another thing. In India you can pretend appearances don't count, although they do. White boys in raggy beards, bare feet and dirty pants may think they look like *sadhu*s, but it is only the *sadhu*s who will give them the time of day. Girls in strappy bra-less tops may feel encouraged by the heat, and fellow tourists, to think that they can let it all hang out, but the Indians will think they are sluts. In *Karma Cola* (1979), Gita Metha writes of Peace Corp workers who buy abused children and then freak because their six-year-old purchase is offering them a head job.

What India has taught me is that contradictions are an essential part of experience. In India you can have the best and worst day of your life in the same 24 hours. You can sit still in the desert night under the stars and be approached by a man playing a flute who will sit and play notes so pure you can hear them soar up to the heavens. Then you can be given a *lassi* with so much *bhung* in it your friends appear to turn into skeletons. Or you can have a moment such as the one I had on my last day in India, in the city then called Calcutta, when I was first there all those years ago. There was a beggar posted out the front of the hostel, it was his patch. His limbs were twisted up behind his torso and he needed a skateboard to drag himself around. Now I realise he had polio, but at the time I didn't know what had knotted him up. He asked me for money and I said I had none, as I was about to leave the country. Then he invited me to join him in some chocolate cake that a Japanese tourist had given to him. I sat with him and we ate cake and he asked me about Australia and we talked about his wife and children.

I left realising that the world was a much more complex place than I had previously understood. I saw the depth of my ignorance and in that was a joy, having seen it I could begin to undo it, though I now see that any process of learning is just a gradual revelation of how deep that ignorance really is. To give up to not knowing, to be uncertain of the name of things, is a revelation. That space is the place where possibility lives. This is another thing India has taught me. Perhaps it is the most important thing.

You can be uncertain whether you have the right to be in India or the right to write about it, but you should do it anyway—just try to do it well. Whatever you choose to do will be both the right and the wrong thing. Be mad in, mad about, India.

I can also tell you that at the cricket on 6 January 2004 I had wanted Waugh to get a century (he went out for 80 and we all leapt to our feet cheering, tears in our eyes) but I had wanted India to win. I did a private dance to the sound of the drums the Indian supporters played throughout the day. It was they, not the Aussie boys muttering about towel heads and making jokes about naan, who moved me.

Works cited

Cunningham, Sophie 1986, 'White on black: the representation of Aborigines in White Australian literature and film, with reference to the works of Patrick White and Peter Weir', Minor thesis, Monash University.

— 2004, *Geography*, Text, *Melbourne*.

Dalrymple, William 1998, *The Age of Kali: Indian travels and encounters*, HarperCollins, London.

Darville, Helen 1995, *The hand that signed the paper*, Allen & Unwin, St Leonards, NSW.

Ginsberg, Allen 1970, *Indian journals*, Grove, New York.

Harper Collins 1991, 'Reading guide', www.harpercollins.com/author/authorExtra.aspx?isbn13=9780060723514&displayType=readingGuide, viewed 12.3.2012

Metha, Gita, 1994, *Karma Cola: marketing the mystic East*, Vintage, New York. (First published in 1979.)

Miles, Barry 2000, *The beat hotel: Ginsberg, Burroughs, and Corso in Paris, 1957–1963*, Grove, New York.

Morgan, Marlo 1991, *Mutant message down under*, HarperCollins/HarperPerennial, New York.

Roche Pharmaceuticals 2002, 'Dear pharmacist', September, www.fda.gov/downloads/Safety/MedWatch/SafetyInformation/SafetyAlertsforHumanMedicalProducts/UCM170905.pdf, viewed 12.3.2012.

Chapter 13

Jackal Eyes[1]

Richard Barz

It was late afternoon on a Wednesday in November 1987. I had spent the day strolling the narrow roads of Keoladeo National Park near Bharatpur in eastern Rajasthan. The park was a tapestry of life. There were cormorants, kingfishers and flamingos, chital, nilgai and sambar. I had even met an impressively big lizard, at least half as long as me. And there had been a large black and white crane not so much eating a fish as playing with it. First he would dart his beak into the pond, snatch the fish and give it three or four hearty shakes. Then he would fling it down into the water and grab it and start the game all over again. Proverbial behaviour for a cat, but a bit unsettling in a bird. The one animal in short supply in the park that day was people. Aside from a scattering of tourists, a ranger or two and a cluster of children on their way home from school, I had met no-one all day.

Then, savouring my solitude in the calm and quiet of twilight, I became aware of something down the road, indistinct in the distance. Gradually, as it came closer I saw that it was not one thing but three. There were three jackals trotting on the road toward me, a leader with two followers slightly behind, one to the left and the other to the right. They came steadily on, looking straight at me but paying me no attention.

What should I do? Nasty thoughts, mostly about rabies, ran through my head: 'At any cost don't be bitten. Just keep walking. Don't let them sense you're afraid. And remember you're a human being. You're the boss. Just keep that clearly in mind and they'll slink off.'

---

[1] I am grateful to my friends and colleagues, Ian Proudfoot and Kuntala Lahiri-Dutt, and my wife Nonie Barz for their comments and suggestions.

But they didn't slink off. They had never read the *Pañcatantra* so they didn't know that they were crafty, craven creatures fit only to skulk around beneath the notice of their betters. Instead, they glowed with wild confidence. And they kept coming unswervingly on without the slightest hesitation.

Now they were so close I could see their eyes. I know that they were bright but I can't say what colour they were. I was transfixed. I could look but not analyse. And then, just as it seemed they must collide with me, the three of them swung as one to the left. Holding formation, with no break in their stride they passed around me and swept back up to the middle of the road and on until they were lost in the evening shadows. I stood there awestruck until at last it occurred to me that the park would be closing and I should leave.

I had spent the day before my visit to Keoladeo going over a Brajbhasha manuscript with a friend in Jaipur. There was no problem about what to do with the manuscript. It was a 19th-century satire on the British written by an anonymous gentleman of Mathura. Either it would be interesting enough to translate into English or it wouldn't. The manuscript belonged to an aspect of the world that was predictable and familiar.

But the jackals and their eyes had not been predictable and were definitely not familiar. They wouldn't go away and couldn't be ignored, but I had no idea what to do with them. In the end they took care of themselves and came out in a way that had quite outgrown the original event:

Keoladeo

Six jackal eyes

in jackal fur

on jackal feet

Came rippling

Bright beauty in the mirror

of my ardour

In the evening.

The jackals and their eyes were not alone. There were other similar experiences for me in India, most to do with places and a few to do with books. Like the encounter with the jackals, each experience grew into a poem with new form and a new substance. Like a lotus flower reflected in its pool but no longer defined by it, each experience has evolved into something far beyond my care or pretension. It's only thanks to that evolution that I can share these poems here:

Prayag
In Jamna stream
With a lovely hyacinth
And a rose Caesar red,
Rowing,
We saw
A kite on a parcel
With two shoulders and a head
Bobbing.

My Love for Govinddas[2]
Bathe in a moment
With clouds in the sky
Around within.

For Kabir, on *Bijak, Sabad* 50[3]
What's going on
In the night out there
And what's it got to do
With the day within
The bud on the tree
That isn't there
That's everything
But the juicy little fruit of sin.

---

[2] Very moving for me was Edward C Dimock and Denise Levertov's English translation of a Govinddas poem (Dimock & Levertov 1968:62); the original Bengali text (poem no. 268) is in Baishnab Padābalī (Mukhopādhyāy 1961:647–648).

[3] Vicārdās Shāstrī gives the original Brajbhasha text with a Hindi translation and commentary in his edition of Kabir's Bījak (Shāstrī 1965:152–153); Ahmad Shah provided in 1917 an English translation of The Bijak of Kabir (Shah 1977:118–119).

Kanpur
Playing cricket on the well
By the Bibi Ghar that isn't
Something to remember
Nana Sahib.

Quick in a Snatch
Quick in a snatch
The bag all gone
Is here again
How can it be
In Lucknow
Sail on upon
The wreck of better times
Unfurled
To catch the breeze of hope astern.

Rickshawallah
A mind made
Good
Stroppy rickshawallah
from Brindaban
For exotic
Dreams.

The mind is
A receptacle
Of what
It's made
To do while
Looking in.

Squeeze
Come in a squeeze
Go in a dodgem
On father's cycle
To Orchha;

Inside
A lingam in
The cosmic countdown
Together in Orchha.

Shakti Pat
Picture
Shakti pat
Fallen on my head
Dayanand
A hundred years dead
In Ajmer.

Ujjain
Wedding marching delirium
Blaring unwoman appearing
Of terror
Coming interior;

Crowing on the line
Between whistle and grime
Ground under Humpty Dumpty
Leaving Ujjain.

Lost and Found in Avadh
The other half of the pig
Found
Dead in the street
Lost in Avadh.

The Tamil Nadu Express 122 up stops at Itarsi for only a couple of minutes in the middle of the night. But that was time enough for jackal eyes:

Tamil Nadu Express
Belle de Jour
Jackal eyes
Unlock
Trust in chains.

The jackal eyes come now and then at odd times and places, wrapped up in the parcel with the kite in the dodgem car by the Bibi Ghar under the tree that isn't there with all the other stuff together with the shakti pat.

That's enough to say.

Works cited

Dimock, Edward C and Denise Levertov 1968, *In praise of Krishna: songs from the Bengali*, Jonathan Cape, London.
Mukhopādhyāy, Harekrshna (ed) 1961, *Baishnab Padābalī*, Sāhity Samsad, Kolkata.
Shah, Ahmad, 1977, *The Bijak of Kabir*, Asian Publication Services, New Delhi.
    (Originally published in 1917.)
Sharma, Vishnu 1993, *Pañcatantra*, translated by Chandra Rajan, Penguin, London.
Shāstrī, Vicārdās 1965, *Bījak*, Rāmnārāyan Lāl Benī, Allahabad.

Chapter 14

Bahut Achhaa in Bharatpur[1]

Linda Neil

I

Like her travel agent in New Delhi, she had expected The Bird Lover's Inn in Bharatpur to be no more than a one-star hotel: a sparse room with a dusty fan, a tap with a bucket in the bathroom, a bed with a thin foam mattress, and perfunctory accessories. But this time the brochure had not lied when it had offered her a 'newly appointed room, off the well-beaten road close to the bird lover's paradise'—well, as far as she knew anyway. It was dark when she arrived from Agra, so she did not know if the road was well-beaten or close to any kind of paradise. But she is both charmed and relieved by the attractive freshness of the new rooms at The Bird Lover's Inn, the marble floors, the blue linen curtains and matching bed covers, especially the size of the bathroom. Her eyes water when she sees the deep bathtub, the shiny new faucets, the stand-up shower. After two months in India she is beginning to be able to smell her own hair, the dust and grime that have settled in its thickness, the premature greyness endowed upon her by the layers of mist and smog through which she has walked every day. The usual handheld showers never offered enough pressure to properly penetrate her thicket of amber curls; for a month now she has relied on surface moisture, perfunctory cleansing and leave-in conditioner. Her hair has developed textures that have nothing to do with hair: inorganic, hybrid, with smells and consistencies that have changed its colour more uniformly than any dye she might have used.

---

[1] Previously published in *M/C Reviews*, 25 May 2008 (http://reviews.media-culture.org.au/modules.php?name=News&file=article&sid=2584) and in *Extempore* 5 (November 2010).

The bath is deep and new; its marble gleams. The showerhead is fixed high to the wall; two plump white towels lie neatly side by side on a bathroom rack. The whole thing is a vision. For weeks she has dreamed about lowering her body into a tub of water, of washing off the grime that is building up daily on her skin. Even the colour of her eyes has changed—from a green to a muddy grey, and her irises are now lined with a ring of dark toxic blue.

Downstairs a fire burns in front of the lodge, encircled by people, dark or light—in the shadows she can't tell—holding their palms towards its warmth. The owner calls out to join them, but at that moment her stomach hears only the call of the kitchen and her haste is indecent as she waves back at the huddled group and calls out 'Thankyou. Later.'

The lights go off almost as soon as she is ushered towards her corner table. In the dark she hears the cook calling out: 'Don't worry, Madam. We cook with gas.' But she is feeling too content to be worried. In India she has become used to things that would have irritated her back home. She likes the way her thoughts form themselves in darkness; the way the lights go out unexpectedly all through the day and night. She likes the waiting, the empty quality of time when it cannot be ordered or controlled; it brings her back to the languid days of childhood, when the slow unfolding of things is both exquisite and excruciating.

'Don't worry, Madam', the cook calls out again. 'We have generator.'

The dark lessens her gnawing hunger. She can hear herself breathe. She thinks about the bath that awaits her, how the lack of something intensifies an experience that has become ordinary. She imagines heat on her spine, water softening the ache of hard beds, rickety buses, the bruising crush of skin against hers.

'I'll just have some dahl', she calls out into the darkness.

'Bread, Madam?'

She wants bread without oil, cooked in dry heat, like the chapattis she buys in the street. There is something honest about fresh heat; she sees red, orange, a slick of blue rising from the centre of a furnace. Feels the quick sharp burning in her stomach.

'Tandoori naan', she calls back.

Has he heard her?

She settles further into the darkness and recalls the various facts about Bharatpur listed in the hotel's brochure that the travel agent in Delhi had told her were 'probably all lies': the town is on the driving route that will take her from Delhi to Agra to Jaipur in just over three days. Indians and foreign tourists come here for bird watching and to find accommodation when all the hotels in Agra are full in high season. There is a national park nearby and a large number of local artists selling paintings of birds in tiny studios dotted around the main hotels. Bharatpur, though, has something even more unexpected than bathtubs, stand-up showers, and birds; something that the brochure neglected to mention: it has silence. Her ears begin to search out peripheral sounds, listening first for familiar honks and beeps, incessant traffic, the underscore of human voices speaking in tongues, but there is nothing familiar in the surrounding silence. Or in the soft aloneness she feels suddenly in the dining room of The Bird Lover's Inn. It comes to her fresh, like a completely new experience.

Only a few seconds pass between the lights stuttering back on and her plate of dahl arriving, along with a basket of tandoori bread, delivered to her personally by the cook. The dahl is yellow and warm and perfectly arranged in a dish shaped like a boat. It has sailed across a vast distance to arrive at her table, gathering its lentils and spices from faraway lands. She pushes her nose down towards it; it seems a gentle dahl, not too oily, lentils lightly swollen in its juices. The cook waits anxiously at her side. She tries to think of how to say very good in Hindi. Another cook, Rahul, from the Institute in New Delhi, where she'd stayed when she first arrived in India, had taught her the word one evening in his kitchen. Rahul had actually taught her three things in Hindi that night: How to say 'how are you?' How to say 'thank you'. And how to say 'very good'. They were useful words and phrases to know in a country where most people would ask her in English: 'How old are you? Are you married?' and 'How many children do you have?'

The word for very good started with a 'b' and sounded like a dance. Rahul was illiterate so she had only learnt to spell it phonetically. Her mind must have gone sleepy along the road from Agra to Bharatpur, because for the moment she can't remember a thing Rahul taught her. She nods her head instead and gives the cook a delighted smile.

'OK Madam? OK?'

She wishes he would not bow. She cannot let him bow to her without her bowing back. It is after all she who is receiving his graces; she who should be bowing to him.

'Where you from, Madam?'

She does an upper body bow at the same time she says 'Australia.'

'Ah, Australia. Number one cricket team in the world.'

'Yes, but India very good too.'

'Australia number one. India number two. You like Sachin Tendulkar.'

Not as much, at the moment, as I like the look of this dahl and bread, she thinks, wondering why in this land of eternal things, she'd had more conversations with Indians about Adam Gilchrist, Ricky Ponting and Shane Warne than she had about almost anything else.

'I like Sachin and Sourav.'

'Ah, Ganguly? A very fine cricketer.'

'And also VVS Laxman.'

'Who can forget his thrilling knock at the Sydney Cricket Ground in that memorable summer series of 2001? Double centuries in both innings. Supported by my personal hero, Mr Rahul Dravid. I was very proud to be an Indian that day, Madam.'

She always liked cricket talk. It reduced everything; it seemed to distil centuries of cultural differences into some simple numbers and concepts: 22 players, two 12th men, three umpires, four consecutive innings. You could hit fours and sixes and not have to run. You could run for twos, threes, fives; score incrementally numbered milestones: half centuries, centuries, double centuries, triple centuries. You could be not out at stumps, declare, retire. Run with a runner. Not run with a runner. Run without a runner. Just run. Appeal. Bowl a yorker, a bouncer, a flipper, a googley. Hit to the boundary and over the top into the crowd. You could stand and field in slips, hit to silly mid on, be caught in leg gully, and bat before pad.

She had met Indians who could recite by heart every score of every innings ever played by Sachin Tendulkar. And by Ricky Ponting as well. Children had been pushed forward to her at gatherings she had attended who could list every wicket ever taken by Shane Warne since he began playing cricket. It was like listening to music sometimes, hearing the numbers roll effortlessly from the lips of these children; like listening to something spiritual, intuitive and irrational, yet utterly logical in its simple and random perfection

Caught behind 67.

LBW 44.

Stumped Gilchrist off Warne for 32.

Clean bowled for ten.

Out for a duck.

Out for a golden duck: a score of zero on the very first ball.

'Anyway Madam', the cook says as the lights stutter and give up completely. 'It thrills my heart that you love our cricketers, because you know Aussies are the best cricket team in the world. Second to none.'

She hopes he is not bowing again as he backs away. The room is so dark she cannot see anything. The renewed silence sinks deeply into her. She waits again, breathing in the blackness, wondering if, as well as not being able to see, she also cannot be seen. Whether she has disappeared completely from view, here in Bharatpur, near a bird-watcher's paradise. What would that be like, she wonders, to disappear from view, to be nothing, to be invisible, to be no-one at all? And in a place that had never dreamed of her existence?

In the darkness outside someone is playing a raga on a sitar. Not brilliantly, she thinks, but not as clumsily as some Westerners she has heard, who come to India for six months of lessons with a sitar master. She had met many of them here and there, in Delhi, in Rishikesh, heading to Varanasi or Kolkata, searching for new sounds, new scales, new disciplines and the surrender that seems to come with it, entwined in the textures of the raga scales and their seemingly endless permutations.

Back in Brisbane, John Rodgers had told her more about those permutations. John was not at all like the Western men she'd met in India, who travelled to the East to answer some kind of call, whether it was the call of meditation, yoga, the mountains, of mysticism, or of drugs. His visit had been professional: as a violinist/composer in the Australian Art Orchestra, a contemporary music ensemble that had travelled to India and toured Europe and Australia in collaboration with some of the best Indian musicians. He had returned from these musical collaborations with a unique insight into India's rich and overwhelming musical traditions.

John confessed he'd felt like 'chucking it all in' when he heard the depth, complexity and brilliance of the Indian masters. Their skill made him question his typically Western multiskilled approach to music; they have 'such a vast and unified musical system', he told her, 'with such a comprehensive way of learning it.' Everyone knew the story of the young Ravi Shankar returning from a future of certain celebrity and fame in the United States to live with his music guru and immerse himself in the traditions of his own musical culture. It was typical of Indian students and teachers, the father/son relationship that formed between the prodigy and the master as they worked together night and day on the infinitesimal intricacies of raga melodies until Ravi had absorbed not just thousands of possible melodic and permutations, but thousands of years of other absorptions: numbers, concepts of time, language, the possibilities of zero, the birth of language, all the things that India, the country Mark Twain had called 'this mother of history, this grandmother of legend, this great grandmother of tradition', had given to the world.

John told her about numbers too: how Indian music did things in threes, unlike Western music, which mostly did things in twos and fours. How it seemed to be based on three principles:

> the principle of doing things in threes

the principle of making things grow
the principle of making them shrink.

'They play three things three times', he told her, 'that shrink while the rhythms inside them grow.'

She'd been dazzled by all the talk of numbers and things growing inside shrinking things; the circularity of it; the idea of things that might not have a beginning nor an end. She thought of the mandalas she had seen from ancient India, the circles resting inside of the squares, or vice versa. Christian writers like Dante obsessed with numbers too, creating pre-Renaissance subsets of numerical symbolism, trinities, holy or otherwise. Indian music seemed to be driven by textural rather than linear imperatives, unlike the climactic impulse that propelled the cadences of Western music. Did this lack of forward movement, this exploring of intricate detail in repeated things signify a state of existence beyond 'progress', when all possibilities of action had been exhausted and the only way forward was down and into, rather than up and on towards something—a conclusion, a cadence, at least some harmonic change? Was the zero that Indian mathematicians had first notated as a big round empty circle with a balanced space inside and a vast never-ending space around the natural signifier of everything that their country's repeated musical rhythms seemed to embody?

That India had come to the idea of zero as an intuitive, spiritual concept made it fundamentally different to the utilitarian abstraction of the Western zero. India's idea of zero was of a nothingness signifying perfect union with everything. Back in Brisbane, John had told her more about numbers; about making tensions against a pulse, about a continuous drone underneath that stretches things out, putting the brain into a trance state while over the top sits intricate and sophisticated rhythms played precisely and brilliantly.

'They do things most Western musicians baulk at: beats subdivided into fives and nines. And they do it completely effortlessly.' John had continued. 'Unlike most Western musicians, who have to learn those subdivisions and practise them painstakingly because, to us, these subdivisions are not natural. Perhaps it relates to their folk melodies', he told her over mugs of chai, which he confessed to disliking. 'Or the mathematical fabric of their religions, social divisions, numerology, the hierarchy of caste; they're probably all to do with numbers too.'

'They never liked the piece I wrote for them anyway', he divulged when she probed further. 'And though we toured with it to Festivals all over Europe and Australia, they wouldn't play it in India. Even though it's got a clear Indian influence, in that it also does things in threes and follows the template of things shrinking and growing, it came out all sounding all wrong, because it engaged too much and did not submit enough.'

'But in many ways it was a logical union between my sensibilities and theirs', John explained, 'on a deeper, conceptual level rather than just on the surface. It was not, however, a surrender of my sensibilities to theirs. That was the problem, I think. If I'd just copied their sensibilities, the music would have been easier for the Indian audiences. It would have just made the music sound like what music normally sounds like when Westerners engage with Indian music: they adopt the raga melodies, the rhythmic rules, the scales, they play sitars and tablas and chant in Sanskrit. But it would have been a surface engagement, like going to India and wearing their clothes and eating the food and studying the yoga and thinking you understand India; never really engaging deeply with the culture while thinking that you have. It's a ridiculous concept, really, to do that, because their tradition is so rich and so ancient. I wanted to go deeper, to engage with their forms and concepts. But it wasn't as easy to grasp, I suppose, because the surface sounds, the melody, the harmonies, just sounded all wrong to them.'

The raga melody stops abruptly; the musician stumbles a few times over the scale and then gives up. She appreciates again the silence. She has stumbled and given up too, many times before. But things are different now. That's what she always tells herself. That's why she returns to places like India. Not to reacquaint herself with the physical surroundings, but with the feelings she experiences within them. To know that things are different now; that another tiny piece of her spirit has been liberated from its bondage, like tiny quarter notes in an Indian scale, released from a dull melody and falling away to nothing.

Things falling away to nothing. To the infinity of a zero. India seemed to promise that.

'Surprising India', the tourist brochures told her. 'Magical India, Mystical India'.

She had never really understood why she came to India; what drew her here. It wasn't the gurus, or the saints or the Brahmins or the Pundits or the gods or the goddesses, not the mountains, the meditations, not the old intelligence that, as Ralph Waldo Emerson had written, 'in another age and climate had pondered and thus disposed of the questions that exercise us'. Not even the music. She did not know why it was to India that she came except that perhaps she was like the thing in their music that shrinks inside the thing that grows; perhaps while India keeps growing in its chaotic, random, yet relentless way, while the pundits and sages and gurus keep pulling it back to its most ancient traditions, she will keep shrinking until she will be reduced to the mysterious zero entity that India had given to the world, and now, in particular, in a dark café in Bharatpur, to her, with all the absence, negation and infinite potential which that most balanced and beautiful number seemed to contain.

II

Bahut aachha.

That was it.

The word for very good.

Very very good

Bahut aachha.

A cha cha cha.

Starts with a b and sounds like a dance.

When she first learned the word from Rahul she had laughed with delight. And so had Rahul. She had repeated the word over and over like the lyric to some nursery rhyme. He had thought her childish. But he had indulged her; laughed along with her. And she had got her violin out for him later and strummed a little song for him, which she spontaneously called 'Bahut aachha a cha cha cha'. She sang for him. Did a little dance for him. It had been a happy moment in Rahul's kitchen. A light, happy, childish, perfect, empty moment.

'*Bahut aachha*', she calls out as she feels her way out of the Bird Lover's Café, touching the solid outlines of chairs and tables as she stumbles like a blind woman across the darkness. She does not even know the direction of the kitchen or where the cook is. She does not know who might hear her as she calls out into the silence that has suddenly descended like something divine onto her world.

'The dahl was *bahut aachha*,'

Later, lying in a warm bath surrounded by candles, she feels embarrassed by how quickly she had devoured the dahl and bread, as if she had been hungry for centuries, a living example of the phrase: 'boy she really wolfed it down'. She wonders what the Hindi word for wolf is and if, in the warm kitchen of The Bird Lover's Inn in Bharatpur, the cook had turned to his assistant and in the shadows of the gas flickering on his big iron oven below icons of the gods, goddesses and Indian cricket heroes that watched over him while he worked, he had said in perfect lilting Hindi: 'Oh my god. Those hungry Western women! That one really wolfed it down. Boy oh boy! She really wolfed it down.'

Chapter 15

Larry in Pondicherry[1]

Inez Baranay

I was having a coffee with Josh in Darlinghurst Road after we'd been to a movie about Andy Warhol at the Chauvel. Josh suddenly went 'oh my god!', interrupting his own monologue on mechanical reproduction and the uncredited work of assistants in the world of art, and called out 'Larry!', and, lo and behold, that's who it was coming in to the café, Larry. This was not long after the astonishing night when freaky bearded Larry turned up on the street, and just after he had turned up at Isabel's in his new clothes, which he was wearing now.

Josh rose as Larry approached and they kissed each other on each cheek. Well!

Then Josh took it in that I knew Larry too, but Larry seemed unfazed.

'Mind if I join you?' he said, 'I think I'll get something to eat.'

'The pasta is good here', said Josh. 'Larry, how long has it been? Where have you been? No-one has seen you for yonks. Not even a postcard. And you didn't tell me you knew him! You did not need to lose weight', and there was a split second of *oh no*, but 'but you look well' said with much meaning.

'I am', smiled Larry.

'You didn't tell me you knew each other!' I said to them.

'I never knew you knew him. We go way back, don't we?'

'Nothing should surprise me', I said.

Larry ate his fettuccine pesto and Josh told him how fantastically his career had gone since they had last seen each other.

And looked at me for substantiation.

---

[1] This is an extract from Baranay's *With the Tiger* (HarperCollins India, New Delhi, 2008).

'It's interesting work', I confirmed. 'There's a lot of interest in Josh's work.'
'I live off it', Josh wanted him to know.
'That's great, Josh', said Larry warmly.
'You must come to the studio, I'll show you what I'm working on, and you must come to this.'

Josh pulled out a flyer, advertising the forthcoming group show that was to include his new piece; Larry put it in his pocket and pulled some money out of his wallet.

'Don't get up like that as if you were going!' said Josh.

'I am', smiled Larry. And suddenly, he had, he'd slipped money under the plate, smiled at us with one of those sweet smiles of his, and disappeared without any memorable exit lines.

'Where is he going in such a hurry at an hour like this.'

'Might have someone waiting for him', I ventured, thinking of those late-night dates with someone finishing their shift in a theatre, restaurant or taxicab.

'I don't know whether to pity them or envy them and ...' Josh paused to make sure I was paying attention and added, 'I should know.'

'What makes you say that?'

'When I was so much younger and naïve, I had a moment of wanting to live with Larry for the rest of my life. I am seriously grateful to whatever fate stepped in; come to think of it, it was Larry himself, who suddenly was going somewhere else right now this minute, no former warning.'

Josh of course liked nothing better than an audience for his stories, the telling of which owed nothing to discretion.

'So where on this planet did you meet Larry?'

'Well I'm not sure it was on this planet. It was when Robert was dying. Larry knew him. He wasn't like some of Robert's friends, it was all too much for them, they didn't want to know, everyone is just so busy with so much to do and what's the point of visiting someone's who's dying, what's in it for you? They'd either been through it before and didn't want to go through it again, or just couldn't face it.

'And I had given up work to look after Robert, there was no-one else to do it, and he was very sick, and sometimes he would be really horrible to me, I knew he didn't mean it but it was awful. And no-one was looking after me, so I was not in a good way, broke, sick, taking too many pills, doing what am I going to do now? Then one day Larry turned up to visit, and he began to come and sit with Robert sometimes and Robert would always sleep peacefully then. And Robert died, and all that was horrible, and Larry just said to me, 'You look like you need to go out for a nice long lunch', and he got hold of my arm and took me right to Watson's Bay, and we sat by the water and he ordered everything, and I just let it all come out, I was broke and rundown and scared and I had to change my life bigtime and the way I looked no-one would even buy me a drink let alone make sure I moved in. All of Robert's money had gone on hospitals and drugs and carers and then his mother turned up after he was dead and took everything that was left, all his work and stuff, I just didn't count, and I was homeless. I didn't think I could go on. Larry! He was so easy to talk to, though he never said much. We spent the whole afternoon there by the Harbour, I felt he'd brought me back to life. You know what, I even told him that I wanted to do my own art. He was the first one I really said it to.

'"What do you need most right now?" he asked me. I just went "ahhh"' and Josh shook his head at me.

'I could hardly say, I needed to get away, have some time, go somewhere different, become what I wanted to be, and Larry just seemed to understand all that and said "I was thinking of going to Pondicherry. You should come with me. As my guest. If you really do just want a quiet time".

'"Larry" I said, just to make sure, "I'm not up to doing anything at all".'

'He realised what I meant. "No, no, as just friends. It would be good for me to have someone with me who wanted a quiet time".'

'I didn't have a clue where Pondicherry was. I realised that Larry was making it easy for me to accept by making it sound like it would be good for him to have someone around, keep other people from intruding. Probably it was. When we were there, I would see people looking at him when we were out together, having a meal or going to lectures or to do group meditation. Doesn't sound like a usual kind of holiday, does it! People would be looking for a way to talk to him, but he would just talk to me, and I was kind of his buffer zone, 'cause he likes to go round in a world of his own. Not that he misses much.'

* * *

Pondicherry, as Josh soon found out, was a quiet little city on the east coast of India. Larry arranged their visas, assured him he didn't need vaccinations or to buy a thing, and in what seemed like mere days, they flew via Singapore to Madras, and from the airport took a taxi to Pondi, a few hours drive down the coast.

Pondicherry had once been part of the French Empire and distinctive traces of its French past remained in the graceful architecture of the old town, the names of the streets, the elegance of the foreign visitors, the baguettes and brioches you could buy at the bakery. They stayed at a guesthouse on the eastern side of town, at the southern end of a long wide boulevard that ran alongside the sea. It was one of a number of lodgings owned and run by the ashram that dominated the area, its various buildings painted a distinguishing pale grey.

Exhausted, unwell, and never having been out of Australia before, feeling so frightened and weak he even wondered if he might die, Josh spent the first days barely venturing out of the guesthouse, sleeping in his room, sitting in the seaside garden, picking at toast and eggs and fruit salad in the dining room and then going to lie down again. As he began to feel stronger, he began to listen to the other guests talk among themselves, chatted to the staff, kind women in blue saris who did not speak fluent English but seemed to communicate warmth and uncanny insight. He picked up books and newsletters in the dining room, and began to wonder who The Mother was, and who Aurobindo was, and to form some idea of what kind of place this was, and why people came here.

Each room had a name, a word on its door, such as Peace, Surrender, Abundance, Forgiveness. Josh's room was called Spirit and Larry's room Knowledge. An Indian couple he talked to over tea one day said that there was always a meaning to the room you had been assigned, and that one should reflect on this.

'Larry was always reading, it was always something strange, spiritual stuff, philosophy, history. He was interested in Aurobindo', said Josh. 'That's what he'd come here for, to find out more about him.'

Sri Aurobindo, born Aurobindo Ghose in Calcutta and educated in England, in the early 20th century had been active in the struggle for Indian self-rule, and eventually, and somewhat inevitably, suffered prosecution and imprisonment as a consequence. Fleeing further prosecution and perhaps with his future calling already clear, he moved south to Pondicherry and began the spiritual work that would be his entire focus for the rest of his life. Here he met the French woman who would become known as The Mother. The Mother and Aurobindo formed a unique alliance. Josh sketched a few of these facts and I would hear more about all this from Larry much later.

What had interested Larry most was the relationship between the political activism of Aurobindo's early life and the spiritual focus of the later years. Was it a matter of progression or retreat? Did the later pursuit negate or affirm the former? What could he learn about the relationship between political activism and the spiritual life? Larry spent a lot of time in the ashram's library, studying in those cool, high-ceilinged rooms, or seeking out people who could talk to him about these matters.

Josh, content to have but a dim apprehension of Larry's project, began in time to venture out of the safe, serene grounds of the guesthouse, walking along the *rues* and peering through high gateways into courtyards to the solid, elegant, cream or pearly-grey buildings of French schools, hospitals and hotels, as well as the ashram's various quarters: residential, workshops, clinics. Bright bougainvillea cascaded over fences, and he stopped to watch some girls kneeling drawing elaborate geometric designs in chalk on the pavement at a doorway. What were they doing? Were those mandalas? They must have been taught at a young age to draw such elaborate, perfectly balanced designs so swiftly and neatly. He began to notice them in all the streets. What did they mean? He bought a notebook and copied some of the designs. Bit by bit he made his way north to an octagonal park where he sat upon a bench and watched workers and tourists walk its paths or rest in its shade, children play, gardeners tend the flowerbeds. He marvelled at his own nerve, though the first excursion so many blocks from the sanctuary of the guesthouse left him so weak that he took an autorickshaw back there. As he grew well and strong, his confidence and curiosity growing, he crossed the canal that divided the town into the quiet, broad, well-tended, European-influenced avenues on the eastern side and on the western side the narrower, far more teeming, bustling Indian streets that stretched into an infinity of Indian urban life that he found daunting to even contemplate. This was a quiet Indian city? Good grief, what must a busy noisy one be like! He had to pick his way over pavements of broken stone, dense crowds and roadside businesses. But he found that if he relaxed and smiled, it was easier. If you smiled at strangers you found the ones that smiled back! A gay man should know this! 'Australia! Coming from Australia', he answered everyone cheerfully. One day he found himself at the main market and was lost there for hours, amazed to see the colourful, unfamiliar produce of the food section, the astonishing varieties of banana and coconut, the piles of spices that the stallholders let him curiously sniff at as he attempted their local names, and the narrow aisles packed with stalls selling cloth, baskets, bangles, mehendi, kohl. He was struck by the pyramids of fine powder in brightest colours, gold, hot pink, blue: what were they for? Ah, for the patterns the girls drew on the ground. Something profound was awoken in him, something to transform him that he could not yet name or comprehend.

Larry took him one evening to the group meditation that was held in the grounds of one of the ashram buildings. People, many people of all ages, mostly Indian but many Westerners too, left their shoes at the gates and fell silent as they passed barefoot through one courtyard into the large courtyard where a large black tomb, the tomb of Aurobindo, sat in the centre, already covered with petals of jasmine, champa and rose. They walked in a procession with tiny shuffling steps around the tomb, some falling to their knees to press their hands or their foreheads to its cool marble surface as if to pray or to draw into themselves some mysterious energy. Sticks of incense added a smoky fragrance. Everyone seated themselves upon the carefully swept grounds around the central tomb, moving up next to each other, sitting very close in rows so that they might all fit there. A bell rang out, the lights were dimmed and all became completely silent. Everyone sat still. Josh was not sure he was meditating correctly; for a while he felt thrilled and puzzled to be part of this, then he began wondering how long it had been and how much longer it would be; then his mind wandered here and there and then he began to feel stiff and sore and wondered how people could sit on the ground for so long with no apparent discomfort. He had heard it was good for you and that the adoption of chairs accounted for widespread troubles with hips and knees in later age. He didn't think meditation was for him, though it had all been very nice to experience, in spite of his embarrassing struggle to get back to his feet and shake out his pins and needles and his cramps. Anyway, afterwards, Larry told him that all he had to do was to sit, and that the stillness of his body would help to still the mind, and what he could do was to observe his own breath, just watch the inhalation and the exhalation, and release any other thoughts that arose. Josh did go back, and tried that, and when the bell rang at the end of the 20 minutes, he found to his surprise that he had not seemed to think of anything at all, but only to experience the scent of the flowers and the *agarbatti*, the sound of his own breath, the soft swirling shades of darkness behind his gently closed eyelids, the sense of a vast unified consciousness that might create a great peace if only it were more widely and often entered. He and Larry went to group meditation night after night.

I could barely have imagined the place Josh was describing to me in Darlinghurst that night, but since then I have been to Indian cities and found even in their miasma and cacophony these beautifully tended oases of stillness and loveliness. If only, they make you think, all our cities contained these spaces dedicated to silence and contemplation.

When they left the *samadhi* grounds, they would stroll in the gently lit streets in the warm air, keeping hold of the silence they had experienced, as if staying a while in a transitional zone as their senses took in the sights of the promenade on the esplanade, the lights on the gentle sea beyond the stone wall, the statue of Gandhi, the families and couples and groups of friends sauntering along or stopping for snacks, the children with their new balloons or bamboo flutes, the sellers of newspaper cones of roasted channa or peanuts. Then they would often have dinner at a garden restaurant, where they ate grilled fish and *pommes frites*, sometimes an onion soup or a cheese soufflé, and maybe a glass of wine. Larry then would begin to talk, opening up and relating some of his experiences of India to a fascinated, even besotted, Josh. On one of those evenings, Larry told Josh the story of his first trip to India, the story of his early adventures and of the friend who'd died, the story I've already told you.

On other occasions, Larry would take him to eat at the ashram dining room, where a crowd of mostly Indian pilgrims lined up for an extremely cheap meal of rice and vegetables, deliciously spiced but not too hot, eaten with the hands—right hand only! Larry instructed him—sitting on the ground, no lingering once you're done, take your plate to be washed.

When Larry disappeared for hours of the day, Josh knew he had gone to read at the ashram library, or to visit people he wanted to talk to. Josh had no interest in accompanying him, nor did he have much of an idea of what Larry's pursuits consisted; he had enough to do, he told me, with recovering his health, forming some new determination, and simply being where he was.

Josh encouraged Larry to read to him. 'I loved hearing that stuff.' Josh became sentimental as he told me this, and carried on for a bit about the way Larry read: 'he didn't put much expression into it but it was so calm and clear, and these beautiful words.'

'I know, it sounds over the top, but I do not regret a moment.'

'I still haven't heard of anything for you to regret', I said.

'Larry had got us two rooms', Josh said. 'I would have shared a room if he wanted to, to save money or whatever, but he said he sometimes read at night and I was there to have a holiday and should keep my own hours. We'd always meet at the end of the day, sometimes I'd see him during the day, sometimes I wouldn't.'

'Sometimes he'd give me a hug when we said goodnight, and I wanted to go on holding him. Finally, one night, as he was letting go of me, I did just hold on, and run my hands down his back and said, "I could try and be very quiet" or whatever I said. We made sure all the windows were closed and then, and let me tell you he is too thin now and he was thin then but he was not bony, he was strong, just naturally slender but hard and smooth and round. Anyway, the earth moved, what do you want to know?'

'Anything you tell me!' I said.

'I thought I'd better go back to my own room afterwards, it was all a bit quiet and ashramy there, they had a curfew and they only had single beds, and I paused and looked back at him as I slipped out the door, and he was picking up an open book, beginning to read it again, and I was forgotten.'

I couldn't help smiling. Yes, a perfect image of Larry, I thought. 'What about the earth moved part?'

'Oh, he was kind of straightforward, no frills, the basic suck and pull, kind of like someone very young would be, vanilla all the way, but not shy at all, not uncertain or anything. I mean, he was really into it, and he was gorgeous. But, basically I had just given him a little break from his reading.'

'Yeah, you can grin like that!' Josh grumbled, but then grinned himself.

'Anyway, act mean and keep 'em keen, not that he was mean, he wasn't mean at all. He was as sweet and generous as anyone could be. But for him, I was just there and one day I wouldn't be, and it wouldn't make much difference to him. But I was hoping he would want to keep me round. Like, really, really hoping. I was waiting for my chance. I wanted him to think he needed me. I thought I was good at that.'

'And then one day he just says, "Look, I'm leaving now, I've paid for your room for the rest of the month and I'll give you this" and he hands over rupees and dollars, "so you can get a place when you go back".'

'I thought, what have I *done*? Was it anything I said? I was devastated. I wanted to beg him not to go, but I couldn't say anything, no way, he didn't have to look after me, he'd always been lovely, whether we had sex or not was always up to me, but I had no idea why he was suddenly leaving or where he was going. I soon realised it had nothing to do with me, that he knew I could look after myself now. There was something new he wanted to do. He confirmed my return flight and then basically didn't need to think about me anymore. He had gone, really, before I could even think what to ask him. I thought, just as well I didn't really have any huge expectations. Lucky for me, cause, really I had no clue.'

We must have talked of other things too, but before we parted that night Josh asked me, 'what do you think of him? You haven't said.'

'You know', I said, 'not many people can claim that they always do and say whatever they want to, but a lot of people would like to. Larry is the only person I know who really just does whatever he wants.'

This didn't really satisfy Josh, who said, 'he does, but you only can tell what he wants to do at any given point in time, I could never get to what he overall basically really *wants*.'

'That', I said, 'was the mystery of Larry.'

Chapter 16

Pandora

A Guided Tour of Various (Non) Fictions

Jayne Fenton Keane

> Pandora was a stranger at a stranger's door. She hesitated, she knocked, she listened for footsteps, glancing around her (Baranay 2003:3).

Jose Dominic extends a coffee-warmed hand, which I shake vigorously. 'Welcome to CGH Earth…':

> She was a foreigner, a stranger, a female stranger—a type you didn't often see around here. A westerner…a stranger with a purpose (Baranay 2003:3).

I'm still trying to process my Indian experience and my surprise at discovering that there was another place in the world where I belonged, that felt like home. It was a strange experience, as residencies are, because on the one hand I was a tourist in the brash, exaggerated landscape of what Mark Twain called the 'most extraordinary country that the sun visits on his rounds' (Paine 1912:1013), and on the other I was isolated from the glare of that sun by my containment within the residency.

I encountered India's imaginary and real spaces through the shutters of the CGH Earth hotel group while on an Asialink Literature residency in 2006. It was a self-made rather than pre-packaged residency. The circle drawn around my experience was deliberately traced because boundaries are sometimes useful for creativity. CGH Earth is an unusual hotel chain based in the southern Indian state of Kerala. I am grateful to them for showing me the best of Indian hospitality. I'm grateful that I did not have to rush around India like a besotted tourist doing this and that in the smoggy facets of India's gilded light.

'What does experience mean to you?' asks Jose.

'To experience is to feel' he thinks. We feel when we are involved. When we are no longer onlookers, but deeply immersed in all that is going on around us' (Dominic 2007).

Immersed in the Dominic family's creative gesture of hospitality I choose to write a hybridised medicinal vegetarian cookbook of poems, photographs and diary notes. I experience firsthand the spirit of Inez Baranay's expression that 'as much as the writer creates the text, the text she writes creates the writer' (Baranay 2004).

Just as the writer creates the text that creates the writer, so does the tourist create the experience that creates the tourist. To add another layer of complexity to the congregation of authors already present at the tourism bazaar, the hotel that creates the experience is in turn created by the experience. In creating a hybridised text, a world within a world, I attempted a rehydration of my parched identity as author. CGH feels like a second home, a place where work and pleasure converge in comfort.

Desperate for a private bathroom, a quiet bed, a door she can shut upon the world, Pandora dares not consider a search for another hotel (Baranay 2003:8).

The pleasure of creative investigation lies in its flexible attitude towards discovery, where 'journeys of research, text and self become harmonious' and integrated (Baranay 2004). India greets me through a series of doorways that open to strange yet familiar scenes and gatherings. 'Don't let the silence disturb you', says the first sign I encounter through Kalari Kovilakom's doorway.

Jose determines that I should begin my Indian pilgrimage in the monastic space of Kalari Kovilakom. I commit to staying for three weeks, even though I have no idea what the property is like. In the end I stay for four. Jose's passion for the newest CGH property is infectious. You can't go on a pilgrimage without surrendering control. Kalari Kovilakom seemed like the perfect place to let go. Some new-age slogan pops to mind, 'let it go, let it unravel, let it be a path on which to travel' or something like that. As the gates close behind me and I step into a portico where I am garlanded with flowers, stripped of my leather and smudged with sandal paste, I feel the history of this place and its long tradition of ayurvedic healing.

> 'Tourism can so often be a window, a space where cocooned in the comforts of technology, people look, snap a picture or two, and move on', says Jose. 'We don't want you to have that kind of experience. We want you to discover your true self. Here is your doorway. Let your pilgrimage begin' (Dominic 2007)

> 'India,' says Lauren, 'you've always wanted to go…Don't get sick, she says, keep well with the thoughts of wellness.' (Baranay 2003:9).

Everything I learned about India, prior to coming here, was from books, movies, music, food, documentaries, travelogues and travel industry promotional material. Even though there are hundreds of Indian students at Griffith University, where I have been studying for the past six years, I did not know any of them. The extent of my ignorance was not fully appreciated until I'd been to India and returned. Now when I pass groups of Indian students I recognise the smell of individual spices in their body odour. I wonder which part of India they are from because now realise that there are differences that relate to place. I assume most of them come from wealthy backgrounds and, although I would like to strike up a conversation with them, circumstances rarely permit it.

It's difficult to speak meaningfully with people who are not in your immediate circle. In the headspace of a traveller, however, there is often a greater openness and willingness to talk to strangers. People make or break a travel experience. 'Did you meet anyone interesting?' asks my mother. Like landscapes and photographs of travel experiences, however, these intimacies cannot be translated adequately. A moment is a brief etching in memory that is sometimes difficult to rejuvenate. This is another of Baranay's gifts.

> Pandora nodded and appreciatively inhaled the aroma of cardamom and ginger from the little cup. Over the blue doorway where the fat man sat brewing and mixing the tea, a faded sign painted green and pink onto a board said 'Jolly Tea House' along with some writing in a beautiful script, some language that surely could not exactly translate (Baranay 2003:56).

The Indian students have become a reminder of a home that I am separated from. They stir up heartache and love at the same time. They are no longer India signified, but individuals who have homes and lives that are very different from the experiences available on the Gold Coast. I wonder what it is like for them and hope they are experiencing the best of Australian hospitality.

> Upstairs, a boy is showing Pandora her room. He picks up a spray can and sprays...He keeps on spraying...he sprays the air with a ghastly chemical. The label calls it jasmine-scented room freshener...The book says this city smells like jasmine (Baranay 2003:11).

I was worried about the toxins in India. Prior to my departure, friends regaled me with stories of slapping wet towels against doors and windows in an effort to keep out the nauseating diesel fumes of New Delhi. A prior near-death experience with pesticides left me with a psychological and physiological aversion to chemicals. As if reading my mind, at our first meeting Jose tells me that CGH resorts 'are chemical-free zones'. I'm sceptical. Jose switches between Malayalam, Hindi and English as he choreographs the various interruptions during our discussions. His eyes dart between the computer screen, the phone, the door and present company. In the middle of booking airline tickets and discussing my project, he manages to segue to ancient tribal wisdom and organic pest-control methods.

Lemongrass oil, that's what they mop the floors and surfaces with at Kalari Kovilakom, dubbed Kalari by those in the know. During my first concert evening I wonder how the mosquito coils fit in with the toxic-free-zone rhetoric. 'Joseph,' I say 'do you have another mosquito management strategy up your sleeve?' I'm not sure if he's laughing or choking until he says, tears hitting his cheeks like monsoon rain on a windscreen, 'I've never heard anyone call it that before.' Mr Joseph Joseph lived with a Germanic sense of humour and is the General Manager of the Kalari during my stay.

> 'Kalari' says Jose with that knack Indians have of rolling their Rs so nimbly 'is a place where opposites meet. It's 19th century luxury. It's monastic. It's austere. It is India from a bygone era.' (Dominic 2007)

I'm anxious about my opposites meeting in public. I prefer them to meet in the sanctuary of my home. It turns out there is more than an architectural truth to Jose's allusion to monasteries. Joseph is quite a character, an occasionally disillusioned evangelist prone to biblical shibboleths that are greeted with raised eyebrows, rolled eyeballs and plenty of lively discussions at meal times.

At Kalari there are no televisions, computers or radios in the rooms. Technological stimulation of any kind is frowned upon, as it supposedly distracts from the effectiveness of the pilgrimage. I'm not convinced of this, as technology is part of the psychological and physical reality that must be processed during any evaluation of contemporary life and its purpose. After all, I am a 21st-century woman embedded in technological tissue. In fact, my pilgrimage begins through technology and the wonders of the internet.

People travel to Kalari to heal, to lose weight, to discover themselves and to experience traditional *ayurveda* principles and methods. The founder of the 'The Land of the Venga Tree', or Vengunad, was Prince Dharmavarman who is said to have travelled to the area in the 10th century seeking a cure for a disfiguring skin ailment. Kalari Kovilakom sits at the base of the stunning foothills of the Annamalai Range that bound the ancient Vengunad Kingdom. Contemporary pilgrims seek relief from high blood pressure, constipation, obesity, exhaustion, pharmaceutical drug-induced problems, depression and a host of other 21st-century ailments. The Annamalai Hills are part of the mountain range known as the Ghats, which travel hundreds of miles along the southwestern coast of India. The Hills are almost permanently capped with clouds and add an enchanting backdrop to morning and afternoon garden walks.

Australians, like Indians, love food and eating out. Indian restaurants are popular. Eating at Indian restaurants in Australia bears little resemblance to dining in Kerala. Fusion permeates the menu. The food in Australian–Indian restaurants is as displaced as the diasporic existence of many Indian migrants and settlers. I ignore the cocked eyebrows, cutting laughter and mild curiosity expressed by peers when I tell them I'm writing a cookbook.

> 'At first,' says Jose, 'you may find the food somewhat bland. But within a day or two, your palate will soften and you will appreciate the subtlety of the flavours' (Dominic 2007).

> [T]hey slowed down to savour a fragrance of a mysterious masala, oil and cumin and chilli. Hissing kerosene lamps cast long shadows around a food cart and the men standing or squatting, eating deep fried spicy pastries (Baranay 2003:187).

My cookbook is a story of food and space told in recipes, photographs and creative excerpts from the journal being written around the cookbook. I have learned to respect creativity's logic and instincts. My scriptwriter, and the forces of destiny that had written this Indian scene for me, compelled me to follow their missions through. 'It'll all make sense later', I reassure myself.

The Queen, whose ferocious portrait peers down the corridors of Kalari, is rumoured to have had at least five consorts or husbands. One of her husbands was a cook in her kitchen. She married him in the traditional way by holding his hand and dipping it in a nearby *ganga*, or river. Perhaps it is the ghost of this husband who inspires me to write a cookbook. There are tales of rattling chains, hair bristling and whispers in corridors as the dark history of the palace is revealed. These are some of the titbits Jaya Jaitly tosses as she reminisces about her visits to the palace when she was a girl. Jaya, political activist and handicrafts expert, is a cousin of one of the palace's original family members. Jaya is also on an ayurvedic detox prescription, along with the former Indian Minister for Defence, George Fernandez.

We congregate for breakfast at 8 am, lunch at 12:30 pm and dinner at 6:30 pm. We compare our individually designed meals dressed in the tailor-made suits provided by the hotel to support the experience of leaving the everyday world behind. George, a legendary socialist politician, is not much of a talker. Jaya is constantly by his side translating the dramas of his life for us. George has his 75th birthday at Kalari and was restored enough to blow out a field of candles. When he first arrived he looked like a man who was about to die. I've never met any genuine radical socialists before, so I spend hours interviewing them in the hope I will be able to create something with their stories and voices to share with the world. I did manage to prepare a three-minute documentary sound poem out of George's famous train-strike story. The piece was published online as part of the '99 Ways to Tell a Story' series run by the Third Coast International Audio Festival in Chicago in 2006. Jaya is a born storyteller who inflates the stiff portraits on the wall with the breath of her stories until they are almost pink with life.

The choice to write a cookbook is a pragmatic one. It emerges from a necessity to compromise, as is too often the case when creativity encounters the world. I feel a responsibility towards CGH to deliver something of value to them. I don't feel compromised by this responsibility as I'm free to write whatever I want anytime (if I could find some) but, as luck and good research would have it, I find myself in the care of a family company that expresses a set of values that resonate with mine. At CGH Earth I notice that my identity and history and that expressed by the hotel's literature and culture are closely aligned. I need more time to consider the implications of this. Sheltering in the open and ambiguous spaces of the CGH properties and its food liberates me from domesticity and the fragmentary existence it provokes. Writing in spaces of leisure helps me encounter this foreign world and its texts. The residency is a kind of poetic habitation where I am liberated from exteriors to become interiorised, to become

> a dreamer of words, of written words. I think I am reading; a word stops me. I leave the page. The syllables of the word begin to move around. Stressed accents begin to invert. The word abandons its meaning like an overload which is too heavy and prevents dreaming. Then words take on other meanings as if they had the right to be young. And the words wander away, looking in the nooks and crannies of vocabulary for new company, bad company in the stuffing of the vocabulary (Bachelard 1969:6).

I tried to feel my way back to the dreaming words after years of cramming them into little suitcases of space between commitments and responsibilities. I can't do it. I don't accomplish the youthful Bachelardian abandon spoken of above because of a commitment to produce product. Production pollutes the space of dreaming and poetic language, though at the end of an open-ended process it can be rewarding; when words are translated into publication for example.

I find the world demands a kind of attention that is contrary to the space of my dreaming: 'The literary image cannot be produced or manufactured, and there is no path that leads directly from the mind or the psyche of the writer to its birth on the page or to its appearance within the horizon of the reader' (Thiboutot 2001:166). As a starched, cockatoo-white napkin perches on my lap, I consider how much more unravelling I would have to do in India to dishevel the ordered space of speech. I will have to hunt for poetry's wild words some other time.

> The lights went out. The sudden blackout came with a sudden silence: the generator had run out of fuel. The little oil lamp on the table barely touched the darkness but in the gently lightened shadows around it a waiter emerged and their food was placed before them (Baranay 2003:193).

Food is the text through which I discover a country while expressing and creating myself in the manner of Baranay's way of thinking of character development 'as much as the writer creates the text, the text she writes creates the writer—not only the part of the writer which writes, but the writer who participates in life, and where and how she does so' (Baranay 2004). Food, like music, literature, dance, drama and the visual arts, is a product of the culture that grows and creates it. If food is a socially produced and reinforcing code which is in turn rendered through food, as suggested by anthropologist Mary Douglas (1972), my writing process has become a kind of archaeological dig.

Ancient recipes and ancient songs punctuate my days as India's soil supports me through travels to indigenous coffee plantations, rural vegetable markets, organic spice farms, worm farms and gardens full of strange vegetables called okra, lady's fingers (not the banana kind) and drumstick leaves. If, as Hosking and Sarwal in their 2007 call for papers for this book say, Indians have been shipping bread to Australia ever since 1791, what could be more natural in the creation of an Indian text than kneading the dough and stoking the ovens of that ancient breadmaking practice? If food is suitable for philosophy, psychology and medicine, why shouldn't an aberrant cookbook pirouette on the edge of interdisciplinary literature?

> So is it a spa? A Palace hotel? An ayurvedic hospital? An ashram? Kalari is beyond these simply because it is a little of all of these (Dominic 2007).

When applying for an Asialink residency I expected to have my PhD wrapped up. My motivation for the residency was a desire to rewrite myself as I faced the post-PhD vacuum that loomed ahead. I planned on escaping the methods of logic and rhetoric that had kidnapped my poetic voice in order to swish around in the exuberant margins of unaccountable imagination. I wanted to pursue Bachelard's idea of '*deforming*' the images of perception; I craved seduction by what Bachelard keys as imagination's open and evasive qualities where transformation's capacities reside (Bachelard 1969:19).

Unfortunately things do not go according to the plans, which were clearly doomed from the start. My dreams are deferred by an awareness that coherence might be called for at any moment. It was never going to possible to be a traveller driven by unaccountable imagination. It was a delusion inspired by a desire to transcend realism and the practical preoccupations of the everyday. To rediscover the joy of writing poetry I have to rediscover poetic consciousness and learn to flex it every day. I desired a return to non-pragmatic texts where the dreamer could pursue her unique language. I have arrived at my own kind of fusion. Delusion and pragmatism resign themselves to living in each other's company in my psyche. As delusion and pragmatism meet over steaming brass bowls of aromatic food, a worldly, conversational poetry begins to emerge.

In the midst of my pilgrimage to the self, I can't take my senses off the world. I am infatuated with the frog calls in deep wells, the light on the belly of the palace's huge wooden pillars at sunset, the bubbled texture of *appam*s and the perfumed taste of drumstick leaves. The oils and milks from the daily massages turn my skin smooth and golden. I exist in a riot of sensation and fight hard to stay coherent and logical in order to write. Pandora's Holy Grail was her neem project. I search for respite and creativity, opposites requiring different energies.

As I wander around the walled gardens I feel my feet step into the story of the palace, the old ways of those who trod the paths before me. Over the fence I watch women scrub themselves and their cows each morning and evening at the local bathing pool. These are not the frolicking nymphs of Norman Lindsay's rock pools, but shy, earthy, saffron-clad women whose calloused hands never get a chance to rest. Inside the treatment rooms overlooking one of the former Queen's bathing pools I receive Pizhichil, a treatment of medicated oil. Molten petals are poured over my body. Warm rivulets of oil spill from the spouts of two ancient brass pots. This is how it feels to be made love to by a flower.

Each morning I am woken at 5 am by the local temple's speakers blasting out a call to prayer. It is not possible to be a spectator of Indian traditions and history at Kalari. I am forced to experience them within my very matter, the molecules and fluids of my material existence. Through the chaos of detoxification I create a new order, a new story based on a holistic sense of myself and my life. Emotional and physical toxins are purged in rituals of cleansing that make me realise how cultural most of these toxins are.

Without stories monuments are simply bricks, stone or mortar, places are only development spaces, and hotels are simply theme parks for recreation. Socrates said that an unexamined life was not worth living but if the life has not been lived richly, there is not much raw material to examine.

The roots of a giant banyan split the concrete outside Jose's office. Inside a CGH computer my cookbook lies dormant. To understand time we must stop for it, linger in its amplitude. By merely using time we become a slave to efficiency and our lives slip by unexamined.

Untouched, the tree stands, its roots burrowing deeper, its spreading branches lifting higher against the smoke burdened sky (Baranay 2003:278).

Works cited

Bachelard, Gaston 1969, *The poetics of reverie*, translated by D Russell, Orion Press, New York.

Baranay, Inez 2003, *Neem dreams*, Rupa, New Delhi,

— 2004, 'It's the other who makes my portrait: writing self, character and the other', *Text* 8(2).

Dominic, Jose 2007, *CGH Earth*, www.cghearth.com, viewed 21.10.2007.

Douglas, Mary 1972, 'Deciphering a meal', *Daedalus* 101.

Paine, Albert Bigelow 1912, *Mark Twain: the personal and literary life of Samuel Langhorne Clemens*, Harper, New York.

Thiboutot, Christian, 2001, 'Some notes on poetry and language in the works of Gaston Bachelard', *Journal of Phenomenological Psychology* 32(2).

Chapter 17

Road to Bangalore[1]

Bernard Whimpress

'Why don't you go?' my wife said.

It was mid-August 2004 and my friend Neville Turner was going to India for the Tests in October. So was Rob Bartlett (a former Adelaide friend, now Melburnian) and his wife Kirsten on a delayed honeymoon. I told Rob that they should catch up with Neville who'd done half a dozen Test series on the subcontinent and knew the ropes.

Hey! Why not?

I'd been to India three times. Never for cricket.

Eighteen years ago was the last time. Australians must be easy to pick because wandering around the big cities a lot of white-collar workers would come up for a chat about cricket. They all wanted to talk about Allan Border and Dennis Lillee.

I had a hit here and a hit there and once batted through an entire lunch hour in Srinagar against a team of clerks. Further afield I took my only overseas wicket, a Kashmiri mountain-villager, with a well-flighted offie within view of K2. Other than that you couldn't help watching the children's cricket on the streets and in the Muslim cemeteries where the headstones were used as wickets. All the bowlers put the ball on a length and all the boys with bats in their hands looked like Dillip Vengsarkar, whipping the ball with a sharp flick of the wrist off their legs. None looked like our kids, attempting to heave cow shots over imaginary fences. India's cricket time would come.

My first trip 30 years ago was at the tail end of the overland hippy trail. Delhi to London and lumping Kerouac along with Richard Brautigan (a

---

[1] Originally published in May 2005 in *Baggy Green* 7(2).

West Coast American LSD writer of limited duration) and Herman Hesse in my rucksack. There wasn't much space for the noble game.

As a historian, I knew almost nothing about Bangalore before leaving this time. As a sports historian, the only sports historical fact I had at my command was that former English cricket captain Colin Cowdrey was born there on Christmas Eve 1932. World populations were once a boyhood hobby of mine before cricket statistics came along. Bangalore didn't make any major lists of big cities.

It would now: 5.7 million people and the fourth biggest city in India, says the *Lonely Planet Guide* which I bought and packed at the last moment; 4.4 million, says one website, and number five in an entry which is curiously out-of-date for the garden city which began as 'a town of boiled beans' in the early 16th century and whose industrial and commercial growth is unequalled in the country.

Sports stadiums are named after politicians in South Asia. The M Chinnaswamy Stadium, formerly the Karnataka State Cricket Association Stadium, commemorates the Board of Control for Cricket in India President from 1977 to 1980. The ground only gained Test status against the West Indies in 1974–1975 and this is only the third Test against Australia played at the stadium. In the first under Kim Hughes in September 1979, the monsoon preventing a result, Australia lost 13 wickets for 410 runs against India's 5–457 declared. In 1997–1998 Sachin Tendulkar posted the highest individual score at the ground (177), but Mark Waugh responded with 153 not out, and Mark Taylor's 102 not out saw Australia to victory by eight wickets for its only win of the three-Test series.

I flew out of Adelaide at 3 pm on Tuesday, 5 October, met Neville at Kuala Lumpur at 10 pm, and caught a late flight to Bangalore, arriving at 11:30 pm. By the time we got through immigration and took a frenetic drive in an Ambassador cab, it was 1 am before we got to the city centre. And we still had to find a bed for the night! The game was only eight hours away and we were tramping up a gloomy street with a few mangy dogs lying about and not much else. Fortunately we didn't tramp far, as the Curzon Court Hotel in Brigade Road beckoned. It proved pristine, cheap enough at 1,000 rupees (around $30), and conveniently located only a kilometre from the ground.

Entry to the cricket was not easy by Australian standards. One thousand police hired by the Karnataka Association were there to keep order, and our first experience is of Neville negotiating forcibly with the constabulary for us to jump 500 locals in the queue to get into the ground in time for the first ball. We didn't quite manage that, but I was impressed by the 40,000-seat stadium. Even though the seats on the cement slabs are hard on the bum after seven hours, they were a great bargain at 50 rupees a ticket.

The first three days were spent in that section, and for the first two we took an American novice (John), whom we had met over breakfast at the Curzon Court, for his initial exposure to cricket. He learned fast, but it was also a great chance to relate to a highly intelligent cricket audience. I back myself against most cricket experts, but a lot of 15-year-old Bangalore lads have a superb appreciation of not only the current game but also of its history. The contrast in ticket prices was remarkable, as on the second day we had a view from the southern end almost straight down the wicket and identical with that of members and special ticketholders in the pavilion, who were paying 20 times our fee. Australia recovered splendidly on the first day, but the police acted ominously with their batons at the end of play as they prodded us out of the arena. After the game we caught up with Indian historian and writer, Ram Guha, at the Koshi Bar, a lovely little Raj-style restaurant within a stone's throw of the ground, for a well-earned Kingfisher beer.

Entering on day two, it was a surprise to be corralled cattle-style between galvanised iron runs. I thought I was smart by purchasing Pepsi bottled water and taking two bottles into the ground in place of the sickly fizz (7 Up, Miranda, Pepsi). To no avail. It was confiscated on entry. Rather than let it go to waste, Neville, American John and I consumed it at the gate. I would be well hydrated for the day.

The cricket is a backdrop to more terrific conversations and the second day started joyfully when Neville and I became kings of the kids by plunging in among a group playing kettle and tabla drums for some wide-angle photos and disco ducking. This brought handshakes galore with about 100 friends, most of whom want to know what we thought of Bangalore, India, Indian food and the cost of things compared with Australia. These questions are asked of travellers the world over, but the questioners were so mature, sophisticated and polite (without deference) that it was fantastic to share their company, even if the pandemonium which celebrated an Australian batsman's fall was in marked contrast to the funereal silence when an Indian batsman was out.

The highlight on the first two days was the exhilarating batting of Michael Clarke and Adam Gilchrist, and both Australians were exuberant in celebrating their tons. For the locals the 400th Test wicket for Anil Kumble (the Smiling Assassin), just ten days short of his 34th birthday, on the ground where he learnt his cricket, had the locals going crazy.

On day two the pendulum swung to Australia as McGrath bowled a brilliant opening spell, breaking through the defence of Rahul Dravid (The Wall) with a superb off-cutter and Shane Warne's big leg-break which knocked over VVS Laxman's off-stump was like a mini-version of the famous Gatting ball of 1993 that set Warne's career on its stellar path.

Amazingly Rob and Kirsten found us exiting Gate G after I'd tried and failed to access their mobile from Australia and from India. Almost simultaneously we bumped into Ram Guha again, whose cricket classic, *A Corner of a Foreign Field* (2002), I'd given Rob as a wedding present only four months before. Again we headed for the Koshi where Ram suggested that Neville and I crash a launch of Rajan Bala's book, *The Covers Are Off* (2004), on India's Test captains.

We were delighted to do so at the absolutely grand Windsor Manor Hotel, an old-style palatial hostelry complete with liveried staff and prints of Victorian notables, not omitting the young Queen herself. We arrived by rickshaw, but got out at the gate to avoid comparisons of the humble mode of our transport with that of those alighting from late model Mercs and BMWs. The launch by major publisher Rupa & Co in lavish surrounds under ornate carved ceilings and hanging chandeliers afforded the opportunity to hobnob with India's professional elite as well as the company of publishers, writers, journalists and cricketers. Among a number of speakers, the most famous was the hero of the hour, Kumble—Mr Elegance personified—whose deep cultured accent suggests film or political opportunities when his cricket finishes.

Mike Coward was the only Australian journalist present but Simon Briggs and John Weaver of the London *Daily Telegraph* and *Guardian* represented the English press. These writers explained that all the English broadsheets were covering the tour. Mike didn't think much of me wearing the egg and bacon Marylebone Cricket Club tie, but my theory, which I expressed, was, 'If you've got it, flaunt it!'

For my part, I was impressed by the *Deccan Herald* reporter, and former opener for Hyderabad, who stated that Rodney Hogg was the most dangerous bowler he'd faced—and he had faced Malcolm Marshall! Turns out he'd driven Hogg's first ball of a match for four on Kim Hughes' 1979 Indian tour and received the next, a bumper from about 17 yards, which knocked his cap off. It was agreed that Hogg could be a bit of a mad bastard. I was also astonished by a man who asked, 'How's the Tea Tree Gully Cricket Club going?' He'd played a half a dozen games for them in Adelaide district cricket in the early 1990s before recommending the great Bhagwhat Chandrasekhar for the following season.

I was up at 6 am on day three, searching and failing to find an early morning coffee house. It's a splendid time as the city teeters to life but, with no coffee discovered, it proved to be a long walk in vain.

Getting into the ground was again awkward as we jostled in the corral. Neville, who always feels that it's sacrilegious to miss a ball, climbed between a cane fence in search of quicker passage and I limboed under it moments later to great applause. Inside the ground Rob and Kirsten had deserted their corporate splendour for the cheap seats and the four of us became the object of attention. One youngster even asked for my autograph, somehow mistaking me for umpire Darrell Hair. Apart from the umpires I seemed to be the only person in Bangalore wearing a panama hat, but maybe I needed to work harder on a paunch. On the other hand I prefer allusions to Graham Greene.

India fought back well to survive half the day in advancing to 246 but Australia at 4–127 was well positioned at the end of play. Even so, the lack of a second-class spinner to support Warne might prove a mistake.

Two Australian wickets fell by the time I arrived on day four, due partly to the thick crowds and slow movement on the way to N gate in an upgraded section, which forced me to remind myself of my whereabouts, think in circular time, and go with the flow. Neville found the best seat in the house outside the pavilion and we were looking straight down the wicket behind the TV cameras. Harbhajan swept through the tail to claim 6–78 and 11 wickets for the game. India's unlikely winning target was 457; the alternative to survive around 135 overs to save the game.

In no time wickets began tumbling and shrewd gamesmanship by Warne in calling three times for the ball to be examined proved a trigger. On one occasion umpires Steve Bucknor and Billy Bowden held up play for eight minutes. Although McGrath and Gillespie bowled superb opening spells, two wickets fell immediately after the stoppages and Ganguly ran himself out in an appalling error of judgment which the captain should be the last person to make. Gilchrist set weird fields, which seemed to owe more to pawn development in chess than cricket, but the bowlers were on top and only a brief partnership of 62 between Dravid and Yuvraj Singh offered any likelihood of resistance. Small pickings. At one stage it appeared as though play might be wound up, but eventually India struggled through to 6–105 at the close.

Saturday night, and we had run into University of Tasmania geographer (and university club stalwart) Bob Cotgrove who invited us to dinner, along with Melbourne Cricket Club library volunteer Ross Perry, in the members' restaurant. Bob, who by good fortune had found himself lodging at the ground, introduced us to a veritable Eden behind the concrete stands, and the exquisite meal, gentle atmosphere and amiable company were spoilt for me only by news of the federal election result from home. Being thousands of miles away and sinking extra Kingfishers helped numb some of the pain.

In Australia the ground would probably have been opened free on the last day. Not so. While there were only about 3,000 spectators present at the beginning the crowd grew to around 10,000. From the outset a six-piece band (bass and two side-drums, two trumpets and tuba) provided wondrous rhythms and, with smaller numbers and more space, it was easier to enjoy the accompaniment.

India was obviously intent on saving the match and Dravid on batting for six hours. The early tactic was for Dravid to take Warne bowling from the southern end, with Irfan Pathan facing the pacemen from the St Mark's Cathedral or pavilion end. Play was slow and this position was maintained for six overs before Gilchrist adopted a chase-the-batsman tactic by bowling five different bowlers in consecutive overs: Lehmann replaced Warne; Warne switched ends to replace Kasprowicz; McGrath replaced Lehmann; Kasprowicz replaced Warne; and Warne replaced McGrath at the southern end. The Indians foiled the plan for a while when Dravid took a single, but the Karnataka hero went lbw to a sharp off-cutter from Kasprowicz for 60 at 7–118 and India's only chance to draw the game sank.

Nevertheless, the tail wagged as in the first innings. Kasprowicz was the pick of the attack, but the attempt to buy the world wicket-taking record for Warne backfired as he bowled poop and came under heavy attack. Pathan, who had been scoreless for the first 40 minutes and whose seven had occupied 100 minutes, began to open out, and when Harbhajan hoisted Warne over long on for a huge six, the leg-spinner's figures read 2/103 out of 8–172, which included 14 extras or just 158 runs from the bat. In fact, Lehmann's orthodox darts looked more dangerous than Warne, who eventually registered 2–120. As a *Times of India* reporter put it on 11 October 2004: 'Not since Abdul Qadir was hammered by a young Sachin Tendulkar 15 years ago has a legendary leg-spinner suffered such humiliation on the cricket field'.

Pathan and Harbhajan added 89 for the ninth wicket and Pathan's 55 lasted 205 minutes before Gillespie, who had not bowled before lunch, had him caught behind by Gilchrist. Even then the last wicket added a further 25 runs, with Zaheer Khan engaging in further lusty hitting before Harbhajan was caught at deep fine leg off Gillespie to give Australia victory by 217 runs.

Neville and I returned to our hotel, ran into American John and had fun explaining the intricacies of the lbw law—boy is he picking things up quickly!—over lassi in the restaurant. Using a glass as the wicket and a Miranda bottle as the batsman, I was in the process of showing how a bowler like Warne cannot pitch outside the leg-stump to hit the bottle and expect a favourable decision when a waiter came up and removed the bottle. 'Hang on', I said, 'you can't get a batsman out like that!' Mirth all round.

We went back to the ground for the second night in a row for more dining under the stars and Tasmanian Bob pointed out that the Aussies were still boozily bonding, singing 'Under the Southern Cross' (plus expletives) at 7 pm, five hours after play had ended. This led to some sober reflections on the historic connections between beer and sport, although it must be said that when we left the restaurant at 11:30 pm it (and us) were gently humming, children were playing and there were no other Australians in sight.

Contributors

Alison Bartlett is Senior Lecturer in Women's Studies and also teaches English and Cultural Studies at the University of Western Australia, and before that at the University of Southern Queensland. She publishes regularly in literary and feminist journals, is co-editor of *Australian Literature and the Public Sphere* (1999) and the author of *Jamming the Machinery: Contemporary Australian Women Writers* (1998). In addition to literary studies her research has included postgraduate supervision and feminist pedagogy, fictocriticism, reading embodiment and modes of activism (including writing). She edits the online journal *Outskirts*.

Amit Sarwal is Assistant Professor in the Department of English, Rajdhani College (University of Delhi), India. From 2006–2007 he was an Honorary Visiting Scholar at the National Centre for Australian Studies and the School of Political and Social Inquiry, Monash University as an Endeavour Asia Award winner (2006). He is the co-editor of: *English Studies, Indian Perspectives* (2006); *Australian Studies Now* (2007); *Fact & Fiction: Readings in Australian Literature* (2008); *Creative Nation: Australian Cinema and Cultural Studies Reader* (2009); *Reading Down Under: Australian Literary Studies Reader* (2009); *Australian Made: A Multicultural Reader* (2010); and *Sold by the Millions: Australia's Bestsellers* (2012).

Bernard Whimpress is one of Australia's leading sports historians and the author of 20 books, mainly on cricket. Among his more important works are *Passport to Nowhere: Aborigines in Australian Cricket* (1999) and *Chuckers: A History of Throwing in Australian Cricket* (2002). His most recent book is *The Official MCC Ashes Treasures* (2002). From 1998 to 2010 he published and edited the Australian cricket history journal, *Baggy Green*. Bernard holds a doctorate in history from Flinders University and is currently associated with the School of Communication, International Studies and Languages at the University of South Australia.

Bruce Bennett was Emeritus Professor at the University of New South Wales Australian Defence Force Academy. He held visiting professorships in Europe, North America and Asia. His books include *Homing In* (2006), *Australian Short Fiction: A History* (2002) and, with Jennifer Strauss, *The Oxford Literary History of Australia* (1998). He is co-editor of the anthology *Of Sadhus and Spinners: Australian Encounters with India* (2009).

Christopher Vernon is an Associate Professor in the Faculty of Architecture, Landscape and Visual Art at the University of Western Australia. His scholarship focuses upon landscape and architecture as collective expressions of identity, especially in the instance of national capital cities. He has also lectured and published widely on Walter Burley Griffin and Marion Mahony Griffin and is presently investigating their Indian work. In parallel, Vernon is comparatively analysing the British Empire capitals, Pretoria, Canberra and New Delhi.

David Walker is Alfred Deakin Professor of Australian Studies at Deakin University, Victoria, Australia. He has written extensively on Australian relations with Asia. Publications include *Anxious Nation: Australia and the Rise of Asia, 1850–1939* (1999) which won the Ernest Scott Prize for History in 2001 and, with Laksiri Jayasuriya and Jan Gothard, *Legacies of White Australia: Race, Culture and Nation* (2003).

Inez Baranay is a well-known Australian writer. Her most recent novel *Always Hungry* was published in 2011. Her previous novel, *With the Tiger* (HarperCollins India 2008), is a rewriting of Somerset Maugham's *The Razor's Edge* (1944). An earlier novel, her seventh book, *Neem Dreams* (Rupa 2003) was also published in India to widespread critical acclaim. A work of nonfiction, *Sun Square Moon: Writings on Yoga and Writing*, was published in 2005 by Writers Workshop, Kolkata. She has been to India many times since 1980, including as writer-in-residence at Madras University and as an Asialink Literature Resident.

Jayne Fenton Keane is a poet, consultant and academic who completed her doctorate in poetics in 2008. She was the first Poet in Residence at the Ornithology and Bio-Acoustics Laboratories at Cornell University in the USA and the first Poet in Residence at the National Science and Technology

Museum in Taiwan. Her research interests include poetics, new media and travel. Jayne's practice and scholarship has a global and interdisciplinary focus resulting in international performances, exhibitions and publications.

Kama Maclean teaches South Asian and World History at the University of New South Wales, Sydney. She completed her BA(Hons) degree at La Trobe University, where she majored in Hindi and Politics with a minor in Sanskrit. She is the author of *Pilgrimage and Power: The Kumbh Mela in Allahabad* (2008).

Linda Neil is a writer, musician, and producer with a PhD in Creative Writing from the University of Queensland, where she has taught creative and academic writing. Her memoir, *Learning How to Breathe* (2009) was long-listed for The Age Book of the Year (non-fiction) in 2010 and her documentaries have twice won gold medals at the New York Radio Festivals and have also been short-listed for the United Nations Media Peace Prize. In 2009, she was the ABC National Radiophonic New Media Artist-in-Residence; in 2010, the recipient of the Peggy Glanville-Hicks' composer's fellowship at the Composer's House in Paddington, Sydney; in 2011, a Writer-in-Residence through Asialink with the Shanghai Writers' Association's International Writers' Program; and in 2012 the Australian Council's Writer-in-Residence at the Cite Internationale des Arts in Paris.

Lisa French is Associate Professor in Cinema Studies, Media and Communication at RMIT University. She is the co-author of the books *Shining a Light: 50 Years of the Australian Film Institute* (2009) and *Womenvision: Women and the Moving Image in Australia* (2003). In her PhD and MA research she was interested in gender and Australian film and she has published widely in these fields in local and international journals. Her film projects include producing *Birth of a Film Festival* (2003), a film about the first Melbourne International Film Festival. Her professional history includes broad experience of screen culture, including three years as director of the St Kilda Film Festival and nine years on the board of the Australian Film Institute.

Margaret Allen is Professor Emerita in Gender Studies, University of Adelaide. She researches transnational, postcolonial and gendered histories. In particular she works on links between India and Australia from about

1880 to 1940. She has published on Indians living in Australia under the White Australia policy and Australian women missionaries in India, among other topics, most recently 'Shadow Letters and the Karnana Letter: Indians Negotiate the White Australia Policy, 1901–1921', *Life Writing* 8(2) in June 2011.

Richard Barz is a Senior Lecturer in Hindi at the Faculty of Asian Studies, Australian National University, Canberra. He teaches courses in Hindi and Urdu. He is currently working on a research project compiling of a grammar of the language of the poetry of Kabir and an inquiry into the history of the major Hindu pilgrimage places in the Uttarakhand Himalaya. His publications include *The Bhakti Sect of Vallabhacarya* (1976 and 1992), *An Introduction to Hindi and Urdu* (1991 and 2000) with Yogendra Yadav, and *Living Texts from India* (1989) with M Thiel-Horstmann.

Rick Hosking recently retired as Associate Professor from the Department of English, Creative Writing and Australian Studies, Flinders University, South Australia, where he worked in all the three areas. His research interests are in Australian cultural history, historical fiction and travel writing. Colonial and postcolonial connections between Australia and India have been a long-standing passion. He is the co-editor of *Fatal Collisions: The South Australian Frontier and the Violence of Memory* (2000), which won the Historical Society of South Australia John Tregenza Award for National Community History.

Roderic Campbell is a Sydney-based, Irish–Scottish poet and writer with particular interests in historical travel writing, who grew up and was educated in Scotland and Ireland. He has worked as a researcher in History at Sydney University since 2002 and has published a biography of a former New South Wales State Governor, *Gordon Samuels Looking Back: A University Chancellor Reflects* (2005).

Sophie Cunningham has worked in publishing for 20 years and is currently the editor of *Meanjin*. Her first novel, *Geography*, was published in 2004 and her second, *Bird*, in June 2008. Her third novel, on Leonard Woolf, is being written under the auspices of a Masters in Creative Writing at Monash University.

Susan Cowan was born in Greenock, Scotland, and is a graduate of the Australian National University in Canberra. She currently works at the University of New South Wales Australian Defence Force Academy, Canberra. Her research interests lie in the Scottish diaspora, Indian–Australian literary links and Australian literature. She has published articles in several journals and is co-editor of *Of Sadhus and Spinners* (2009) and *Resistance and Reconciliation: Writing in the Commonwealth* (2003).

Index

Note: Page numbers followed by n indicates footnote.

abjection 158–9, 160n18
Aboriginal people
    destitution of 44–5
    exclusion from representations of colonial life 43–4
    missions to 46, 48
    representations of 44–5, 46
    and settler women 37–8, 44
    Stolen Generations 131
Across the Sea Wall (Koch) 76–7, 145–6
Adams, Phillip 159
The Adventures of Priscilla, Queen of the Desert (film) 153, 155
The Age of Kali (Dalrymple) 172
The Age (newspaper) 12, 87
Ali, Mushtaq 66
All India Radio 67
Ambrose, Ethel 41
Ambrose, Lily 41
An Angel at My Table (film) 153, 156
Anderson, Austin 140
Anderson, Ethel xix, 80–1, 140–2, 147
Anglo-Indians
    as 'heaven-born' 91
    migration to Australia 4–5
Angus, Joseph 45
Annamalai Hills 202
anti-imperialist nationalism 84
antimalarial drugs 168
antique India, appeal of 8–17
Argus newspaper 105
Armanath, Lala 66
Armstrong, Louis 151
Arnold, Edwin 15
Arnold, Ellen 39, 41–2, 46, 47, 48
Aryan origins 13
Ash, Susan 129, 131
'Asia and the Australian Imagination' (Koch) 145
Asia Education Foundation (AEF) 31–2

Asia–Pacific Economic Cooperation (APEC), Australia's resistance to Indian membership 30
Asialink 31, 198, 205
Asian Studies, in Australia 27
Asian 'Tiger' economies 30
Association for the Protection of Coloured Races 38
Aurobindo 192–3, 194
Australia–India Council 31
Australia–India cricket matches
    Australian tours of India
        first visit by team of Australians 65–6
        Lindsay Hassett's Services side in 1945 66
        in 1956 67
        in 1959–60 67
        in 1964 67–8
        in 1970 68
        in 1979 68–9, 209, 210–14
        in 1998 70
        in 1999–2000 71
        in 2001 71, 184
        in 2004 71, 208
    Indian tours of Australia
        in 1947–48 66–7
        in 1967–68 68
        in 1977–78 68
        in 1980–81 69
        in 1991–92 70
        in 2003–2004 71, 167, 174
        in 2007–08 71–2
    limited-over competitions 70
    one-day cricket 69
    Titan Cup 70
    World Cup in 1987 69–70
Australia–India cricketing relationship
    Australian cricketers playing for Indian teams 74

controversies 30–1, 68, 70–1, 72
as a cultural bridge 65, 73–4, 183–4, 208, 210, 211, 212
disputes over umpiring decisions 72
gambling 70–1
Indian cricket nationalism 73
Indian cricketers playing for teams in Australia 211
Indian involvement in World Series Cup 69
national game in India and Australia 65
the 'New Ashes' 71–2
racial abuse 72
strengthening of ties in 1980s 69–70
Australia–India relationship
1990 Senate Committee Report 31
1998 parliamentary report 30
need to cultivate 32
The Australian Abroad on Branches From the Main Routes Round the World (Hingston) 8, 79, 105–6
Australian Art Orchestra 185
Australian Board of Control for Cricket 65–6, 72
Australian cinema 153–5, 156n9, 159
Australian Cricket Board (ACB) 70–1
The Australian Town and Country Journal 79, 80, 82
Australian–India connection, from earliest day of British settlement of Australia 3
autostereotypes 75

Bachelard, Gaston 205
Badami, Sunil 142–3
Baedeker guidebooks 106
Baker, Herbert 53, 57
Bala, Rajan 211
Bangalore 209
Banks, Joseph 75
Baptist Missionary Society (BMS) 45–6
Baranay, Inez
   attitude to academy and contemporary theory 126, 129–30
   biographical details 133–4
   critical acclaim in India 126, 127–8
   critical reception of *Neem Dreams* 127–8
   critical reception of *Rascal Rain* 126, 128–31
   engagement with academic criticism

and postcolonial theory 128, 131–2, 135–6
   literary career 126–7, 132–6
   'Theory Couldn't Help Me' 129, 136
Barjrang Dal 173
Bartlett, Kirsten 208, 211, 212
Bartlett, Rob 208, 211, 212
Bascham, AL 27
bathing at the *sangam* 20–4
Battle of Ferozeshah 100
Battle of Gwalior 94
The Beat Hotel (Miles) 169
Beat Poets 169
Beato, Felice 121–2
Bedi, Bishen 68
Benares 113–17
Benaud, Richie 67, 68
Bennett, Bruce 146
Bennett, Mary Montgomery 38
Benson, Mark 72
Bentinck, Lord William 99
Beyond the Echo: Multicultural Women's Writing (Gunew & Mahyuddin) 133
Bhabha, Homi 86, 98
Bharatpur 182–3
Bhartiya Janta Party (BJP) 173
Bhosle, Asha 31
Bihar state 172
bilateral relations
   during latter 20th century 25–6
   educational linkages 31
   factors that require attention 31
The Bird Lover's Inn (Bharatpur) 181–5
birdwatching 182–3
Biswas, Punchanon 41
'Black and Blue' (Lang) 90, 93, 94
'Black and White' (Strangman) 85–6
Blavatsy, Madam 17, 115n3
Board of Control for Cricket in India 209
Board for the Cricket Council of India (BCCI) 73
Bodhi temple, and World Heritage status 172
Boldrewood, Rolf 89
Bollywood 152
'Bombardier Gwyllam's Night Out' (Anderson) 140
Bond, Ruskin xiii
Boon, David 69

Border, Allan   31, 68, 69, 70, 208
Bose, Mihir   66
Botham, Ian   69
Bowden, Billy   212
The Boy in the Bush (Lawrence & Skinner)   81, 82
Brabourne Stadium (Bombay)
  cricket nationalism   73
  East Stand   73
  riot during Test match   68
Bradman, Don   67
Brautigan, Richard   208–9
Briggs, Simon   211
Bringing Them Home report   131
British Commonwealth League   38
British Empire
  gender and race hierarchies   49, 78
  importance of India   110–11
  privileged position of Australian settlers   37
  relationships between colonies   38, 40
  unequal status of India and Australia   25, 37
British presence in India   7–8
Bruzzi, Stella   162
Bucknor, Steve   72, 212
Buddhism   171
Buddhist pilgrims   172
Bulletin   79
Butler, Harcourt   60
Butters, John   58
Byerly, Alison   90

Calcutta *see* Kolkata
Campbell, Robert   3–4
Campion, Anna   150
Campion, Jane   149, 150, 151, 151n4, 153, 154, 155–6, 157, 158–62
Canberra
  changes to the Griffins' plan   57–8
  the Griffins' winning plan for   53, 54–7
  international competition for city plan   53, 55
  naming of   57
  nomenclature scheme   58
  origins of   53
  political commitment to   59
The Canterbury Tales (Chaucer)   99
Carey, William   45

Carmody, Keith   66, 73
Carter, David   132, 133
Cashman, Richard   73
The Castle (film)   153, 154
Cawnpore massacre   7–8, 10, 113, 122
Ceylon   3, 6
CGH Earth hotel chain   198, 201, 203–4
Chandrasekhar, Bhagwat   68, 211
Chatterjee, Piya   156
Chaucer, Geoffrey   99
child labour   172
child marriage   48
China, Australia's relationship with   76
Chinnaswamy, M.   209
Chisholm, Caroline   xvii, 4
Christian missionaries   11
Chutter Munzil, Lucknow   118, 120
cinema
  in Australia   153–5, 156n9, 159
  glitter-cycle films   153–4
  gothic form   159
  in India   152
Clark, Greg   76
Clark, Manning   143–4
Clarke, Michael   210
climate
  affinities between tropical Queensland and India   16–17
  and health   4–5
Clive, Robert   91n5
clothing trade   6
Cold War politics   25–6
colonial womanhood in Australia   42–5
colonialism, and whiteness   36–7
contradictions   173
Cook, James   75
A Corner of a Foreign Field (Guha)   211
Cory, Arthur   123–4
Cotgrove, Bob   212, 214
counterculture of 1960s   26
Coverdale, John   4
The Covers Are Off (Bala)   211
Coward, Mike   211
Cowdrey, Colin   209
cricket
  Barmy Army   72
  bodyline   72
  Champions Trophy award ceremony   31
  Indian Cricket League (ICL)   74

Indian Premier League (IPL) 74
  national game in India and Australia 65
  roots in Australia 65
  roots in the *maidan* in India 65
  sledging and racial taunts 30
  Titan Cup 70
  World Cup 69–70
  see also Australia–India cricket matches; Australia–India cricketing relationship
Crittenden, Victor xiii, 89
Crossings 127
culinary items, import of 6
cult-exiting 150
cultural interaction, Deakin's views on Australia–India relations 14–15
cultural relations, with countries of Asia 77
cultural representation
  politics of 131–2
  theoretical debates 130
  see also representations of India and its people
Cumming, Constance 22
Curzon Court Hotel 209

Dalit people 76
Dalrymple, William 172
Darville, Helen 169–70
Davidson, Alan 67, 68
Dawkins Revolution 27
Deakin, Alfred 11–15, 87, 115
Demidenko, Helen 169–70
'A Democrat on the Ganges' (Clark) 143
Dev, Kapil 69
Devaranjan, Padmini 128
Dharamsala 171–2
Diamond, Neil 151
Dickens, Charles xii, 89, 89n2, 90
disease 5
Dorrington, Albert 82–3
Doshi, Dilip 69
Dowling, James Sheen x
Dowling, James (Sir) x
Dravid, Rahul 71, 184, 211, 212, 213
dumping of dangerous products 168

East India Company 9, 95, 100, 112
Eastern religions 171
  growing interest in 15–16
  influence on New Age spirituality 29
  see also Buddhism; Hinduism
economic growth, in India 30
economic protectionism
  in Australia 26
  in India 26
education, funding cuts 27–8
educational linkages, broadening scope of 31–2
Eighteen Fifty-Seven (Sen) 90
Elkington, Mary C. 85
Elliott, Stephan 153
Emerson, Ralph Waldo 187
Empire Day 8
Esson, Louis 83–4
'The Eurasian' (Anderson) 80–1, 142
Eurasian community 81
Evans, Matilda Jan 42–3, 48
Evatt, H.V. 66
An Exercise in Discipline (film) 158
expatriate life, absurdities of 79
exports to India, in 19th century 5–6
Eyre, Edward John 40

fakirs 115
famine 5
Fazal Mahmood 66
female experience, and 'girlshine' 155–6
female *jouissance* 157
female will 159, 159n15
feminism 133
feminist theory 130
Fernandez, George 203
First Anglo-Sikh War 100
First Fleet ix, 25
First War of Indian Independence 60
Fischer, TB 11
food 205
'For Kabir, on *Bijak, Sabad* 50' (poem) (Barz) 177
Forbes-Mitchell, William xii
Forster, E.M. 85
Franc, Maud Jeanne 42
Fraser's Magazine 78
'Fraught Territories' (Baranay) 131
French, Patrick 172
Friedlander, Peter 29
Friedman, Thomas 25
Furphy, Joseph 15
Fyans, Foster 4

Gabay, Al   12
Gandhi, Mahatma   85
Ganguly, Sourav   184, 212
Ganhi, Indira   29n13
Gatting, Michael   211
Gavaskar, Sunil   68, 69
gender   155
Geography (Cunningham)   xix, 170
George V, King of England   54–5
Ghats (mountain range)   202
Ghose, Aurobindo   192
Gilbert, Marie   40, 41–2, 46, 47, 48
Gilchrist, Adam   71, 184, 210, 212, 213
Gillespie, Jason   71, 212
Ginsberg, A.   167
'girlshine'
    and female experience   155–6
    shadow aspect of   157
glitter-cycle films   153–4
global financial crisis (gfc)   32
globalisation studies   75
Go8 institutions   28
goddessess   152
Golden Gifts, an Australian Tale (Evans)   44, 47
Gooden, Rosalind   41
gothic form   159
Green, H.M.   140
greenhouse gas emissions   25, 26
Griffin, Marion Mahony
    move to India   60
    plan for Canberra   53, 54, 55–7
    return to US   62
Griffin, Walter Burley
    death   53, 62
    design for University of Lucknow library   58, 61
    as Federal Capital Director of Design and Construction   57
    move to India   58
    on New Delhi   59
    plan for Canberra   53, 55–7
Grosz, Elizabeth   130
Grout, Wally   68
Guha, Ram   210, 211
Gunew, Sneja   133
Gupta, Pratul Chandra   90

'Haan, Main Tumhara Hoon/(Yes, I'm Yours)' (song)   31
Hack, Wilton   15–16
Hadlee, Richard   69
Hair, Darrell   212
Hall, Catherine   36, 40
Haneef, Mohammed   29
Hansen, John J   72–3
Harbhajan Singh   71, 72, 212, 213
Hardinge, Henry   xi–xii
Harris, John   ix, 46
Harvey, Neil   67–8
Hassett, Lindsay   66
Hawke–Keating governments, push to Asian engagement   29–30
Hayden, Matthew   71
health, and climate   4–5
'heaven-born'   91
Hendry, 'Stork'   66
Hentry, James   4, 6
Henty, Francis   6
Hesse, Herman   209
Hessey, Ruth   161–2
higher education
    funding cuts   27–8
    'Marsupial Model'   28
'The Himalaya Club' (Lang)   91–3
Hindi language studies   29
The Hindu   127, 134
Hinduism   14–15, 114, 115, 152, 172
Hindustan Times (newspaper)   127
Hingston, James   8–10, 79
    arrival in Madras   107–9
    background   105
    on Benares   113–17
    in Calcutta   112
    on cremation   116–17
    on former architectural splendours   118–19
    on Hinduism   113–17
    imperial viewpoint   123–4
    on Indian Mutiny   112–13
    on jugglers and magicians   107
    on Kootub Minar in Delhi   119–20
    on Lucknow and Delhi   117–23
    objection to guidebooks   105, 106
    on opium trade   110
    overseas travels   105
    representations of Indian people   113

on travel as self-education 107–9
travel writings 105–6
travels up the Hooghley River 110–13
view of unchanging nature of the East 113
writing style and tone 106
hippy trail 208–9
A History of Indian Cricket (Bose) 66
Hogan, Paul J. 153
Hogg, Rodney 211
Holly Holy (song) (Diamond) 151
Holy Smoke! (film) xix, 149, 150, 151, 153, 154, 155, 157, 159–62
Holy Smoke! (novel) (Campion & Campion) 150
Hope, Laura 39
horse trade 5–6
Hosking, Rick 78
hospitality 39
Household Words (magazine) xii, xvii, 89, 90, 94
housing, Indian bungalows 4
Howard government 29
  cuts to education funding 27–8
  response to Indian nuclear tests 30
Howard, John 24–5, 26
Hughes, Kim 68, 209, 211
human communication, men and women in the world 157–62
humiliation 161–2

The Illustrated Australian Medical Guide (Muskett) 5
imperial connection
  kin networks 38
  and trade 2–4, 5–6, 38
  unequal terms of membership of Empire 25, 37
imports from India, during 18th and 19th century 6
In Fear of China (Clark) 76
Independence Movement 7, 25
'India', lexical effects on Southern Hemisphere 75–6
India, as metaphor for spirituality 151–2
'India', as a name for Australian girls 76
Indian asceticism
  and media coverage of the Kumbh Mela 21–4

and technology 22
Indian Association for the Study of Australia (IASA) 31
Indian bungalows 4
Indian diaspora in Australia, growth rate 32
Indian Famine Relief Fund 5
Indian language study 27, 28–9
Indian Mutiny 7–8, 9–10, 89, 89n1, 97n11, 112, 121–2, 140–1
Indian restaurants 202
'Indian Society' (Lang) 100
Indian students in Australia 32, 200–1
  Deakin's vision for 14, 87
Indian Subcontinental Studies 27–9
Indian Tales (Anderson) 80
Indian women, relationships with European men 93–4
Indo-Australian plate xvii, 77
Inglis, James 6
International Cricket Council (ICC) 70, 72
invasion-scare novels 76
Irish Sketch Book (Thackeray) 90
Ironmonger, Bert 66
Irrigated India (Deakin) 12, 13, 87
Irving, Washington 90

jackals 175–6
Jaitly, Jaya 203
James, Clive 79
Japan
  Australia's relationship with 76
  as trading partner 28
Japanese Studies 28
Jardine, Douglas 72
Jeffrey Report 27, 28
Jeffrey, Robin xx, 27
Jhansi, Rani of 94–6
Johnston, Bill 67
Jones, Dean 69
jouissance 157, 157n10

Kaiser Bagh gardens, Lucknow 118, 121
Kalari Kovilakom 199, 201–2, 203
'Kanpur' (poem) (Barz) 178
Karma Cola (Metha) 173
Karnataka Association 209
Karnataka State Cricket Association Stadium 209
Kasprowicz, Michael 213

Kauffman, Stanley 159
Keoladeo National Park 175–6
'Keoladeo' (poem) (Barz) 176
Kerouac, Jack 208
Kerry, George 40–1
Khan, Imran 69
Khan, Mizra 141, 142
Khan, Zaheer 213
Kingston, Beverley 6
Kipling, Rudyard 104, 140
Kippax, Allan 66
Klawans, Stuart 159
Koch, Christopher 76–7, 87, 145–6
Kolkata (previously Calcutta) 55
    Black Hole of Calcutta 112
Kootub Minar, Delhi 119
Koshi Bar, Bangalore 210
Kristeva, Julia 158, 160n18, 161
Kumar, Meenakshi 127–8
Kumar, Ravinder 27
Kumbh Mela
    ban on photography 22–3
    media coverage of 20–4
Kumble, Anil 71, 210, 211
Kyoto protocol 25, 26

La Nauze, JA 12
La Trobe University, Hindi language studies 29
Lakhshmibai 94
Lalla Rookh (Moore) 9, 118–19, 120, 122–3, 123n5, 123n6
landscape, in Australian cinema 155, 155n6
Lang, John George
    on common soldiers 103
    death and burial xiii
    Eurocentrism 98
    family background ix, 138
    first marriage x
    his newspaper *The Mofussilite* x–xi, xvii, 78, 89, 90
    on imperial practices in India 103
    on instant experts on India 103–4
    as lawyer in India xii, 94–5, 96, 100–1
    as lawyer in Sydney x
    meeting with Lall Singh 100–2
    meeting with the Rani of Jhansi 94–5
    move to Calcutta x
    move to Meerut, Uttar Pradesh xi
    publications 89, 138–9
    representations of the British in India 92–3, 147
    representations of India and Indians 98
    reputation in Australia x
    reputation in England ix–x
    reputation in India xi–xii
    return to India xiii
    second marriage xiii, 93
    studies in England ix–x
    on transracial relationships 94, 147
    travel writing 96–103
    as writer in London xii–xiii, 89–90
Lang, Lucy (née Peterson) x
Lariam 168
'Last Mango in Pondicherry' (Badami) 142–3
Lawrence, D.H. 81, 82
Lawry, Bill 68
Laxman, VVS. 71, 184, 211
Lee, Brett 31, 73
Lee, Sophie 154
Legends of Australia (Lang) x, 139
Lehmann, Darren 74, 213
Leunig, Michael 24
The Light of Asia (Arnold) 15
Lillee, Dennis 208
Lindwall, Ray 67
LiNQ journal 129, 131
Little Ghosts (Anderson) 80, 140
Llewellyn-Jones, Rosie 53
The Lone Hand 79, 84
'Lost and Found in Avadh' (poem) (Barz) 179
Love, Hammy 66
Low, DA 27
Lucknow
    architectural projects by Walter Burley Griffin 60–2
    British transformation of urban fabric in 19th century 60
    First War of Indian Independence 60
    former glory 117–18
    Indian Mutiny 7, 10
    urban erasure in 21st century 62
Luhrmann, Baz 153
Luketic, Robert 154
Lutyens, Edwin 53, 57, 58

M Chinnaswamy Stadium   209, 210
Macartney, Charlie   66
Macauley, Thomas   7
McDermott, Craig   70
McGrath, Glenn   71, 211, 212, 213
Macquarie, Lachlan   4
Madras   107–9
Maharaha Peishwa Bahadoor   97
Maharaja of Patiala, Team of Australian Cricketers   65–6
Mahyuddin, Jan   133
Majarajahs, fascination with lives of   83–4
Mallet, Ashley   68
mandalas   193
'mango novels'   xix, 143, 147
Maninder Singh   69
Manohar, Vasha   73
A Manual of Family Medicine for India (Moore)   5
Marian; Or The Light of Someone's Home (Evans)   42–3
maritime links, in 19th century   8
Marshall, Malcolm   211
Martyn, Damien   31, 71
masculinity, in Australian writing about India   80
Matthews, Greg   69
Maugham, Somerset   xx
Mayavati   152
Mead, Silas   45–6
Meanjin   131, 132
Medcalf, Rory   xiii
media coverage
    of Indian news stories in Australia   24–5
    of Kumbh Mela   20–4
meditation   194
mefloquine   168
Mela Rules, ban on photography   22–3
Merchant, Vijay   66, 73
Metha, Gita   173
middle class culture   128
migration, of Anglo-Indians to Australia   4–5
Miles, Barry   169
military presence in colonial India   79–80, 139–40
Miller, Keith   66, 67
mind/body split   159, 159*n*14
missionaries in Australia   45, 46

missionaries in India   11, 38–9
    Baptist women from Australia   39–42, 47–8, 49
    in Bengal   45
    support for   38, 40
Mistry, Rohinton   xix, 143
Modi, Rusi   66
Modjeska, Drusilla   131
Moffatt, Tracey   155
The Mofussilite (newspaper)   x–xi, xvii, 78, 89, 90
'The Mohammedan Mother' (Lang)   93–4, 147
Mohanty, Chandra   130
Moore, Robin   27
Moore, Thomas   9, 118–19, 120, 122–3, 123*n*5
Moore, William   5
Moore-Gilbert, Bart   86
Morissette, Alanis   156
Mother, The   192
'The Mouth of the Moon-God' (Dorrington)   82
'Mrs James Greene' (Anderson)   140–2
Müller, Max   14–15, 114, 115
multiculturalism   133, 134, 135
Murdoch, Walter   12, 87
Muriel's Wedding (film)   153, 154
Murphy, Kathleen   151
music   185–6
Muskett, Phillip   5
mutability of civilisations   9
Mutant Message Down Under (Morgan)   170
'My Friend, the Maharajah' (Esson)   83–4
'My Love for Govinddas' (poem) (Barz)   177

naga sadhus   21–3
Nana Sahib   97
Nana Sahib and the Rising at Cawnpore (Gupta)   90
Narain Singh House (Varansai)   61
Narasimhaiah, C.D.   78
national images, study of   75
Neem Dreams (Baranay)   xix, xx, 126, 127–8, 135
Neroni, Hilary   157
New Age spirituality, influence of Indian religions   29
New Delhi   201

design of   53
    as seat of Indian government   55
Night Cries, A Rural Tragedy (film)   155
nonviolent confrontation   85
nuclear testing by India   24, 30
numbers   185–6

O'Dowd, Bernard   16
onomastics   99
opium trade   110
Oudh Kingdom   9, 112
Our Bond (missionary publication)   39
Oxenham, Ron   66

Pal, Swati   128
Pappin, Alice   41, 42
The Paris Sketchbook (Thackeray)   90
Parsees' Towers of Silence (Mumbai)   79
Parsons, Amy   41, 42
Partition   173
A Passage to India (Forster)   85
Pataudi, Nawab of   68
Patel, Jasu   67
Pathan, Irfan   213
Patrons, Players and the Crowd (Cashman)   73
Pawar, Sharad   31
Pepper, Cec   66
Perry, Ross   212
Pershad, Ajoodia   xii, 96, 100–1
Pesman, Ros   38
Peterson, Andrew Turton   x
The Piano (film)   153, 158, 159n15, 159n16
picturesqueness, appeal of   22
pilgrims   172, 202
Pinto, Eugenie   127
Pioneer   140
Playford, Thomas   11
Pokhran II nuclear tests   30
Polan, Dana   160
political extremism   173
Pondicherry   191–2, 193
Ponsford, Bill   66
Ponting, Ricky   71, 72, 184
postcolonial theory   75, 131–2
poverty   26, 171
Prabhu, K.N.   73
Prasanna, Erapally   68
Pratt, Mary Louise   91
'Prayag' (poem) (Barz)   177

Proctor, Mike   72
promontary view in travel writing   91
Proyas, Alex   155
publishing industry, market-driven nature of   135
Pullinger, Kate   151, 161

Qadir, Abdul   213
Queensland, and emergence of new race   17
'Quick in a Snatch' (poem) (Barz)   178

ragas   185, 187
rail network in India   112–13
railway stations India   112
Ram, Alur Janaki   144
Ramsay, Balcarres D Wardlaw   xi–xii
'The Ranee of Jhansi' (Lang)   94–6
Rascal Rain (Baranay)   126, 128–31
Rati   152
The Razor's Edge (Maugham)   xx
Red Fort, Delhi   118
Reeves, Peter   27
religion *see* Eastern religions; spirituality; Theosophy
representations of India and its people
    adventure, excitement and exotica   82–3, 119, 128
    by Alfred Deakin   11–15, 87
    colonial relations   85–7
    life of Majarajahs and their retinues   83–4
    life on the streets   84–5
    military life and masculinity   79–80
    and postcolonial theory   131–2
    sociocultural history of   76
    travel stories   78–9
    in women's fiction   80–2
Reva   152
'Rickshawallah' (poem) (Barz)   178
Rigby's Romance (Furphy)   15
Rivett, Eleanor   11
Rodgers, John   185–7
Roe, Jill   15, 16, 38
Rorke, Gordon   67
Rushdie, Salman   xix, 143
Russia, threat of imperial ambitions   7
Ryder, Jack   65, 66

Taj Mahal   99, 120, 193

Tarrant, Frank 65, 66
Taylor, Mark 70, 209
tea trade 6
Tea Tree Gully Cricket Club 211
Temple and Tomb in India (Deakin) 12, 13, 87
Tendulkar, Sachin 30, 70, 183, 184, 209, 213
Tenniel, John 122
Tent Life in Tigerland (Inglis) 6
Thackeray, Williiam 90
'Theory Couldn't Help Me' (Baranay) 129
Theosophy 15–17, 38
Thirwell, Mark 32
The Thousand and One Nights 120
Three Sydney Novels (Baranay) 135
Tibet, Tibet (French) 172
Tibetan refugees 171–2
Tiffin, Helen 146
time, understanding of 206
'Tirhoot, Lucknow, Bhitoor, ETC.' (Lang) 96
Titan Cup 70
Titsiana Booberini (film) 154
Toshack, Ernie 67
tourism, by Westerners 26
tourist's view of India 150–1
trade
  Australia–Japan 28
  benefits of 13
  and imperial connection 3–4, 5–6
transracial relationships 93–4, 140–2
travel writing 79, 90, 91
travels through India, by Australians in 19th century 8–12, 14
The Triad 85
tropical heat, impact of 4, 5
Truth and Progress (Baptist publication) 47
tsunami, in December 2004 77
Tuck, Bertha 42
Tucker Sees India (Skinner) 80, 81–2, 139–40
Turcotte, Gerry 159
Turner, Neville 208, 209, 210, 211, 212
Twain, Mark 8, 185, 198

Udayan, children's leprosy home 70
'Ujjain' (poem) (Barz) 179
UKraine 169
'Under Western Eyes' (Mohanty) 130

Underwood, Joseph ix
United Provinces Industrial and Agricultural Exhibition 61
University of Lucknow, architectural designs by Walter Burley Griffin 58, 61
urination scene in *Holy Smoke!* 157–60

Varma, Shanta Nedungadi 31
Vengsarkar, Dilip 208
Vengunad Kingdom 202
Venkataraghavan, Srinivasaranghavan 68
Victoria, Queen of England 76, 146
village life, biblical nature of 11–12
Vishwa Hindu Parishad (VHP) 173
Viswanath, Gundappa 69

Walker, David 79, 84
Wanderings in India (Lang) x, xx, 89, 90, 91, 92, 93, 94, 104
Warne, Shane 70–1, 184, 211, 212, 213
Waugh, Mark 71, 209
Waugh, Steve 31, 70, 71, 167
Weaver, John 211
Weber, Tom 27
Well of Knowledge 115
Well of Purification 115
Wellek, Rene 75
Westall, Richard 122
The Wetherbys, Father and Son; Or, Sundry Chapters of Indian Experience (Lang) 78, 147
Wetter, Margaret xiii, 93
White Australia policy 25
Windsor Manor Hotel 211
Winslet, Kate 149, 156
With the Tiger (Baranay) xx
women
  colonial womanhood in Australia 42–5
  female experience and 'girlshine' 155–6
  female *jouissance* 157
  female sexuality and spirituality 156
  and female will 159, 159n15
  missionaries in India 11, 38–42, 47–8, 49
  settlers and Aboriginal people 37–8, 43, 44
women's fiction, representations of India and its people 80–2
Woodfull, 66

Woolacott, Angela   38, 48
World Series Cup   69
writer–text relationship   199
writings about India by expatriates, 'mango novels'   xix, 143, 147
writings about India by non-Indians
    ambivalence about   170–1
    in colonial era   138–42
    contemporary works   126–8
    in post-colonial era   142–6
    see also Hingston, James; Lang, John George
Wyllie, Dan   153

'You Oughta Know' (song) (Morissette)   156, 156*n*8
youth, passing of   154

Zach, Wolfgang   75
zenana   47
zero, idea of   186, 187–8